ABHANDLUNGEN
DER NORDRHEIN-WESTFÄLISCHEN AKADEMIE DER WISSENSCHAFTEN

Sonderreihe
PAPYROLOGICA COLONIENSIA
Herausgegeben von der
Nordrhein-Westfälischen Akademie der Wissenschaften
in Verbindung mit der Universität zu Köln
Vol. XXVI/1

PAPYROLOGICA COLONIENSIA · Vol. XXVI/1

THE ARCHIVE OF AMMON SCHOLASTICUS OF PANOPOLIS

(P. Ammon)

Volume I: The Legacy of Harpocration

Texts from the Collections of Duke University and the Universität zu Köln

Edited by William H. Willis
Duke University

and Klaus Maresch
Universität zu Köln

Westdeutscher Verlag

In Zusammenarbeit mit der Arbeitsstelle für Papyrusforschung im
Institut für Altertumskunde der Universität zu Köln
Leiter: Professor Dr. Wolfgang D. Lebek

Die Deutsche Bibliothek – CIP-Einheitsaufnahme

The archive of Ammon Scholasticus of Panopolis: (P. Ammon) /
[in Zusammenarbeit mit der Arbeitsstelle für Papyrusforschung
im Institut für Altertumskunde der Universität zu Köln]. –
Opladen: Westdt. Verl.
(Abhandlungen der Nordrhein-Westfälischen Akademie der Wissenschaften:
Sonderreihe Papyrologica Coloniensia; Vol. 26)
Vol. 1. The legacy of Harpocration: texts from the collection of Duke University and
the Universität zu Köln / ed. by William H. Willis and Klaus Maresch. – 1997
ISBN 3-531-09943-4

Der Westdeutsche Verlag ist ein Unternehmen der
Bertelsmann Fachinformation GmbH.

Herstellung: Westdeutscher Verlag
Druck und buchbinderische Verarbeitung: B.o.s.s Druck und Medien, Kleve
Printed in Germany

ISSN 0944-8837
ISBN 3-531-09943-4

In memoriam

HERBERT CHAYYIM YOUTIE

ΜΥΘΟΣ

A story is told in Achmim, whose burghers believe it to be the oldest continuously inhabited city in the world, that on a certain dark night of the year a native adventurer may at midnight in the center of the town encounter a large black dog with gleaming eyes who will silently lead him through tortuous alleys to a stair descending deep into the ground. If the brave adventurer will but follow quietly, he will emerge onto a resplendent plaza brilliant with marble pavement and temples ornamented with objects of gold. If he withholds his hands, the dog will lead him back to the upper town and disappear. There his neighbors next day will admire and celebrate his dream. But if in greed he grasp even a single object, there the dog will abandon him, and he will disappear forever.

— as told by Mishmish, schoolboy of Achmim, March 1981

FOREWORD

On an extended visit to Achmim in 1968 to study the Coptic Church and its liturgy, our Duke University colleague Professor O.S. Wintermute became acquainted with a local merchant, who eventually showed him some papyri that he said he had unearthed in his garden. Those he would part with Wintermute acquired and on his return donated to the Duke University Library, sixteen fragments altogether of which nine are in hands of the III or IV century and were later seen to derive from the archive of Ammon Scholasticus of Panopolis. Since all were fragmentary, though one was large (P. Duke inv. 18), none revealed its context. Only after other papyri from the Ammon archive came to light in 1971 did their source become apparent: three joined Cologne papyri (P.Köln inv. 4532, 4535 and 4539), three others papyri acquired by Duke in 1971 (P.Duke inv. 179, 182 and 193 respectively).

In Cairo in 1969, when I acquired from a dealer a small fragment (P.Duke inv. 6) later recognized as belonging to the archive, I was informed that a large group of papyri had a month earlier been sold to a Swiss collector, whom I unsuccessfully sought to contact. Two years later I learned that this find had been transferred to a museum in Germany, on a visit to which in 1971 I negotiated their acquisition by the Duke University Library (P.Duke inv. nos. 176 to 229, plus about 100 unnumbered tiny fragments). These, as it turned out, were a substantial part of the Ammon archive. When at the XIV International Congress of Papyrologists at Oxford in 1974 I announced this find and presented a series of *apographai*, I learned from colleagues that a number of related documents belong to the collections at the Universität zu Köln (P.Köln inv. nos. 4531 to 4557) and the Istituto Papirologico G. Vitelli in Florence.[1] As a result it was agreed that Duke and Cologne should collaborate in the publication of their respective holdings of the archive. Through the good offices of Professors Reinhold Merkelbach and Ludwig Koenen the Cologne pieces were deposited on loan at Duke University in 1976 so that I might rejoin *disjecta membra*, as indeed many have been. Dr Klaus Maresch,

---

[1] Other papyri from the Ammon archive are preserved in the PSI collection in Florence, not available to the present editors. Whether these include fragments adjoining those published in this volume is at present unknown.

my collaborator at Cologne, spent the year 1987–88 at Duke, where we worked together on texts from the archive and other papyri shared by the two collections.

The family archive, comprising several hundred fragmentary papyri from very small to quite large and including texts dated from A.D. 281 to 372 (from the time of his parents to his own old age), is the legacy of Aurelius Ammon, son of Petearbeschinis, advocate (σχολαστικός) from Panopolis. The earliest texts preserved in the archive had already been assigned for publication to Professor G.M. Browne of the University of Illinois, who in 1976 published two documents dated A.D. 281 and 289 concerning property of Ammon's father Petearbeschinis and his first wife Senpasis (*P.Coll.Youtie* II nos. 71–73). In 1977 he published the first of Ammon's documents of A.D. 348 (*ICS* II pp.184–96), revised and republished as no. **6** in this volume. The only two literary texts found with the archive I published in *ICS* III (1978) pp.140–53 as presented at a conference in 1976 before an additional fragment of each was recognized in the archive; the rejoined expanded text of one appeared in 1989 as *CPF* I.1.1 and is republished in this volume as no. **1**, the expanded text of the other is here no. **2**. Ammon's long letter to his mother that I reconstituted from fragments at both Duke and Cologne and presented to the Brussels Congress in 1977, was published in the *Actes du XV Congrès International de Papyrologie* II (1979) no. 22, has been revised and is republished here as no. **3**; the present text owes many of its improvements to the advice and suggestions of my colleague Peter van Minnen.

A new text, no. **4**, is a petition to the prefect concerning Ammon's vain effort to obtain from the *archiereus* of Alexandria and All Egypt the appointment of his nephew Horion II to the *propheteia* in succession to Horion's deceased father, an effort that is discussed in no. **3**. Thereafter nos. 5–25 are all the papyri preserved in the two collections pertaining to the case before the *catholicus* (*rationalis*) in A.D. 348 concerning the litigation between Ammon and a *delator* for possession of the slaves of Ammon's deceased brother Harpocration, a rhetor with the imperial court.

In preparation of this first volume of the archive, I identified, sorted and joined the Duke fragments and made preliminary transcriptions. Maresch revised the transcriptions of nos. **5–24**, drafted some of the introductions and contributed some of the notes. I then revised all transcriptions from reexamination of the papyri and rewrote the introductions and commentary.

Maresch supplied most of that which pertains to Roman law. He also has prepared the indices and along with my Duke colleague Peter van Minnen has supplied useful advice on readings and bibliography.

The collaborators at Duke and Cologne propose to publish the texts of the archive in a series of volumes entitled *P.Ammon*, of which this first volume comprises all the papyri related to Ammon's case before the *catholicus* in Alexandria in A.D. 348. A second volume is projected to contain all the texts concerned with the family's property, with other volumes to follow. It is hoped that our Florentine colleagues will wish to include in the series volumes presenting their own holdings of texts from the archive.

I gratefully acknowledge the support by the late Dr Benjamin E. Powell, then director of the Duke University Libraries, for the acquisition of the Duke portion of the Ammon Archive, and of the John Simon Guggenheim Memorial Foundation for the opportunity to explore Achmim for the origin of the archive and to study the holdings at the Universität zu Köln. Maresch wishes to thank the Deutsche Forschungsgemeinschaft for support of his stay at Duke from October 1987 until March 1988. In reading the texts, searches of CD ROM "D" issued by the Thesaurus Linguae Graecae and of the Duke Data Bank of Documentary Papyri on CD ROMs 6 and 7 issued by the Packard Humanities Institute have proved indispensable.

William H. Willis
Duke University

15 December 1995

EDITORIAL SYMBOLS

[ ]	Lacuna on the papyrus
[...]	Lacuna with estimate of the number of lost letters
ca 10	Editor's estimate of number of letters unread or lost
....	Approximate number of letters unread by the editor
αβγδ	Doubtful letters postulated by the editor
⟦ ⟧	Deletion by the scribe
{ }	Editor's suppression of superfluous letters
`αβγδ´	Letters added by the scribe above the line
´αβγδ`	Letters added by the scribe below the line
< >	Letters added by the editor
vacat	Uninscribed space on the papyrus
( )	Editor's resolution of a scribal suspension
l	Beginning of a new line on the papyrus
—>	Horizontal direction of the fibers of the papyrus
↑	Vertical direction of the fibers of the papyrus
r	Recto of the papyrus
v	Verso of the papyrus

CONTENTS

INTRODUCTION

The archive to be published in the projected series of volumes entitled *P.Ammon* comprises the family papers collected and preserved by the fourth-century advocate Aurelius Ammon Scholasticus,[1] son of Petearbeschinis, of Panopolis in the Thebaid. A well educated lawyer who professes and exhibits interest in rhetoric and philosophy, he was born during probably the first or second decade of the IV century to Petearbeschinis and his second wife Senpetechensis also called Nike; he was the mainstay of his family and presumably in mid-career in 348 when he wrote most of the texts contained in this volume. He is last attested in 372 when he championed his daughter and son-in-law Helladios in litigation. The archive includes not only his own papers but many from other members of the family. The earliest dated text is a purchase of property in 281 by his father's first wife, census returns of 303 and 308 by his parents and in 299 by his elder half-brother Horion I, and many undated papers including farming accounts and receipts. The family possessed or drew income from extensive holdings scattered throughout the Panopolite nome.

Head of a family of high-ranking hereditary priests, Petearbeschinis was priest of the principal temples of the nome, his first wife Senpasis was a priestess and daughter of a priest, and their son Horion I was priest and *archiprophetes* of the temples of the nome, to whose account accrued one-tenth of all their vast temple lands. Of the five ranks of the traditional college of priests, the *archiprophetes* stood alone in the first rank, exercising authority analogous to that of bishop or archbishop, while the higher-ranking priests constituted the second tier, in which Petearbeschinis was apparently senior. Horion II, son of Horion I and so Ammon's nephew, was expected

---

[1] The title σχολαστικός designates a person of advanced education in rhetoric, law and philosophy, much like a modern higher degree, and one carried by Ammon with great pride. On the profession of *scholasticus* see A. Claus, Ὁ Σχολαστικός, Diss. Köln 1964, and more recent examples collected by P.J. Sijpesteijn, *ZPE* 70 (1987) 143ff. Although 'advocate' is a frequent meaning, J.A. Crook, *Legal Advocacy in the Roman World* (Ithaca/New York 1995) does not mention the title, nor does W. Kunkel, *Herkunft und soziale Stellung der römischen Juristen*[2] (Graz/Wien/Köln 1967).

to succeed his father in the hereditary *propheteia*. The family was therefore quite distinguished and wealthy, a priestly aristocracy.

Other members of the family, though not priests so far as we know, were educated and prominent in other pursuits. Most notable was Ammon's full brother Aurelius Harpocration, who styled himself σοφιστὴς δημόσιος, was at times a member of the Imperial *comitatus*[2] delivering panegyrics in honor of the emperors, meanwhile serving as *curator* and *procurator* of the principal cities of Greece,[3] and who died abroad unexpectedly in 348. Both Harpocration and Ammon were on intimate terms with the "ἡγεμών of the Ethiopians," presumably the ruler of the Meroitic kingdom in its last days. Apollon, a nephew of Ammon, was a poet who had received audience in Panopolis with the high magistrate Flavius Sisinnius, who was later promoted to *catholicus* in Alexandria where he became arbiter of the litigation documented in our texts nos. **5–15**; Apollon, however, is not attested elsewhere. In any case the family is clearly well known in very high circles. Evidence from the texts in this volume yields a stemma of the family shown in Figure 1:

---

[2] For accounts of the *comitatus*, the imperial court and entourage that accompanied the emperor on his travels, see especially A.H.M. Jones, *The Later Roman Empire* I (Oxford/ Norman 1964, repr. Baltimore 1986) pp.49–51 and 366–68; also F. Millar, *The Emperor in the Roman World*[2] (Cornell 1992) pp.42ff. In addition to military contingents and financial officials were included the three palatine civil secretariats, first of which was *officium* (or *scrinium*) *memoriae*, headed by the *magister memoriae*. Cf. 3.26, 9.6f and 13.23–26, and Millar pp.265f.

[3] Cited as no. 63 by R. Delmaire, "Le personnel de l'administration financière en Égypte sous le Bas-Empire romain," *CRIPEL* 10 (1988) pp.132f, as attested by a preliminary citation from P.Köln inv. 4533 first published hereinafter as no. **13** (Delmaire's reference to *SB* 11929 is in error).

FAMILY OF AURELIUS AMMON SCHOLASTICUS OF PANOPOLIS
(A.D. 281–372?)

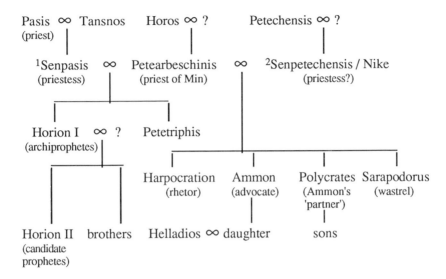

alii:: Macaria (elder relative of Ammon, perhaps his maternal grandmother)
   Kanea(?) (elder relative of Ammon)
   Apollon (poet, Ammon's nephew, son of Polycrates, Horion I or Pete-
      triphis?)

FIGURE 1

   Obviously Harpocration, Ammon, Apollon and presumably Horion II had
all received advanced education well beyond the level of *grammaticus*, and
there is no indication that such higher education would not have been available to them in Panopolis, although we lack direct evidence of such a school
or professor there.[4] That Panopolis was the cultural center of the Thebaid
has been widely recognized by commentators from Herodotus (2.91) to the

---

   [4] See, however, J.-L. Fournet, *ZPE* 92 (1992) pp.253f with nn.1 and 2, who argues for
rhetorical schools in Panopolis. *P.Berl.Bork.* lists two *rhetores* in the city, Theodotus at
ii.4 and Theon at A.i.2f, who may be professors of the art (see *infra* n.8). For *rhetores* as
advanced teachers see R.A. Kaster, *Guardians of Language: the Grammarian and Society in
Late Antiquity* (Berkeley 1988) pp.34, 104f, 204f.

present.[5] In a document of A.D. 289 (*Pap.Agon.* 3) citing the "sacred, tri-
umphant, international, Pythian, scenic and athletic games of Perseus Oura-
nios at the great festival of Pan," the city is styled ἡ λαμπρὰ καὶ λογιμω-
τάτη καὶ σεμνοτάτη Πανοπολιτῶν πόλις and λαμπροτάτη καὶ εὐσε-
βεστάτη, hyperbole typical of the privileged society of athletes and Diony-
siac artists.

In the "great city called Chemmis" Herodotus describes a square temple of
Perseus ... The colonnade before this temple is of stone, very great, and at
the entrance stand two great stone statues." He makes no separate mention of
the great temple of Min, chief god of the city, perhaps because he had not yet
been identified with Pan by the Greeks, or Herodotus himself identified Min
with Perseus. In any case it was of such πρωτολόγιμα ἱερά that Petearbeschinis was a ranking priest. Alongside the temenos of the great temple of
Pan and extending onward to the sacred lake of Phoebus (Horus) was a fine
garden or grove planted with περσέαι, established in the II or III century.[6]

Besides its splendid temples, the city possessed a theater, at least three
public baths, a gymnasium, a comasterion, a praetorium and other public
buildings. As a nome capital Panopolis was no doubt awarded a *boule* in the
reform of Septimius Severus near the beginning of the third century. No. **3**
line 2 with its mention of a former *bouleutes* is belated confirmation that the
boule existed there prior to 348; hitherto the only attestations of *bouleutai* in
Panopolis were *P.Lips.* 45.r.6, 59.5 and 60.r.3 all dated 371, *PSI* XII

---

[5] For discussion see Alan Cameron, "Wandering Poets: a Literary Movement in Byzantine Egypt," *Historia* 14 (1965) 470–509, esp. 472, 473 n.17 "The fact that so many of
these poets came from the Thebaid suggests that there were some very competent schools
and teachers there to foster the tradition; it is most unlikely that they *all* received their
instruction in Alexandria," and 508. See H.J. Thissen, "Der verkommene Harfenspieler,"
ZPE 77 (1989) pp.238ff; see also E.G. Turner, *Greek Papyri*[2] (Oxford 1980, rp. 1988) 51–
53, 201 addenda to ch. iv with references cited there; also E. Wipszycka, "La Christia-
nisation de l'Égypte," *Aegyptus* 68 (1988) p.163, and "Le nationalisme a-t-il existé dans
l'Égypte byzantine?" *JJP* 22 (1992) esp. p.100 with n.45 and p.107 with n.68; and R.S.
Bagnall, *Egypt in Late Antiquity* (Princeton 1993) 103f, 109, 265 and 272f (to be modified
now by texts in this volume, esp. **3** and **4**).

[6] C.B. Welles, "The Garden of Ptolemagrius at Panopolis," *TAPA* 77 (1946) pp.192–
206. On the history and documentation of Apou/Chemmis/Panopolis/Achmim, see F. von
Känel, "Achmîm et le IXe nome de Haute Égypte (de la XXVe Dynastie à la époque
copte)," *L'Égyptologie en 1979* I (1982) pp.235ff, where a more extensive work is announced. Numerous statues and stelae from the city are now lodged in the Egyptian Museum Cairo and principal museums in Europe and North America.

1233.2 dated 323/24,[7] and duplicate documents from the Ammon archive dated 281, *P.Coll.Youtie* II 71 and 72.

The remarkable but fragmentary topographical register of the city dating from the first third of the IV century,[8] in a street-by-street, house-by-house inventory of a quarter containing more than 300 houses (one of which belonged to Petearbeschinis' son Petetriphis), lists also nine smaller temples or shrines and one Christian church. Panopolis was a center of textile weaving (as indeed Achmim continues to be today), metal-working (particularly goldsmithy) and shipbuilding[9]; stonemasons (or sculptors) are mentioned by Strabo (17.1.42). The city-register lists two *rhetores*, two physicians, and eight priests, one of whom is named Petetriphis; whether he is the Petetriphis son of Petearbeschinis is impossible to determine since there are four others by that name, and the six of that name in *P.Panop.Beatty* 1 are identified by Greek patronymics appropriate to an official register, while we do not know Petearbeschinis' Greek alias.[10]

All but one (no. **2**) of the texts in this volume were written by Ammon himself in 348 or near it, in the middle of a century which began when the old religion was as yet virtually unchallenged and ended with the triumph of Christianity.[11] Like most of the elite, Ammon's family were unquestioningly pagan, especially since they were a family of priests. But by midcentury the shadows were encroaching. Nos. **3, 4** and **7–15** reveal both the anxiety of

---

[7] An offer to lease agricultural land addressed to the former *bouleutai* Eulogios and a Harpocration, possibly of Ammon's family although there is no evidence to connect him: *P.Berl.Bork.* has five entries of that name, of whom at least three are different persons, but no entry of a Eulogios.

[8] See Z. Borkowski, *Une description topographique des immeubles à Panopolis* (Warsaw 1975) [*P.Berl.Bork.*].

[9] T.C. Skeat in the introduction to *P.Panop.Beatty* pp.xxxiff.

[10] Some names similar to those in the archive appear in the very fragmentary texts from Panopolis published in *CPR* XVIIB of the late II and early III century, too early to afford connections with names appearing in Ammon's archive. In fragments securely dated to A.D. 184/5 a Pekysis (1.54) and a Petetriphis (3.2) occur; in those dated 217/8 we find an Aurelius Paniscus (13.16), a Petearbeschinis as someone's father (13.8), a Horion father of Castor (23.17) and a Horos son of Chemsneus (18.1). None of them, however, is further identified. The texts derive from a banker's archive.

[11] On this see L. Kákosy, "Das Ende des Heidentums in Ägypten," in P. Nagel, ed. *Graeco-Coptica* (Halle 1984) 61–76, and *idem* in *ANRW* II 18.5 (1995) esp. pp.2934ff; see also F. Zucker, "Priester und Tempel in Ägypten in den Zeiten nach der decianischen Christenverfolgung," *Akten des VIII. Int. Kongresses für Papyrologie* (MPER n.s. V, 1956) 167–73; Z. Borkowski, "Local Cults and the Resistance to Christianity," *JJP* 20 (1990) pp.25f; and Bagnall (*op.cit.* n.5) pp.261–73 and 278–89.

devout adherents of the old cults and their anxious belief that the gods and the wheel of Fortune would soon restore their world. They throw a rare and striking light on the cultural life of their class shortly before the final victory of Christianity, providing documentation of pagan piety, priestly activity and temple income at least a half-century later than documentary evidence available hitherto.[12]

---

[12] Bagnall (*op.cit.* n.5) assigned an early IV-cent. date to the letter republished here as no. **3** (pp.272f), lacking the evidence for its redating provided by nos. **4–15** and the as yet unpublished *apographai* of 299, 303 and 308. No evidence was then available to him for temple income after the middle of the III century (pp.267f) nor datable IV-cent. evidence for festivals (p.269) or piety (p.271).

I. Literary Papyri

1. Ammon's List of Scholarchs

P.Duke inv. 178   (9.9 x 22.0 cm)   Panopolis, IV cent.
Plate I

In the preambles to two of the drafts of his petition to the *catholicus* Flavius Sisinnius in December A.D. 348 (**7**.3f and **13**.9f) Ammon says of himself "While I myself, to be sure, know that a quiet life free from intrigue befits those educated in philosophy and rhetoric..." As if to document his claim, he has left us in his archive the fragments of a private memorandum written in his own informal hand listing the principal philosophers with whose works he had become acquainted in the advanced education he had received, presumably in Panopolis, in preparation for his profession as *scholasticus*. The hand of the memorandum is so similar to that of his drafts of 348 that it appears to have been written not long before. The verso is uninscribed.

The originally square sheet (*ca* 22 x 22 cm) bore three narrow columns and was apparently folded vertically into six panels, of which only the top half of the second, most of the third and the lower part of the fourth survive, so that only parts of the first two columns remain. The right half of col. i, broken off after twelve lines, has lost its lower sixteen, col. ii its first four lines, and col. iii is altogether missing. The names are grouped by school or period, separated by *paragraphoi*.

After a title, col. i begins with Thales and continues through Diogenes of Apollonia in master-pupil sequence; thereafter the lost lines would have provided space for at least eight additional Presocratics. The top of col. ii probably named Socrates (though he might have come at the foot of col. i) and surely Plato, since the first surviving line lists Speusippus; then follow Academics, early Cynics, Peripatetics, and just above the lower margin the subtitle 'Stoics with Cynics'. The lost col. iii presumably continued with the later Cynics and Stoics together, with room also for Epicureans. These later Cynics were likely to have most influenced Ammon, since he is much given to *sententiae* of a Cynic flavor, none of which is traceable in extant literature.

Apparently Ammon's *philosophorum index* is unique in that its only purpose was to list the principal philosophers, each with his polis, in teacher-pupil sequence, and from the Academy onward by school citing only the scholarchs. Other ancient lists additionally attribute works or summarize doctrines, as exemplified in H. Diels, *Doxographi graeci*[2] (Berlin/Leipzig 1929) and the *Corpus dei papiri filosofici greci e latini (CPF)* I.1 (Firenze 1989) pp.15–78 (*P.Herc.*) and 85–114. No other list presents the same names and schools in precisely the same order. Clearly he is following a doxographic tradition, but one differing at several points from all traditions attested in earlier and contemporary sources. In selection and order the closest parallel is provided by the *de Fide* of Epiphanius, a Palestinian and slightly younger contemporary of Ammon, bishop of Constantia in Cyprus from A.D. 367 and earlier a monk in Egypt; for the text, written some thirty years after Ammon's index, see *de Fide* 9.5–48 (ed. K. Holl vol. 3 pp.505–09) and Diels, *Dox.Gr.* pp.589–593. The object of Epiphanius' compilation, however, was to epitomize and disparage individual doctrines; he does not designate the philosophical schools.

AMMON i	EPIPHANIUS	AMMON ii	EPIPHANIUS	(EPIPHANIUS)
Scholarchs		[Socrates]		
Thales	Thales	[Plato]	Plato	Cleanthes
Anaximander	Anaximander	Speusippus	Aristippus	Persaeus
Anaximenes	Anaximenes	Xenocrates	Theodorus	Chrysippus
Anaxagoras	Anaxagoras	Polemon	Hegesias	Diogenes Bab.
Archelaos	Archelaos		Antisthenes	Panaetius
	Socrates	_Arcesilaos		Posidonius
Pherecydes	Pherecydes	Carneades		Athenodorus
	Pythagoras	Clitomachus		Epicurus
	Xenophanes	Philion		
Parmenides	Parmenides	_Antiochus		
Diogenes Ap.		Diogenes Cyn.	Diogenes Cyn.	
- - - - - -	Zeno El.	Monimus		
	Melissus	_Crates Cyn.	Crates Cyn.	
	Leucippus		Arcesilaos	
	Democritus		Carneades	
	Metrodorus	Aristotle	Aristotle	
	Protagoras	Theophrastus	Theophrastus	
	Diogenes Smyr.	Strato	Strato	
	Pyrrho	Praxiphanes	Praxiphanes	
	Empedocles	_Critolaos	Critolaos	
	Heraclitus	Zeno Stoic.	Zeno Stoic.	
	Prodicus	(*margin*)		
[(*margin*)]		[*col. iii lost*]		

Unlike Epiphanius, Ammon's *paragraphoi* (preserved only in col. ii) separate his list by school. Although he recognizes three phases of the Academy, from the Old Academy he omits Crates of Athens (*RE s.n.* Krates 8) after Polemon but assigns Arcesilaos, whom Galen and Diogenes Laertius call the founder of the Middle (or New) Academy. No *paragraphos* divides the Middle Academy from the Third; Carneades, who Galen says founded the 'New' Academy, is assigned here to the Middle (or Second?). The following rubric 'Third Academy' (col. ii.16) is apparently intended to group the three preceding names, Clitomachus, Philion and Antiochus. From the Cynics he omits Antisthenes, though includes the rarely met Monimus; but he and Epiphanius, alone among doxographers, list Crates the Cynic. Uniquely, Epiphanius defers Arcesilaos and Carneades to a position after the Cynics and preceding Aristotle. Like Epiphanius and no othe doxographer, Ammon gives the same list of Peripatetics in the same order, including the less well known Praxiphanes but omitting the more notable Lycon and Ariston.

Since there can be no question of either Ammon or Epiphanius as a source for the other, it seems inescapable that both are indebted to a lost common source current in the third or early fourth century, one available to Ammon in the course of his higher education in Panopolis. For Epiphanius it was a vehicle for attack on the pagan philosophers, for Ammon a personal memorandum of the philosophers he admired.

The first edition of **1**, published before an additional fragment was recognized (now col. i.1–4), appeared in *Illinois Classical Studies* 3 (1978) pp.145–51 with plate p.153. The expanded text was republished as no. 1 in *CPF* I.1 pp.81–84, together with a commentary by T. Dorandi. Since the new fragment preserves its top margin, a recalculation provides the overall dimensions of the original sheet and indicates that the loss at the top of col. ii allows space for four lines (instead of two as previously hypothesized), so that col. ii probably began with Socrates, followed by Plato, each occupying two lines.

Text

col. i

1	[φιλοσό]φων ἀρ[χηγέται?]
	[ ] *vacat*
	[Θαλῆς Μι]λήσιος
	['Αναξί]μανδρ[ος]
5	[Μιλ]ή[σι]ος
	['Αναξιμέ]νης Μιλήσ(ιος)
	['Αναξαγόρα]ς ἐκ Κλαζο-
	[*vacat*] μενῶν
	['Αρχέλαο]ς 'Αθηναῖος
10	[Φερεκύδ]ης Σύριος
	[Παρμεν]ίδης 'Ελεά[τη]ς
	[Διογένης ἐξ 'Απολλω]νίας

- - - - - - - - - - - - -

col. ii

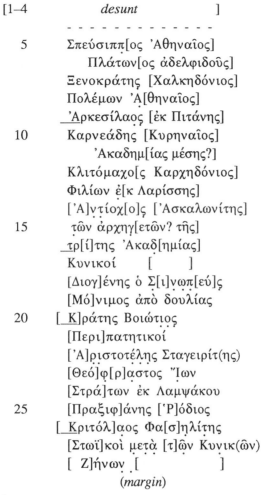

<pre>
        [1–4   desunt   ]
                    - - - - - - - - - - -
          5   Σπεύσιππ[ος 'Αθηναῖος]
                 Πλάτων[ος ἀδελφιδοῦς]
                 Ξενοκράτης [Χαλκηδόνιος]
                 Πολέμων 'Α[θηναῖος]
                 'Αρκεσίλαος [ἐκ Πιτάνης]
         10   Καρνεάδης [Κυρηναῖος]
                 'Ακαδημ[ίας μέσης?]
                 Κλιτόμαχο[ς Καρχηδόνιος]
                 Φιλίων ἐ[κ Λαρίσσης]
                 ['Α]ντίοχ[ο]ς ['Ασκαλωνίτης]
         15   τῶν ἀρχηγ[ετῶν? τῆς]
                 τρ[ί]της 'Ακαδ[ημίας]
                 Κυνικοί   [   ]
                 [Διογ]ένης ὁ Σ[ι]νωπ[εύ]ς
                 [Μό]νιμος ἀπὸ δουλίας
         20   [Κ]ράτης Βοιώτιος
                 [Περι]πατητικοί
                 ['Α]ριστοτέλης Σταγειρίτ(ης)
                 [Θεό]φ[ρ]αστος Ἴων
                 [Στρά]των ἐκ Λαμψάκου
         25   [Πραξιφ]άνης ['Ρ]όδιος
                 [Κριτόλ]αος Φα[σ]ηλίτης
                 [Στωϊ]κοὶ μετὰ [τ]ῶν Κυνικ(ῶν)
                 [Ζ]ήνων [   ]
                          (margin)
</pre>

[col. iii lost]

Notes

col. i

1. Because of the loss of the top of col. ii we cannot determine whether the title for the list extended across two columns or doubled back in the lacuna of line 2. The surviving αρ[may be supplemented ἀρχηγοί or ἀρχηγέται, with which cf. ii.15 αρχηγ[.

7f. Anaxagoras is the only early candidate from Clazomenae. Some doxographers name him as a pupil of Anaximenes and teacher of Archelaos.

10. Pherecydes is unexpected here, though as an early cosmogonist, contemporary and possibly a pupil of Anaximander, he is the only candidate from Syros. There is no testimony that he was a teacher of Parmenides.

col. ii

[1–4.] Here one would expect Σωκράτης and Πλάτων, whether in single lines 3 and 4 if the heading at i.1 extended over two columns or if not, each occupying two lines with ethnic or other epithet.

9. ἐκ Πιτάνης or Πιταναῖος. As elsewhere in this list, the *paragraphos* separates the preceding group from the ensuing, here dividing the Old Academy, to which Arcesilaos is attributed, from the Middle (or New), which begins with Carneades.

11. μέσης or δευτέρας.

12–16. Although no *paragraphos* is visible, apparently Clitomachus (12), Philion (13) and Antiochus (14) are grouped as among the scholarchs of the Third Academy (15f), and are separated by the second surviving *paragraphos* from the ensuing Cynics.

13. Φιλίων (of Larissa), so Ammon; the name is commonly spelled Φίλων. Ammon's orthography is in agreement with the codices of Eusebius, *Praep. Ev.* at 14.8.15, 9.1–3; "given Ammon's education, it may be presumed that it is not a matter of an error but of a form that he correctly retained" (Dorandi).

19. Monimus of Syracuse is named by no doxographer in Diels, *Dox.Gr.*, though he figures in Menander (fr. 215 Kö.), Sextus Empiricus (*adv.Math.* 7.48, 88; 8.5) and Diogenes Laertius (6.82f), who cites Sosicrates as saying that he was a pupil of Diogenes Cynicus and was once slave to a Corinthian banker until he feigned madness and was dismissed— hence Ammon's ἀπὸ δουλίας. He is credited with two books, Περὶ ὁρμῶν and a *Protrepticus*.

20. Of the doxographers only Epiphanius lists Crates, next after Diogenes, and styles him ἀπὸ Θηβῶν. Diogenes Laertius (7.4) calls him a teacher of the Stoic Zeno, one of whose books was entitled (Κράτητος) Ἀπομνημονεύματα.

23. Theophrastus is identified not by his native city on Lesbos as Ἐρέ-σιος but as Ἴων, as though Ammon thought of the Aegean as simply Ionia. Even so, the commoner Ἰώνιος might have been expected.

27f. As in Epiphanius' list, Zeno and the Stoics come next after Critolaos, but Ammon associates with them the later Cynics, who are often so attached and by whom he was probably particularly influenced to judge from the character of his frequent *sententiae*. On the lineal relation of the Cynics and Stoics see J.M. Rist, *Stoic Philosophy* (Cambridge 1969, rp. 1980) esp. pp.54–80. At 28 Ζήνων is unexpectedly indented (possibly so as to accommodate a definite article), but no other name with this termination is available.

Translation

col. i   (margin)

[1]SCHOLARCHS OF (THE) PHILOSOPHERS: [Thales] of Miletus, [Anaxi]-mander [5]of Miletus, [Anaxime]nes of Miletus, [Anaxagora]s from Clazo-menae, [Archelao]s of Athens, [10][Pherecyd]es of Syria, [Parmen]ides of Elea, [Diogenes from Apollo]nia, [*column breaks off, ca 16 lines lost*]

col. ii [*four lines lost*]

[5]Speusippus [of Athens] Plato's [nephew], Xenocrates [of Chalcedon], Po-lemon of A[thens], Arcesilaos [from Pitane]. (*paragraphos*) [10]Carneades [of Cyrene] [of the MIDDLE or NEW?] ACADEMY. Clitomachus [of Carthage], Philion from [Larissa], [15]Antiochus [of Ascalon] of the scholarchs [of the] THIRD ACADEMY. (*paragraphos*) CYNICS: [Diog]enes the Sinopean, [20]Moni-mus up from slavery, Crates of Boeotia. (*paragraphos*) PERIPATETICS: Aristotle of Stagira, Theophrastus of Ionia, [25][Stra]ton from Lampsacus, [Praxiph]anes of Rhodes, [Critol]aos of Phaselis. (*paragraphos*) [STOI]CS WITH THE CYNICS: Zeno [of Cyprus?]   (*margin*)

[*col. iii lost*]

2. HOMER, *ODYSSEY*

P.Duke inv. 176   frr.A (4.8 x 22.0), B (4.1 x 4.8)   III cent.
          [codex *ca* 16.5 x 29.5]   Plates II and III

Although these fragments of a papyrus codex containing the *Odyssey* have no connection with the other papyri in this volume, they are included here because as part of the archive they may further illuminate Ammon's literary interests. Their text is written in a small third-century bookhand unlike any other represented in the archive. Fr. A is revised from its first publication in *Illinois Classical Studies* 3 (Urbana 1978) pp.142–45 + plate p.152. Fr. B, recognized later among papyri in the archive, is hitherto unpublished; it is a fragment of the tenth leaf following fr. A.

As described in greater detail in the *editio princeps*, the codex was nearly twice as tall as broad, falling within Turner's Group 6, characteristic of early codices of the third and fourth centuries.[1] Its computed 54 lines per page again indicate an early date, as shown by Turner's list of 33 papyrus codices with fifty or more lines: 20 are assigned to the II or III centuries, 9 more to the III or IV.[2] Given the calculated page dimensions of Ammon's codex, the entire *Odyssey* would have filled 112 leaves or 224 pages. Since the two surviving fragments derive from Books 9 and 11, perhaps their source contained only the first half of the poem.

The text is a properly written copy of the vulgate, except that the scribe has added *nu*-movable at the end of 9.301 and has written line 354 twice by dittography. At 9.302 our text reads ἔρ]υκε[ν], the correct reading accepted by modern editors; the ἀνῆκεν of some Mss, found first in scholia, was falsely imported into the *Odyssey* from its occurrences at *Iliad* 7.25, 21.395 and 22.252 (an observation I owe to H. van Thiel). In line 370 the scribe corrected his omission of *delta* by inserting it in place just under the line. The false *iota*-adscript at-

---

[1] E.G. Turner, *The Typology of the Early Codex* (Philadelphia 1977) Table 1 p.18.
[2] *ibid.*, Table 14 pp.96f.

tached to τῇ at 347, omitted by modern editors, is common in Homeric papyri and manuscripts. The preserved parts of fr. B agree with modern editions. Two other papyri overlap parts of the text of fr. A (see Pack[2]); fr. B is thus far the sole representative of its text among papyri.

Text

Fr. A, *recto* (↑) *Od.* 9.295–309

    desunt ca 5 lineae

- -

1   [   ]．．   295

    [   ]．．

    [   ]．．

    [κεῖτ' ἔντοσθ' ἄντροιο τανυσσάμενος διὰ μήλ]ων.

5   [τὸν μὲν ἐγὼ βούλευσα κατὰ μεγαλήτορ]α θυμὸν

    [ἆσσον ἰών, ξίφος ὀξὺ ἐρυσσάμενος παρὰ] μηροῦ   300

    [οὐτάμεναι πρὸς στῆθος, ὅτι φρένες ἧπα]ρ ἔχουσιν,

    [χείρ' ἐπιμασσάμενος· ἕτερος δέ με θυμὸς ἔρ]υκε[ν].

    [αὐτοῦ γάρ κε καὶ ἄμμες ἀπωλόμεθ' αἰπὺν ὄλεθ]ρον·

10 [   ]．．

    [χερσὶν ἀπώσασθαι λίθον ὄβριμον, ὃν προσέθη]κεν. 305

    [ὣς τότε μὲν στενάχοντες ἐμείναμεν Ἠῶ δῖ]αν.

    [   ]

    [   ]

15 [πάντα κατὰ μοῖραν, καὶ ὑπ' ἔμβρυον ἧκεν ἑκάστ]ηι.

- -

    desunt ca 34 lineae

    verso (—>) *Od.* 9.344–84

         (*margin*)

1   σὺν [δ' ὅ γε δὴ αὖτε δύω μάρψας ὁπλίσσατο δόρπον.]

    καὶ τό[τ' ἐγὼ Κύκλωπα προσηύδων ἄγχι παραστάς,] 345

    κι[σ]σύ[βιον μετὰ χερσὶν ἔχων μέλανος οἴνοιο.]

    Κύκλωψ, τῆι, π[ίε οἶνον, ἐπεὶ φάγες ἀνδρόμεα κρέα,]

5   ὄφρ' εἰδῇις οἷόν [τι ποτὸν τόδε νηῦς ἐκεκεύθει]
     ἡμετέρη· σοὶ δ[' αὖ λοιβὴν φέρον, εἴ μ' ἐλεήσας]
     οἴκαδε πέμψεια[ς· σὺ δὲ μαίνεαι οὐκέτ' ἀνεκτῶς.]   350
     σχέτλιε, πῶς κέ[ν τίς σε καὶ ὕστερον ἄλλος ἵκοιτο]
     ἀνθρώπων πολ[έων; ἐπεὶ οὐ κατὰ μοῖραν ἔρεξας.]
10   ὣς ἐφάμην, ὁ δὲ [δέκτο καὶ ἔκπιεν· ἥσατο δ' αἰνῶς]
     ἡδὺ ποτὸν πίν[ων, καί μ' ᾔτεε δεύτερον αὖτις·]   354
     {ἡδὺ ποτὸν πιν[   ]}   354 bis
     δός μοι ἔτι πρ[όφρων, καί μοι τεὸν οὔνομα εἰπὲ]   355
     αὐτίκα νῦν, ἵνα [τοι δῶ ξείνιον, ᾧ κε σὺ χαίρῃς.]
15   καὶ γὰρ Κυκλώπ[εσσι φέρει ζείδωρος ἄρουρα]
     οἶνον ἐρισταφυ[λον, καί σφιν Διὸς ὄμβρος ἀέξει·]
     ἀλλὰ τό[δ' ἀ]μβρ[οσίης καὶ νέκταρός ἐστιν ἀπορρώξ.]
     [   ]   360
     τρὶς μ[ὲν] ἔδ[ωκα φέρων, τρὶς δ' ἔκπιεν ἀφραδίῃσιν.]
20   αὐτὰρ ἐπεὶ Κύ[κλωπα περὶ φρένας ἤλυθεν οἶνος,]
     καὶ τότε δή μ[ιν ἔπεσσι προσηύδων μειλιχίοισι·]
     Κύκλωψ, εἰρω[τᾷς μ' ὄνομα κλυτόν; αὐτὰρ ἐγώ τοι]
     ἐξερέω· σὺ δ[έ μοι δὸς ξείνιον, ὥς περ ὑπέστης.]   365
     Οὖτις ἐμοί γ['] ὄ[νομα· Οὖτιν δέ με κικλήσκουσι]
25   μήτηρ ἠδὲ [πατὴρ ἠδ' ἄλλοι πάντες ἑταῖροι.]
     ὣς ἐφάμην, [ὁ δέ μ' αὐτίκ' ἀμείβετο νηλέϊ θυμῷ·]
     Οὖτιν ἐγὼ π[ύματον ἔδομαι μετὰ οἷς ἑτάροισι,]
     τοὺς δ᾽ ἄλλους [πρόσθεν· τὸ δέ τοι ξεινήϊον ἔσται.]   370
     ἦ κ[αὶ ἀνακλινθεὶς πέσεν ὕπτιος, αὐτὰρ ἔπειτα]
30   κεῖ[τ' ἀποδοχμώσας παχὺν αὐχένα, κὰδ δέ μιν ὕπνος]
     ᾕρει π[ανδαμάτωρ· φάρυγος δ' ἐξέσσυτο οἶνος]
     ψωμ[οί τ' ἀνδρόμεοι· ὁ δ' ἐρεύγετο οἰνοβαρείων.]
     καὶ τό[τ' ἐγὼ τὸν μοχλὸν ὑπὸ σποδοῦ ἤλασα πολλῆς,]   375
     εἵω[ς θερμαίνοιτο· ἔπεσσί τε πάντας ἑταίρους]
35   θάρσυ[νον, μή τίς μοι ὑποδείσας ἀναδύη.]
     ἀλ[λ' ὅτε δὴ τάχ' ὁ μοχλὸς ἐλάϊνος ἐν πυρὶ μέλλεν]
     ἅψε[σθαι, χλωρός περ ἐών, διεφαίνετο δ' αἰνῶς,]

καὶ τ[ότ᾽ ἐγὼν ἆσσον φέρον ἐκ πυρός, ἀμφὶ δ᾽ ἑταῖροι] 380
ἵστα[ντ᾽· αὐτὰρ θάρσος ἐνέπνευσεν μέγα δαίμων.]
40 οἱ μ[ὲν μοχλὸν ἑλόντες ἐλάϊνον, ὀξὺν ἐπ᾽ ἄκρῳ,]
ὀφθ[αλμῷ ἐνέρεισαν· ἐγὼ δ᾽ ἐφύπερθεν ἐρεισθεὶς]
δίν[εον, ὡς ὅτε τις τρυπῷ δόρυ νήϊον ἀνὴρ]

- -

desunt ca 12 lineae

---

301 ἔχουσι *codd.* 302 ἔρυκε(ν) *codd. plur., schol.* BT B 5, Z 524 : ἀνῆκεν *Paris.* 2894, *schol.* AB A 173, *Et. Mag.* 458.15. 347 τῇ *codd. nonnulli* : τῇ *codd. plur.*, Apoll.Soph., Herod., *edd.* 348 οφρ᾽ ειδηις *pap.*, ὄφρ᾽ εἰδῇς *codd.*, Ludwich : ὄφρα ἰδῇς Allen. 351 ἄν *codd. pauci*, Eust. : κέν *codd. complur., edd.* 353 δὲ δέκτο *codd. complur.* : δ᾽ ἔδεκτο *codd. pauci.* : δὲ ἔδεκτο *schol.* (*scriptio plena*). 354 bis *dittogr.* 370 τοὺς δ᾽ ἄλλους *codd., edd.* 376 εἵως *codd.*, Ludwich : εἷος, ἧος *corr. edd. plur.* 379 ἄψεσθαι P[21] (Pack[2] 1081), *codd. plur.* : ἅψασθαι *codd. nonnulli.*

Fr. B, *recto*? (↑), *Od.* 11.273-82

- -

1 [γημαμένη ᾧ υἷι· ὁ δ᾽] ὃν πατέρ᾽ ἐξεναρίξ[ας]
[γῆμεν· ἄφαρ δ᾽ ἀνάπυστ]α θεοὶ θέσαν ἀνθρώ[ποισιν.]
[ἀλλ᾽ ὁ μὲν ἐν Θήβῃ πο]λυηράτωι ἄλγεα πά[σχων] 275
[Καδμείων ἤνασσε θεῶ]ν ὀλοὰς διὰ βουλάς·
5 [ἡ δ᾽ ἔβη εἰς Ἀίδαο πυλάρ]ταο κρα[τεροῖο,]
[ἀψαμένη βρόχον αἰπὺν ἀ]φ᾽ ὑψηλοῖο μελάθ[ρου]
[ᾧ ἄχεϊ σχομένη· τῶι δ᾽ ἄλγ]εα κάλλιπ᾽ [ὀπίσσω]
[πολλὰ μάλ᾽, ὅσσα τε μητρὸ]ς Ἐρινύες ἐκ[τελέουσι.] 280
[καὶ Χλῶριν εἶδον περικα]λλέα, τήν π[οτε Νηλεὺς]
10 [γῆμεν ἑὸν διὰ κάλλος, ἐπεὶ πό]ρε μ[υρία ἕδνα,]

- -

---

273 ὃν *codd. plur.*, αὖ *conj.* Bekker[2]. 275f *damnat.* Duentzer. 276 βολὰς *Vindob.* 56, *Lond. Harl.* 5674 (*corr. m[2]*). 278 ἀφ᾽ *om. Hamb.* 56, μελάθρου *codd.*, δόμοιο Plut. *De cur.* 516b. 280 *om. Vratisl.* 28, ἐρινύες *codd. pauci.*

verso? (—>) *traces of ink*

II. DOCUMENTS OF A.D. 348 PRECEDING AMMON'S CASE AGAINST EUGENEIOS

3. AMMON'S LETTER TO HIS MOTHER

P.Duke inv. 177r	frr. A 9.5 x 24.5 cm	From Alexandria to Panopolis
+ P.Köln inv. 4534r and 4538r	B 4.5 x 24.5	May/June?, A.D. 348
	C 60.2 x 24.5 = 75.0 x 24.5 as recombined	Plates XV and XVI

In what, as far as I have ascertained, is the longest private letter surviving among the papyri, Ammon writes from Alexandria to his mother (Senpetechensis, whose Greek name is Nike [**13**.49], the second wife of his father Petearbeschinis[1]) in Panopolis, apparently the matriarch of the family. She has sent Ammon to Alexandria to negotiate pending matters of family concern, and the letter is his report on his progress thus far together with news of his brother Harpocration. His stay in Alexandria on his current mission was clearly quite extended (col. ii.13).

Since the letter anticipates and confirms details and phrases repeated in several drafts of Ammon's petition to the *catholicus* composed in December 348, it must have been written earlier in that same year. It is not only our principal source of information about Ammon's family but is the only independent source for the antecedents of the subsequent court case about the inheritance of Harpocration's slaves.

Fragmentary, much abraded and discolored in some areas, five of the original columns are substantially preserved. These are preceded at the left edge of the

---

[1] Petearbeschinis, high-ranking priest of the Panopolite nome and scion of a line of priests and priestesses, bears a name previously known only from *CPR* XVII B 13.8 (A.D. 217/8) and from the early IV-cent. city-register of Panopolis: V. Martin, *Relevé topographique des immeubles d'une métropole* (*Recherches de Papyrologie* II [1962]) 37–73 = P.Gen. inv. 108, and Z. Borkowski, *Une description topographique des immeubles à Panopolis* (Warsaw 1975) = P.Berl. inv. 16365 I 23. These papyri comprise fragments of 18 columns of the same roll, a topographical register listing the buildings and plots of Panopolis dating probably A.D. 315–320 but possibly 298–330 (Borkowski p.13). Petearbeschinis is there named as father of Petetriphis, who would therefore be a full brother of Horion the *archiprophetes*; a Petetriphis is named three times in Ammon's list of property holdings on the verso of his letter.

papyrus by the righthand margin of a preceding column (here designated col. i) of which only final scattered letters are visible. While it is possible that preceding this there were one or more columns now lost without trace, the tenor of col. ii seems near the beginning of the main substance of the letter. An unrelated text on the verso justifies the supposition that col. i was detached and discarded by Ammon himself, for the verso text, written in the large informal hand he used for his drafts, appears to be complete. With ample right and left margins, it comprises six narrow columns of a list of landholdings, apparently an inventory of the family estate.

The letter is carefully written in Ammon's 'formal' hand, consistently punctuated by a high dot (*stigme*) for full stop and low dot (*hypostigme*) to mark off subordinate clauses; the following transcription reproduces Ammon's dots, the commas are my editorial insertions. Usually he writes final *iota*-adscript for dative singular and third-person singular subjunctive endings but not in medial position. Uniquely and nearly always, even in texts in his draft hand, he marks the final *iota*-adscript of the dative singular ending -αι with a *macron* to distinguish it from short -αι of verbal and first-declension nominative plural endings, possibly revealing a distinction in pronunciation. The transcription again reproduces Ammon's practice. Only rarely does he employ a *koine* form: κατα-λήμψομεν at iii.8, μαθέτωσαν at iv.21 (within a quotation) and παρήμην at vi.14.

As col. ii becomes legible, the family has suffered a reversal of fortune for which Ammon consoles his mother with philosophical assurances that the revolving cycle of fortune will return the family (and all mankind) to prosperity. (Perhaps one may detect here the encroachment of Christianity upon the hieratic family's pagan heritage.) Their problems seem to entail payment of taxes and his mother's difficulties in managing their large estate in Ammon's absence.

Cols. iii and iv contain the heart of the letter, revealing that the chief purpose of Ammon's mission to Alexandria is to deal with the *archiereus* of Egypt on behalf of Horion Junior, whose deceased father, Ammon's elder half-brother Horion, had been *archiprophetes* of the Panopolite nome. No. **4**, a petition to the prefect complaining of malfeasance by the high-priest, is closely related to the account in this letter, but precisely when and how remain unclear because of lacunae in both texts.

From col. iii we learn also that Harpocration is expected to return home invested with high honors and assigned to a very important enterprise. Following immediately is mention of 'the *hegemon* of the Ethiopians', a close friend and daily dinner-companion of Harpocration who has apparently sought Harpocration's aid in appealing to the emperor; juxtaposition suggests that the 'very important enterprise' is somehow directly connected with the Ethiopian's appeal.

At this period 'Aithiopia' would still have meant the Meroitic kingdom of Kush just south of Hiera Sykaminos, between which and Roman Egypt lay the Dodecaschoenus, which in 298 Diocletian had abandoned to the nomad Blemmyes by withdrawing the Roman army northward to Philae.[2] While the latest dated Meroitic document is an inscription at Philae of A.D. 265 and the earliest recording the demise of Meroe is an Axumite inscription of the Christian king Aezanes dated variously *ca* 350–370, whose adversaries in Kush were already the people of Noba, the last of the Kushite pharaohs is believed to have reigned well into the IV century.[3] Presumably in 348 at the time of Ammon's letter, the Meroitic kingdom after its thousand-year history was in final decline, beset by nomadic invaders from east and west and bereft of Roman support on the north. Ammon's letter is thus one of the latest surviving testimonials of the dying kingdom, and the Ethiopian *hegemon* may well have been seeking Roman aid through Harpocration's advocacy.

Col. iv returns to Harpocration's instructions at his departure from Alexandria on 28 April and his promise, never to be fulfilled, to return home to Panopolis in August before the harvest. Of special interest (10–14) is information that he has left with Ammon his three female slaves (παιδία) to be conveyed to Panopolis

---

2 Diocletian's withdrawal of Roman garrisons from the Dodecaschoenus, commonly dated to 297, must be redated to 298 in light of *P.Panop.Beatty* 1; see T.C. Skeat's introduction p.xiv.

3 See W.Y. Adams, *Nubia, Corridor to Africa* (Princeton 1977) ch.13, pp.382–90; P.L. Shinnie, *Meroe, a Civilization of the Sudan* (New York 1967) 52–57; L. Török, "Geschichte Meroes" in *ANRW* II.10.1 (Berlin/New York 1988) 107–341, esp. 284ff. D. Dunham (*Royal Cemeteries of Kush* IV [Boston 1957] 7) hypothesizes the date of the last pharaoh's death as 339, F. Hintze (*Abh.Berlin* 1959.2 p.31) as 320. See also W.B. Emery, *Egypt in Nubia* (London 1965) ch.10 pp.232ff, on the Blemmyes and the Nobatae.

when he returned home and that Ammon meanwhile has consigned them to 'the landlord' to work for their keep; no doubt they were domestics. These are presumably the slaves who after Harpocration's death were claimed by the *delator* Eugeneios, the subject of Ammon's case before the court of the *catholicus* the ensuing December and who appear in several drafts of his petitions published later in this volume: **5**.11f, **6**.6f, **7**.16–20,23,39, **9**.3,30, **10a**.4,17, **10b**.3f,10, **11c**.8,11, **12**.12–17,23,25, **13**.19,40,43f,52,61f, **16b**.3, **18b**.8 (all ἀνδράποδα); **9**.11, **11d**.1, **13**.30ff,65–70, **15**.1, **23b**.4 (all δοῦλοι). At **13**.69f and perhaps at **15**.1 (see notes) there are three δοῦλοι, and at **15**.1 they παρθενεύονται, presumably maid-servants.[4] In the drafts the landlord's name is given as Konon, an Alexandrian friend of Harpocration; perhaps it is with him that Ammon lodges when in Alexandria.

Most urgent of Harpocration's instructions to Ammon concern the appointment of Horion Junior to the *propheteia* formerly held by his deceased father Horion the *archiprophetes*, an appointment Ammon has been pursuing in the normal way by payment of a fee to the *archiereus* of Egypt. Harpocration urges that there is no need to spend more in this pursuit because he will secure the appointment directly from the emperor, relying on the emperor's good will (Constantius II?) and on an otherwise unattested rescript of Diocletian concerning the *propheteia*, of which Ammon gives a copy to his brother. Ammon's effort is documented by his petition to the prefect concerning the *archiereus*, the surviving fragments of which constitute no. **4**.

Col. v returns to domestic problems in Panopolis about which his mother had written. His brother Sarapodoros has spent or lost some part of the family's fortune, for which Ammon tries to console and reassure her with a litany of philosophical declarations derived perhaps from Stoic or Cynic sources. Through ten very lacunose lines col. vi continues in this vein before closing with a long roll-call of greetings to numerous members of his family, especially, after his mother, another 'mother' named Makaria, perhaps his grandmother or an aunt;

---

[4] A small problem is posed by the number of the slaves. In **13**.62f and **16b**.2–4 (cf. **6**.7) they are said to be divided (see p. 63). Since the agreement stipulates equal division, it would seem to follow that there was an even number (four or six) of slaves. If the number of slaves was indeed odd, then possibly the equivalent of half a slave was to be paid in money.

Sarapodoros; still another 'mother' named perhaps Kanea; his nephew Horion Junior with his brothers and mother; his brother and 'partner' Polycrates and his sons. In each case he greets also τὰ παιδία τῆς οἰκίας, no doubt the household servants since at iv.11 he has called Harpocration's household slaves παιδία. Nine more very lacunose lines afford room for greetings to still others.

The numerous improvements in the text from that presented in the *editio princeps* (*P.Congr.XV* 22) have been aided by use of Packard Humanities Institute CD ROM 7, an imaging computer, a binocular microscope, and the useful queries and suggestions of my colleague Peter van Minnen.

Text

col. i

    desunt ca 12 lineae

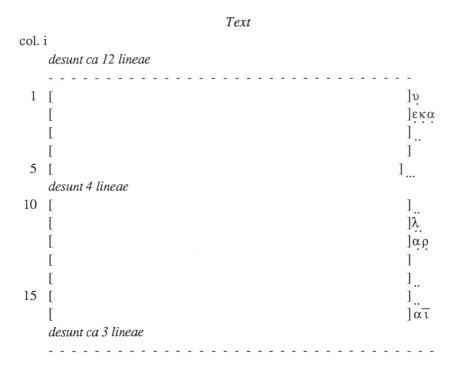

- -

1 [   ]υ

    [   ]εκα

    [   ]..

    [   ]

5 [   ]...

    desunt 4 lineae

10 [   ]..

    [   ]λ

    [   ]αρ

    [   ]

    [   ]..

15 [   ]..

    [   ]α̅ι̅

    desunt ca 3 lineae

- -

col. ii

(margin)

1   ἡ αὐτὴ χ.[   ] του αι[   ]
    ταύτης καὶ [   ]μ φ.[   ]
    [λ]ύπη ετ[.].[   ].ουν.[.].[   ]
    δα γὰρ πο.α.[   ]η καὶ καταγρ[   ]
5   .τας ἀθυμ[   ] διὰ τὴν ἡμ[   ]
    δ.. · οἶδα.[   ] πάλιν αὐτὴν.[   ]
    τηση· αισθ[   ] σὺ μὴ γράψῃς [   ]
    [δ]ύναται τι[   ]ν ἄνω τὴν τ[ύχην πάντων]
    κρατοῦσαν καὶ πᾶσιν πάντα ὁριζο[μένη]ν δεσ[.].[.]ρ[κύκλους]
10 τούτων τῶν ἐ[π]άνω ἡμῶν τοὺς π[αρὰ ἀ]νθρώποις ποτὲ μ[ὲν
        ἀγα]-
    θούς, ποτὲ δὲ καὶ δυσκόλους· ὥσπερ ν[ῦν ἡ]μῖν ὁ κύκλος οὗτος
        δύ[σκολος],
    μετ' ὀλίγον δὲ ἡ[μ]ῖν εἰσέρχεται ὁ βελ[τίω]ν· ἢ σὺ κατὰ σεαυτὴ[ν
        γινώ]-
    σκεις, ὦ μῆτερ, ὅτι καὶ ἀπὸ πρώτου μ[ηνὸς] ἀφ' οὗ ἐξῆλθον τῆς
        πα[τρίδος]
    ἤθελον αὖθις ἐπανελθεῖν πρὸς ὑμῖ[ν, ἀλλ'] οὐχ οὕτως ἔδοξεν τῆι
        [τύχηι]
15 ἀλλ' ἔκρινεν πρὸ[ς] χρόνον με ἀποστῆ[ναι τῆς] πατρίδος· λογίζου
        ο[ὖν ὅτι]
    σὺ τὴν τῆς τύχης ἀνάγκην καὶ [ca 6] ἀθυμοῦσα καὶ φέρε
        τ[·]
    λογίζου ὅτι οὐδὲν ἐφ' ἡμῖν· καὶ ἐπιμε[λοῦ μὲ]ν σεαυτῆς,
        ἐπιμελ[ήσομαι δὲ]
    τῶν πραγμάτων· ⟦γινώσκουσα⟧ ʿκαὶ μάθεʾ ὅτι τ[ύχη ἔ]μπαλιν
        πάντα τἄλλ[α ἡμῖν ἀνα]-
    λύει· εὐθυμ[εῖ]ν οὖν σε χρὴ λ[ο]γιζομ[ένην ὅτι οὐ]κ ἀνεκτός, ὦ
        μῆ[τερ, ὁ κύ]-
20 κλος. ὅμως [ἡσ]υχάζωμεν· οὐκ ἐν δε[   ]ωι ἐσμὲν οὐδὲ
        πε[   ]

Translation

col. ii

... [Fortune] [9]holding sway [over all] and determining all things for all men ... [the cycles] [10]of those above us, sometimes beneficent, sometimes also harsh towards men. Just as now this cycle is harsh to us, but soon a better cycle is coming for us. Surely you realize, Mother, that from the first month of my absence from my homeland I wanted to return again to you, but Fortune did not so decree [15]but decided that I remain absent from my homeland for some time. Consider therefore, that as you [have borne without?] despair the necessity of Fortune, so bear [the present circumstances]. Consider that nothing is in our power. And take care of yourself and I shall look after our affairs. And understand that [Fortune?] again is going to resolve all other affairs [for us]. Therefore you must be of good heart (though) reckoning, Mother, that the cycle is unendurable. [20]Nevertheless, let us be calm. We are not in [prison?] nor

οὐδὲ ἐν χερ[σ]ὶ λῃστῶν· ἀλλ᾽ ἐν ἐχ[υρότητι] πάσῃι· εἰ δὲ διὰ
　　τὰ [　　　]
ἀθυμεῖς ὡ[ς τ]αῦτα διοικεῖν οὐ δύν[ασαι ὑπὲρ τῶ]ν υἱῶν. λέγω
　　μη[　　]
ὅταν χρεία σ[οι] ἦι μεταπέμψαι [　　　　　　]ων τῶν ἐμῶν
　　κα[　]
[　]υ τὸ νόμιμ[ο]ν ἀπαιτηταῖς καὶ[　　　　　]εσται προσ [.]...
　　[　　]
25 ἕκαστος ἰδ[ί]αν [φ]ροντίδα ἔχει [　　　　] σὺ πέμψῃς
　　ἐπιτη[　　]
χρείᾱ σοι· οὐδ[ε]ὶς ἀφ᾽ ἑαυτο[ῦ　　]ται ἐλθεῖν πρ [.] [　　　]
ἑαυτοῦ λέσχας· μάλιστα π[　　]ι πάντες ἀνετράπη[σαν διὰ]
τὰς π[α]ραγραφὰς καὶ τα[　　τῶ]ν λοιπάδων· μὴ ὀκ[νήσῃς]
μηδὲ αἰδεσ[θ]ῇς μετ[απέμψαι　　ο]υς ὅταν σοι χρεία ἦι [　　]
30 ἀποδημοῦντο[ς ἐμοῦ　　　　]αι μετὰ τα[ῦτα] καὶ η [　　]
υἱῶι ἀναβῶμ[εν　　　　] καὶ ἔτι [　]οι[　] [　　]
[　]ησαι περὶ τ[　　　　] οὐκ ἐρα[　]ην μ[.] [　　]
[　] χ υἱὸν· δι[　　　　]α καὶ π[...] ησα [　　]
　　　　(margin)

———

21 αλλ᾽ pap.　　25 ϊδ[ ]αν pap.

col. iii
　　　　(margin)
1 [.]πι φ ὅστις γὰρ ....[　　　　　　]
ἀπαιτηθήσεται· οὐ γὰρ [.] ...[　　　　　]
μὴ τὰς ὕβρεις καὶ τὰς ἀδικίας τὰς [　　　]
[.] πονηρὰν φημοσύνην ἀγοντι [　　　　]
5 [　　　]α μανθάνει ὅτι εἰς κακ [　　　　]
[　　σ]τρατ[η]γῶι ἃ ὤφειλεν διὰ τ[　　　]
[　　　] ηι· ἀλλ᾽ εἰ ... ἐγχωρεῖ [　　　　]
λαβω[　] · ἤδη δὲ καταλήμψομεν [　　πρᾶ]-
γμα τὸ τοῦ [　]ιου ἐκπλέκεται ἡμῖν· ἦν γὰρ πρὸ τούτου τ[....]..

... nor in the hands of brigands but are in complete security. But if you are discouraged because of the ... that you are not able to manage these affairs for your sons, I say do not [hesitate], whenever you have need, to send for some?] of my [friends/brothers?] and ... [pay?] to the tax-collectors what is lawful and ... 25each person has his own concern ... [that] you send ... at your need. Nobody of his own accord [wants?] to encounter vain talk [about] himself. Especially ... all were upset [because of] the marginal entries and the [... with the] arrears. Don't hesitate and don't be embarrassed to [send for my friends/brothers?] whenever you have need. ... 30while I am away from home ... after this and ... [*Remnants of three lines*]

col. iii

1... whoever ..... 2will be demanded, for not ... 3lest the outrages and and the wrongs which ... 4grievous pronouncement ... 5he is learning that to ... 6to the *strategos* what he owed because of ..., 7but if he allows ..., 8and already we shall find ... 9the matter of the ... is being untangled for us, for before this ...

10   ὁ ἀρχιερεὺς περὶ τὰ μέρη τῆς κάτω χ[ώρα]ς· ἐξῆλθεν γὰρ ἀπ[ὸ
       Φα]μενὼθ κ̄.

    εἰσῆλθεν δὲ εἰς Ἀλεξάνδρειαν τῆι ἑ[ορτῆ]ι τῆ λ̄ Φαρμοῦθι· κ[αὶ]
       μετὰ τὴν

    ἑορτὴν [ ]⳹⳹ διοικηθῆναι τὸ πρᾶγμα ποιήσω· καὶ ἤδη
       διο[ικ]ηθήσεται

    ἐν ταῖ[ς ⳹⳹] αὐταῖς ἡμέραις· καὶ τὰ γράμματα παραλαβὼν ⳹⳹ σ᾽
       εὐθέως

    καταλαμβάνω θεῶν βουλομένων, εἰδέναι δέ σε ἀνὰ [μέσ]ον καὶ
       τοῦ -

15   το, ὅτι μετ᾽ ἀξιώματος πολλοῦ ὁ Ἁρποκρᾶς εἰς τὴν πατρίδα τ[ὴν]
       ἑαυτοῦ ἐπαν-

    ελθεῖν μέλλει· καὶ πάλιν ἤρξατο ἡ τύχη [α]ὐτὸν ἀνεγεῖραι·
       τοῖ[ς γ]ὰρ ἀεὶ θεοῖς

    [ἔ]στι φ[ίλο]ς οὗτος· καὶ ὅταν μὲν κατωθῆι. εἰς μέτρι[α δ᾽]
       ἀναβαίνει·

    [κ]αὶ [ὅ]ταν [⳹⳹]ησῃ. εἰς μεγάλα πάλ[ιν] ἀναβαίνει· γράμ[ματ]α
       οὖν αὐτῶι

    [ἐπέ]μ[φθ]η ἀπὸ φίλων τινων πα[ρ]ά τινων μεγά[λων
       ἀ]νθρώπων

20   [   ]⳹⳹ ταῦτα τὰ γράμματα ἐπὶ πρᾶξιν μεγίστην· ἤ[δ]η γὰρ καὶ
       αὐτὸς

    [   ] [γρά]μματα τῶι ἡγεμ[όν]ι τῶν Αἰθιόπων ⳹⳹ ομένωι πρὸς
       τ[ὸν]

    [βασιλ]έα· καὶ γὰρ πάνυ φίλος αὐ[το]ῦ γέγονεν καὶ καθ᾽ ἡ[μ]έραν
       μετ᾽ αὐτοῦ

    [συνεδ]είπνει· καὶ οἶδεν ῾τ᾽αὖ[τα] ὁ Πεκῦσις· καὶ πρὸς τοὺ[ς
       φί]λους σὺν τοῖς ἐμο[ῖς]

    [α]ὐτῶι γράμματα καὶ [ ] [⳹⳹]κα ἵνα αὐτῶι πρα[   ] ⳹⳹⳹

25   [   ] καὶ παρὰ τῶν φίλων Αἰθιόπων πρὸς αὐτὸν [τὰ γράμ]ματα
       παρ᾽ ὑ[μῶν]

    [   ]῾καὶ παρὰ [τ]οῦ Αἰθίοπος·᾽ καὶ ἤδη πάλιν ἐξῆλθεν εἰς τὸ
       κομιτᾶτο[ν·   ]ν δ᾽ ἐβουλό-

[10]the high-priest was [occupied] in the regions of the low country, for he had been gone since the 20th? of Phamenoth (16 March?). But he came to Alexandria for the festival on the 30th of Pharmouthi (25 April), and after the festival I myself shall cause the matter to be settled; and now it will be settled during these same days. And as soon as I receive the documents I will meet you the gods willing; meanwhile <I want> you know this too, that [15]with great honor Harpokras is about to return to his own homeland. And Fortune has again begun to raise him up, for he is dear to the eternal gods. And whenever everything abases him, he rises to moderate success, and whenever [that happens], he rises up again to greatness. So letters from certain friends [sent to] him from certain great persons [20]... these letters [summon him?] to a very important mission. For already he himself too [has written?] a letter for the governor of the Ethiopians ... to [the emperor?], for he has become his close friend and dined with him daily. Pekusis too knows this. And to his friends together with my own [I have shown] the letters to him in order that [they may act?] for him [25]... and from the Ethiopian friends the letters from you and from the Ethiopian. And already he (Harpocration) has returned to the imperial court (*comitatus*).

[μην αὐτὸ]ν κατασχεῖν καὶ οὐκ [ἐ]δ[υν]ήθην· ο̣ι̣ [   ]ν̣·
       οὐδ̣.[.]

[   ]ωι ἔλεγον ἐπὶ μεγάλα α̣[ὐ]τὸν καλοῦ[ντες   ].̣.[.]

[   ] ταῦτ᾿ [ο]ὐδ[.]   *traces*   [   ].̣.̣.[   ]

30 [   ]ομένου̣ .[.].̣[.̣.̣.[.̣[.].̣[   ]

[   ] εἰς πραγ[.̣.̣]..̣.̣[   ].̣[   ]

[   ] ἀνθρωπ[.̣.̣.].̣[.].̣[.].̣[   ]

[   ]θ̣ιουκ[.].̣.̣[.].̣.̣[   ].̣[   ]

[   ].̣αρ̣.[.].̣[   ]

(margin)

---

7 αλλ᾿ pap.   24 ϊνα pap.   25 πα̣ϋ[pap.

col. iv

(margin)

1 [*ca 23*   ].̣.̣εντ̣[.̣]λ̣[.̣.̣].̣.̣[.].̣[   ]

[   ] τῆς οἰ[κ]ίας ε[.̣.̣].̣[.̣.̣]ιουχ̣[.]̣[.̣.̣[.̣.̣.̣]δρα[   ]

[   ]ει τοῦτο ὑπα[.̣] [.̣.̣]σας αρ[*ca 8*   ]αν[   ]

[   ]ποτηι οἵ τε [πα]ρ̣᾿ Ἀ[πί]ωνος [ἡγεμ]ονεύσαν[τ]ο̣ς

5 [   ] τοῦτο ἀπο[*ca 8*   ]ειας̣ [.̣]̣[.̣.̣.̣] ἡμερῶν

       τῶ]ν ἡμερῶν [.̣.̣]λ̣[.̣]μο̣.̣[   ].̣ [ἐ]ὰν δὲ π[.̣]̣υ̣

[   ]ν ἐστιν ω[.̣.̣.] μουσα̣.̣[   ]ν ναυτικὸν

[πολ]υπραγμον[εῖ]ν καὶ ἐξετάσαι ε̣[.̣.̣.̣]πεν αὐτάς·

ἔλεγεν οὖν καὶ [*ca 10*   ].̣[.̣]ς ὅτι ἐὰν θεὸς θέληι κατα[λαμβ]άνω
       ὑμᾶς

10 εἰς Πανὸς ἄχρι Μ[εσο]ρὴ πρὸ τῆς τρύγης· γ̅ γὰρ τοῦ Παχὼν
       ἀπε[λθὼ]ν̣ κατέλει-

[π]εν δέ μοι ἐντα[ῦθα] τὰ παιδία αὐτοῦ ἐπεὶ θ[η]λυκά ἐστιν·
       [επει] ἐπ[ε]νετείλατό

μοι ἀνενεγκεῖν αὐτὰ̣ εἰς Πανὸς μετ᾿ ἐμ̣[ο]ῦ· τρεῖς δέ εἰσιν Φοί[νικ]ε̣ς
       καὶ ἀνα-

φέρω αὐτὰς ἀνερχόμενος· τέως μέντοι παρὰ τῶι σταθμούχ[ωι]
       εἰσιν ἐργαζό-

At that time I wished to hold him back and I couldn't. [*Remnants of seven lines*]

col. iv

[*Remnants of three lines*]

[4]... to the [emperor?/prefect?] both the (agents?) of Apion the former prefect [*remnants of three more lines*]

... the sailor [8]... to be busy and to investigate whether he [left?] them. He said therefore ... "if god wills I (shall) meet you [10]in Panopolis in Mesore (August) before the harvest." For departing on the 3rd of Pachon (28 April) he left his slaves behind here with me since they are female. He directcd me to bring them up with me to Panopolis. There are three, Phoenicians, and I am bringing them up when I come. Meanwhile, however, they are with the landlord

μεναι εἰς τὰς τροφὰς ἑαυτῶν· μέλλων δὲ ἐξελθεῖν πολλά [μοι]
    ἐ[π]ετρέψατο
15 ἀναβῆναι ἤδη εἰς Πανὸς λέγων ὅτι εἰς τί [κ]αὶ ἀναλίσκεις ἄλλα
    τινὰ ἐπὶ τοῦ
ἀρχιερέως ἕως λάβῃς τὴν τάξιν τῶι [π]αιδί· τί δὲ ὅλως [ ] διάγεις
    προσ-
ελθεῖν τάξει ἀρχ[ιερ]έως περὶ τούτου· δεῖ γάρ με πάντως ἔξω
    π[αρ]ὰ τοῦ βασιλέως
λαβεῖν αὐτῶ[ι, καὶ] ὤμοσεν ἐπάνω τῆς θαλάσσης μέλλω[ν
    ε]ἰσβῆναι εἰς τὸ
πλοῖον ὅτι κἂν λάβῃς παρὰ ἀρχιερέως ἐ[ά]ν τε μή, ἐγὼ παρ[ὰ
    το]ῦ βασιλέως
20 λαμβάνω τῶι παιδὶ τὴν τάξιν· καὶ οὐδεὶς ἄλλος φανήσετα[ι ἐν]
    Πανὸς πόλει
προφήτης Ὠ[ρί]ωνος ἀποθανόντος εἰ μὴ ὁ παῖς Ὠρ[ί]ω[νος]·
    μαθέτωσ[α]ν
οὖν τὴν ἑαυτῶν [τ]ύχην ἐκεῖνοι οἱ θεοῖς ἐχθροί· καὶ γὰρ [ἔλαβ]εν
    παρ' ἐμοῦ
τὰ ἴσα τῶν γ[ρα]μ[μ]άτων τῶν βασιλικῶν τῶν περὶ τῆ[ς
    προ]φητείας· οὐ-
[δε]⸢δὲν δὲ ἰσχύει [πρὸ]ς τὰ γράμματα τὰ Διοκλητιανοῦ· ἐγὼ δὲ′
    τέως αὐτ[ὸς παρὰ] τοῦ ἀρχιερέως λαμβάνω τὸ
    μέρος [κα]τὰ [τ]ὰ γράμματ[α]
25 τὰ Διοκλητ[ιανοῦ] καὶ ἤδη λαμβάνω· α[ὐ]τὸς γάρ μοι ὁ
    ἀρ[χιερεὺς] προσέπεμψεν
μετανοήσα[ς διότι] καὶ ἐχύλωσεν προστάτου τὸν χρόνο[ν
    ca 6   ]ν δὲ καὶ αὐτὸς
φοβηθεὶς [τὰ γρά]μματα τὰ βα[σιλ]ικὰ π[ρο]σδοκᾷ οὐδ[   ]   ἐὰν
    θεὸς θέλῃ
ἐμοῦ μ[ca 6   π]αρουσίαν με[ ]π[   ] [ ] καὶ τοῦ ἀδ[ελφοῦ
    ἀφ]ιξομένου τοῦ κ[   ]
εχ [   ] [ ] υκε[   ]α[   ] [ ]ντες· ε [τ]ὴν δὲ σ[ο]ὶ
    ἐπιστο-

working for their own keep. As he was about to depart he gave me many instructions, [15]to go up now to Panopolis, saying "Why are you spending still more money with the high-priest in order to get the office for the boy, why in short ... do you continue to approach the high-priest's office [for the boy?] about this? For I ought to get it abroad from the emperor for him," and at the sea when he was about to embark on the boat he swore, "Whether you receive it from the high-priest or not, [20]I (will) get the office for the boy from the emperor; and after Horion's death no other person will be appointed prophet in Panopolis except the son of Horion. Let those hostile to the gods therefore learn their own fate." For he received from me the copies of the imperial rescript about the office of prophet. Nothing prevails against the letter of Diocletian. I myself meanwhile shall get the portion from the high-priest in accordance with [25]Diocletian's rescript, and already I am receiving it. For the high-priest himself has sent to me after changing his mind [because] he had also used up(?) the term(?) of an administrator. But now also he himself in fear awaits the imperial document ... if god wills, my ... presence ... and (my) brother about to arrive ...[*Remnants of six lines*]

30 [λὴν   ] φείσασ[θ]α[ι ͙ ͙ ͙] ασι ͙[   ]ν ἀποδ[ ] ͙[ ]η[   ]
   [ἀν]αγκαίου [   ] ͙[   ] ͙λη ͙[ ] ͙[   ]
   [   ]εχων δ[   ] ͙[   ] ιον ͙[   ]
   [   ] ͙ ͙ τα ͙[͙]͙[   ]αῑ κα[   ]
   [   ]α ͙[   ]μιν ο ͙[   ]

(margin)

---

16 *supra* ολως *spir.asp.* (Type 2 Turner) pap.   23 ϊσα pap.   24 ϊσχυει pap.

col. v

(margin)

1   ͙ ͙[͙ ͙] ει[͙] ͙[͙]αν ` ͙ ͙[ ]′ μεν[   ] ͙[   ] ει ͙[   ]
   [͙ ͙ ͙ ͙]το[͙] ͙[͙] ͙ ͙ αὐτου[͙]ι[   ]κα[   ]εις ͙[   ]
   [͙ ͙]ω γραψ[ὅ]τι ὑγιῆ κλα ͙[*ca 8*]θ ͙[*ca 6*]τηδ[   ]
   [͙ ͙] χρεία ε[*ca 6*] ὡς ἀναβάντος [͙ ͙]οδ[͙ ͙] στη ͙[͙] ͙[   ]
5 ἔγραψας δέ [μοι ὦ μ]ῆτερ ἐν ταῖς αὐ[ταῖς ͙ ͙ ͙] ἐπ[ιστο]λαῖς ὅτι
                Σα[ραπόδωρός τινα]
   ἀνήλωσ[ε] τ[ῶν] πατρῴων· ε[*ca 9*] ͙[*ca 7*]ελει τῶν α ͙[   ]
   οὐ[δ]ὲν γὰρ ἴ[διον ἄ]νθρωπος ἔχει [*ca 6*]α[*ca 6*]η[͙]· καὶ αὐτὴ
         [*ca 10*   ]
   ὅτε βούλετα[ι ͙ ͙ ͙ ͙] καὶ ἀφαιρεῖται [πάλ]ιν · ἐάν τ[ις εὐλα]βηθῇ τὰ
                πατρ[ῷα   , οὐ]
   πάντως εὐ[τυχεῖ] εἰς ὅλον τὸν βί[ον· οὐ]δὲ ὁ μὴ σ[ῴζω]ν ταῦτα
                πάν[τως ἄπο]ρο[ς]
10 γίνεται εἰς τ[ὸν βί]ον σύμπαντ[α] ἀλλὰ καὶ πολλ[οὶ μ]ηδὲν ἐκ τῶν
                π[ατρ]ῴων παρ[α]-
   λαβόντες η[ὐτύ]χησαν καὶ εὐπορώτατοι ἐν τῶι [βίω]ι γεγόνασιν·
                ὥ[στ]ε οὐ πάν[τως]
   λυποῦμαι διό[τι] ἀπώλεσά τινα [τῶ]ν πατρῴων[· ο]ὐδ᾽ ἐὰν εἴπῃς
                ὅτι σοὶ ἀποδώσω
   ταῦτα παρηγορ[εῖς] με ἐν τούτωι· ἀλλὰ μόνον μοι γίνοιτο ἰδεῖν σέ
                γ[ε] καὶ πάντα
   ἔχω· γένοιτ[ο σὲ] ἐν τῆι οἰκίαῑ τῆι ἐμῆι εὑρεθῆναι ἔτι κ[α]ὶ οὐδὲν
                ἀπώλεσα· εὐτυχῶ

col. v

[Remnants of four lines]

[5]You wrote [to me] in the same letters that Sa[rapodoros] had spent [some] of the patrimony ... For a man has nothing of his own ... [apart from Fortune?], and she [gives] when she wishes and takes away again. If one takes care [not to lose] his patrimony [he is not] completely fortunate throughout his entire life. He who fails to preserve it does not become altogether without means [10]for his whole life, but also many who have inherited nothing from their patrimony have had good fortune and have been very prosperous in life; and so I do not altogether grieve that I have lost some of the patrimony. Not even if you say "I shall repay you" do you console me in this. But only may it be granted at least to see you and I shall have everything. May it befall [me] to be found in my own household again and I shall have lost nothing. I am fortunate

15 πάντα καὶ ηὐ[δαιμόν]ησα ἐὰν εὐρωστοῦσάν σε εὕρω[· το]ῦτο γὰρ
        ἀεὶ εὔχ[ο]μαι ὦ μῆ[τ]ερ,
    ʽμαρτυροῦσιν [οἱ θε]οὶ οἱ τὰ πάντα ὁ[ρ]ῶντες· αὕτη᾽ μοι μόνη ἡ
        [. . .]τη ἐλπίς· τοῦ[τό] μοι μέγιστον [εὐτύ]χημα ἐὰν
        ὑγι[αίν]ουσαν τὴν
    μητέρα εὕρω [ἐπι]δημήσας τῆ[ι πα]τρίδι· διὰ σὲ π[αρ]ὰ τῆς
        πατρίδος ἀπ[εδ]ήμησα· διὰ
    σὲ καὶ [[εἰς]] τὴν οἰ[κία]ν μου πάνυ ʽκα[τελθ]εῖν᾽ ἐζ[ήτη]σα καὶ
        ζητῶ [· τόδ]ε μόνον σε ὑπ[ομι]μνήσκω,
    ὦ μῆτερ· ἐπε[ὶ ἄ]λλα αὐτὸς ἐκάμ[νον] εἰς τὸν λάκ[κον ὅτ]ι σχεδὸν
        διὰ τὴν ἐμὴν ἐπ[ι]-
20 μέλειαν ἀνά[γκ]η φροντίζεσ[θαι ὡ]ς μὴ τοὺς [ἡμετέ]ρ[ο]υς
        καρποὺς [π]αραλάβω[σ]ι
    μόνοι· πολυπρ[α]γμόνει οὖν περ[ὶ τῶ]ν φόρων κ[αὶ] πέμψον ἐκεῖ
        τ[ιν]α ἐπισκέψα-
    σθαι· καὶ τ[ο]ὺς [κ]οινωνούς μου [ἤ]δη μετάπεμ[ψα]ι Πολυκράτη
        τε κ[αὶ] τὸν
    προστά[τη]ν [ὡς] ὑπομνησο[μένο]υς καὶ περ[ὶ τ]οῦ ἡμετέρου
        [ca 7   ]
    πονεῖ[ν], τοὺς μὲν πόνους [ ]αυ[ ]ης ὑποστῆ[σαι] σύμπαντας
        [. .][ ][. .] , [τοὺς]
25 δ᾽ ἐμοὺ[ς ἐπὶ] τῶν καρπῶν· [γρ]άψω δὲ ἤδη [χει]ρὶ ἰδίαι τοῖς φ[ίλοις
        ἵνα ἡμῖν κοι]-
    νωνῶ[σ]ι περὶ τού[τ]ου· ἐ[πεὶ] ἤδη καὶ ὁ και[ρὸ]ς τῆς συγκο-
        μιδῆ[ς   ]
    καὶ τάχ[α] συμβαίνει μὴ ἀπολ⟨ε⟩ιφθῆναι τηνι[κάδ]ε καὶ
        καταλαμ[βάνειν σε κατὰ τὸν τῆς]
    συγκ[ομι]δῆς καιρόν· ἀλλὰ [ἴ]σως μὴ α[. . .]· [. . .]χε σὲ καὶ τὸν
        ἀδε[λ]φ[όν] μ[ου]
    Σαραπ[όδω]ρον εἰς τὰς ἀπαιτήσε[ις τ]ῶν φ[όρων ἀπὸ] τῆς
        Ἀραβίας ο [. .] [   ]
30 . [.] ʽ [ ]᾽ [. .]α· καὶ ἐάν σοι φῇ κ[α]ὶ ἐμοὶ . . [. π]αρόντος
        ἀποδ . [. .] . . [   ]

[15]in all things and have become truly happy if I find you in strong health. For I ever pray for this, Mother, the gods who see all things are my witness, (you) alone my [greatest] hope: this will be my greatest good fortune if I find my mother well when I return to my homeland. Because of you I departed from my native city; also because of you I have eagerly sought and do seek to return to my house.

But [now?] this only do I call to your attention, Mother; when [on other occasions?] I worked at the silo, it is necessary [20]because of my own concern so to speak I had to take heed that they on their own do not appropriate our harvests, therefore busy yourself about the revenues and send someone there to investigate. And do you now send for my partners, both Polycrates and the steward, that they may be mindful also to be diligent about our ..., to support all your own efforts ... [25]and my own [concerning] the harvest. I shall write now in my own hand to my friends [that they may] act in concert [with us] about this. Since now too the time of the harvest [approaches], perhaps it (will) turn out that (I/he) not be left behind then and (will) meet [you/us?] at harvest-time. But perhaps ... And [dispatch?] my brother Sarapodoros to the collection of the rents from Arabia ... [30]and if he says to you

```
[        ]ωι τὰς ἀμ[ο]ιβὰς ἐξ[        ] · οἶδεν γὰρ καὶ α[        ]
[        ] μὴ ὀκνή[σ]ῃς ε [        ]ισαι ἄλλους τινὰς [        ]
[        ]α ἦι· οἶδα δ[ὲ ὅ]τι [        ] ὑπὸ σοῦ κληθε[        ]
[        ]θανομε [        τοῖ]ς φίλοις ἰδίοι[ς        ]
35 [        ]  ̣  ̣ ̣̣  ̣`ἐγὼ [        Τ]αυρίνωι νῦν´  ̣  ̣ ̣̣[        ]νον
                  ὅτι σὺ [        ]
```

(margin)

---

7 ϊ[pap.   13 ϊδειν pap.   16 ἀυτη pap.   25 ϊδιαϊ pap.   34 ϊδιοι[pap.

col. vi

(margin)

```
1   ειν  ̣ ̣[τὰ]ς ἐμὰς μερίμνας ἔχει.  ̣ισ [ ̣] ̣[        ]
    τραπ ̣[ ̣] καὶ ἀδελφικαὶ φι[λίαι]  ̣ ̣ ̣[ ca 6 ] [        ]
    ἔγραψα ἵνα μὴ ὑμᾶς καὶ [ἄ]λλα[ς  ̣ ̣] ἀδελφ[ ̣ ̣] ̣ ̣[        ]
    [ ̣]ημ  ̣ · ἐπεὶ οὖν σὺ καὶ  ̣[  ̣ ̣ ἄ]λλο [ ̣] [        ]
5    ̣ριους καὶ πάσας ἄλ[λα]ς· π  ̣[ ̣ ̣ ̣]ις τὰ[ς ἐπισ]τολὰς
    τὰ[ς] ἐμὰς διὰ  ̣ ̣ ̣ ̣ ̣[ ̣ ̣] γράφω ἵνα σοι  ̣[ ̣] ̣ ̣[        ]
     ̣[ ̣] ̣[ ̣] οἶδα [γὰ]ρ [ ̣] σ ̣ν πο ̣ ς κολ ̣ ̣ ̣ ̣[        ]
     ̣ ̣ ̣ικω[ ̣] ̣ τουπ ̣ λως εὑρήσεις·        traces
    ιν[  ̣]ωνων [ ̣] ἴστε· καὶ παρηγορήσει ̣ ̣ ̣ ι τὴν μητέρα
10   ̣[ ̣] καὶ γ[ ̣ ̣ ̣]ου σχεδὸν πάρεστιν· καὶ παραβαλῶ
    αὐτῆι συνεχῶς· καὶ μηδὲ ὅλως αὐτὴν ἀθύμω[ς]  ̣[        ] -
    σῃς· τὸ αὐτὸ δὲ τοῦτ[ο] καὶ τῆι κυρίᾱ μου μ[ητ]ρὶ
    Μακαρίᾱ ἐντέλλομαι. εἰ μὴ ἄρα ἡμῶν ἐπελάθετο·
    καὶ ἐνετειλάμην πολλάκις καὶ ὅτε παρήμην καὶ
15  διὰ γραμμάτων ὅτε [ἀ]πεδήμησα παρηγορήσα[ς τ]ὴν
    μητέρα ἕως σὺν θε[οῖ]ς αὐτὴν καταλάβωμεν·
            ἐρρῶσθα[ί σε ε]ὔχομαι, μῆτερ κυρία,
    ἀσπάζομαι πολλὰ [τὸ]ν κύριόν μου ἀδελφὸν
    Σαραπόδωρον καὶ [ἀσπ]άζομαι τὴν μητέρα μου
20  Μακαρίαν καὶ τὴν μητέρα Κα ̣αν καὶ Ὡρίωνα
    τὸν νεώτερον [σὺ]ν τοῖς ἀ[δελ]φ[ο]ῖς καὶ [τῆι]
    μητρὶ καὶ τὰ [πα]ιδία τῆς οἰκίας, ἀσπαζο-
```

... the payments ..., for he knows also ... do not hesitate ... some others ... ;
but I know that ... called by you ... to the personal friends [35]... I myself ... to
Taurinos now ... that you ...

col. vi

[1]... to have my concerns ... and brotherly affections ... I have written in order
that [he?] may not ... you and other ... Since therefore you also [5]... and all
others; ... my letters? through the sailor? I write in order to ... to you ... For I
know ... you will find; ... he will comfort ... [your?] mother [10]and ... he is
almost present and I/he? will come to her forthwith; and do not let her be altogether disheartened. This same thing I enjoin also my revered mother Makaria, if
indeed she has not forgotten us; and I have often enjoined her both when I was
present and [15]through letters when I was away, consoling my mother until with
the gods' help we may meet her.

I pray for your health, honored Mother. I send many greetings to my
honored brother Sarapodoros and I greet my mother [20]Makaria and mother
Ka..a and Horion the younger together with his brothers and his mother
and the slaves of his house;

μαι καὶ τὸν ἀδελφόν μου Π[ολ]υ[κρά]τη καὶ [το]ὺ[ς]
υἱοὺς καὶ τὰ π[αιδ]ία τ[ῆς] οἰκ[ίας α]ὐτο[ῦ]
25 κ[α]ὶ κατὰ δύναμιν σὺν κ ̣ [̣] α ̣ [   ]
καὶ [   ] ̣ ας κα[ὶ ἀσπ]άζομα[ι   ca 6   ] ̣ ̣ ̣
[   ] ̣ ̣ [τ]οὺς φ[ι]λ[ο]ῦντάς σε πάντας·
[   ] ̣ [   ]δ[̣] [̣] ̣ [̣] [̣] [̣] ̣ ̣ ̣
[   ]ν φ[   ]της πρ ̣ [̣]   ca 7   [   ]
30 [   ]ια ̣ η ̣ [̣] ̣ μη· ̣ [̣] [̣] ̣ ̣ [   ]
[   ] ̣ [̣] [̣]   ca 6   [   ]
[   ] ̣ [̣] ηι ̣ ̣ ̣ [   ]
[   ] ̣ ̣ [   ]

- -

———
6 ϊνα pap.   9 ϊστε· pap.

Notes

col. ii

8. τι̣[or η[.

8f. Context suggests that the participles modify τύχην (or μοῖραν) lost at the end of line 8. At the end of 9 possibly δέσπ[ο]ιναν, after which the long descender suggests *rho* or *phi*; δεσπότειραν might also be possible, though a much rarer word; Maresch suggests possibly ὀρίζο[υσα]ν δεσ[μοῦσαν τοὺς κύκλους]. In three VI-cent. papyri from Aphrodito the phrase ἡ κρατοῦσα τύχη means the emperor (cf. *P.Lond.* V 1663.8 n.), a meaning possible but unlikely here; to date ὁριζομένη has not occurred elsewhere with τύχη.

10ff. Probably [ἀγα]|θούς, modifying κύκλους restored at the end of line 9. Though κύκλος can mean 'circle' of men or 'cycle' of time or events, the latter seems appropriate here. The cycle of Fortune is presaged in the tract *Asclepius* from the *Corpus Hermeticum*, of which a Latin translation of the Greek original was known and quoted by Lactantius at the beginning of the IV century: cf. *Corp. Herm.* ed. by A.D. Nock and A.-J. Festugière II (Budé ed., Paris 1945) pp.327–31. Cf. also Marcus Aurelius, *Med.* 9.28 ταῦτά ἐστι τὰ τοῦ κόσμου ἐγκύκλια, ἄνω κάτω, ἐξ αἰῶνος εἰς αἰῶνα.

I greet also my brother Polycrates and his sons and the slaves of his house, 25and ... as possible with ... and I greet ... all those who love you. .....

[*Remnants of six lines*]

13. Ammon's business in Alexandria has occupied at least two months.

14. At end the traces of τῆι might equally fit τῶι, but [τύχηι], suggested by H. Maehler, is conjectured from context; J. Shelton proposed τῶι [δαίμονι].

15f. At end, ὅτι] or ὅπως]; cf. 17 λογίζου ὅτι; Maresch suggests rather καὶ]. At 16 preceding ἀθυμοῦσα, perhaps [ἤνεγκας οὐκ] and at end τ[ὰ νῦν] or τ[αῦτα]; cf. Men. *Sent.* 657 (Jaekel, 812 Kock) πειρῶ τύχης ἄνοιαν ἀνδρείως (εὐχερῶς Meineke) φέρειν. If ὅτι] is omitted at 15, perhaps [λῆγε] or [παύου] ἀθυμοῦσα (Maresch).

19f. Perhaps ὁ κύ]ικλος may be supplied, but there is no room for a verb; as 18f are reconstructed, a pronoun like οὗτος would have no antecedent. An alternative word-division might be] κἂν ἐκτός.

20. δ[εσμωτηρί]ωι would fit the space.

22. Perhaps μὴ [ὀκνήσηις] or simply μῆ[τερ.

23f. Perhaps κα[ὶ καταβα]ι[λο]ῦ 'and pay'. On ἀπαιτηταί see B. Palme, *Das Amt des ἀπαιτητής in Ägypten* (MPER 20, 1989) pp.67–77; the source and date of his no.478 p.217 should now be revised.

24. At mid-line either]εσται or]σθαι.

25. Perhaps ἐπιτή[δεια τῆι].

26. Possibly βούλε]ται and πρὸ[ς] τ[ὰς περὶ].

28. Perhaps μετὰ τῶ]ν λοιπάδων, a common phrase.

31. ἀναβῶμ[εν or ἀναβῶ μ[ετὰ e.g.; ἔτι [or ἐγρ [or ἐτρ [.

31ff. Here the main purpose of Ammon's mission to Alexandria may be introduced, for υἱῶι at 31 and υἱὸν at 33 probably refer to Horion II, the son of Horion the *archiprophetes*, perhaps recently deceased.

col. iii

3. Perhaps wrongs committed (or expected to be committed) by the *archiereus*; cf. **4**.30.

4. Though φημοσύνη is a very rare word, no other reading appears to fit the surviving traces.

6. The *strategos* served as local representative of the *archiereus* and as a conduit for fees paid by priests such as the initiation fee, the *eiskritikon*.

9. Following the prior lacuna either]ιου or]ρου, for in this hand a long descender with a leftward finial is characteristic of only *iota* and *rho*; if the former, ἱε[ροταμ]ίου 'temple treasurer' may be possible. At line-end perhaps τ[οῦ μην]ὸς.

10. No doubt the *archiereus* of Alexandria and All Egypt is meant, the high Roman official who from the middle of the III century had inherited the authority to award priesthoods to the highest bidder regardless of the hereditary rights of priests. As the high-ranking civil, not religious, official responsible to the imperial government for fiscal control of the temples and their clergy, his religious allegiance, possibly even Christian at this time, would have been immaterial. In col. iv Ammon negotiates with him seeking the appointment of Horion II to succeed his father as *prophetes* and about interim payment of τὸ μέρος of the *propheteia*. χ[ώρα]ς was first suggested by H. Maehler. On this controversy with the high-priest see further no. **4**, a petition for redress from him.

11. The restoration ἑ[ορτῆ]ι was suggested by J. Shelton. The festival was presumably the Sarapeia, celebrated in many parts of Egypt and beginning on 30 Pharmouthi (cf. *P.Stras.* VI 559.14 n. [*ca* A.D. 315]). See F. Perpillou-Thomas, *Fêtes d'Égypte ptolémaïque et romaine d'après la documentation papyrologique grecque* (Studia Hellenistica 31, 1993) pp.129–36.

12. Possibly [α]ὐτὸς 'I myself'.

13. τὰ γράμματα are probably documents expected to confirm Horion II's appointment, which would thus fulfill Ammon's mission to Alexandria.

14. An expected ἐθέλω to govern εἰδέναι may be concealed in the scattered flecks of ink above the infinitive.

15. 'Harpocras' is the family's hypocoristic for Harpocration as he is called in all the official documents.

17. After μέτρι[α Maresch reads κ]αταβαίνει.

18. Perhaps ὅταν [τυχ]ήσῃ 'whenever that happens (to him)', or [ἀναζ]ή-σῃ or [κρατ]ήσῃ (Maresch).

18ff. Apparently Harpocration has received letters from high-ranking officials appointing him to a higher post in the imperial service. It is not clear whether Ammon has received these letters for Harpocration and has shown them to his brother's friends (lines 23–26). At 19 preceding ἀπὸ Maresch suggests -επέ]μ-[φθ]η and to begin 20 [καλοῦντα].

21ff. For the Ethiopian *hegemon* see the introduction. In the phrase inserted above line 26 he is specifically called an Ethiopian. After Αἰθιόπων Maresch suggests [στελλ]ομένωι πρὸς τ[ὸν] | [βασιλ]έα.

23. Pekysis is not identified nor mentioned anywhere else in this letter nor in the archive.

26. Although it is not certain whether the subject of ἐξῆλθεν is Harpocration or the Ethiopian, most likely it is the former, and he had returned to Alexandria, has been seen by Ammon and has already gone back to the *comitatus* (see p.2, n.2 and cf. iv.9f), from which he is expected to return home to Panopolis in autumn of the current year. It is less probable that the Ethiopian as envoy to the court may have come to Alexandria, bringing to Ammon the news of Harpocration reported above, and had now returned to court. In the following translation I have taken Harpocration to be the subject. In the final lacuna ἔνθε]ν δ' or ἐνθέ]νδ' would fit.

col. iv

4. By δεσ]πότηι either the emperor or the prefect could be meant, but perhaps simply 'master' since the slaves are mentioned soon below. If [ἡγεμ]ονεύσαν-[τ]ος 'former prefect' is right, a former prefect whose name ends in -ων must

be sought. Only two such are known since Diocletian's accession, Septimios Zenon A.D. 328/29 and Aurelios Apion between 323 and 328, and of these only Apion will fit here.

7. Possibly ... τὸ]ν ναυτικὸν 'the sailor'.

8. αὐτάς are doubtless the slave girls of lines 11–14; before the preceding lacuna, ε or α followed by ι, ν or π.

9–15. Presumably Harpocration is the subject of ἔλεγεν (9) and of κατέ-λειl[π]εν (10f), as verified by the similar statements in the drafts of Ammon's subsequent petition to the *catholicus* at **7.**15ff, **12.**12ff and **13.**19; so also of ἐ[π]ετρέψατο (14) and λέγων (15).

15–22. Where Harpocration's discourse ends, whether in line 18 or, as assumed at line 22 of the translation, is by no means certain. In any case doubtless Ammon is to be understood as the subject of ἀναλίσκεις (15). The subject of [ἔλαβ]εν (22), if rightly restored, is presumably Harpocration.

21. Ammon's older half-brother Horion, *archiprophetes* of the Panopolite nome, is last attested by his *apographe* dated A.D. 299 (P.Duke inv. 181), but apparently he has died recently. The family has been seeking for his son Horion Junior an appointment as *prophetes* (ostensibly his hereditary due) by license purchased from the *archiereus*, a Roman revenue-producing and temple-control procedure which would be obviated by imperial intervention.

22. οἱ θεοῖς ἐχθροί 'antagonists, opponents' = ἀσεβεῖς; cf. L. Koenen, ΘΕΟΙΣΙΝ ΕΧΘΡΟΙ, *Cd'É* 34 (1959) 103–19, esp. 115. Here it is conceivably a reference to Christians attempting to thwart clerical tradition.

23. Such a letter or constitution of Diocletian concerning the *propheteia* is otherwise not recorded. Presumably it would have regulated the right of succession to the *propheteia* (restricted to direct descent) and entitlement to its proceeds (one-tenth of the income of all temple lands in the nome held in common by the *pentaphylia* of priests, according to Horion's *apographe*, apparently reduced from the one-fifth that had been prescribed by the *Gnomon of the Idios Logos* [*BGU* 1210] par. 79). It is this μέρος (line 25), doubtless interrupted upon Horion's death, that Ammon is seeking to have restored to the family by the succession of Horion II to the *propheteia*.

26. ἐχύλωσεν, a rare verb found elsewhere only in its literal sense (LSJ 'convert into juice, extract the juice of'), must here be metaphorical, perhaps 'drain, exhaust'. Though 'Prostates' is a well-established personal name at this time in Panopolis, as attested by four persons of that name in *P.Panop.Beatty* 1, here προστάτου (without any previous identification) may be the noun 'administrator, steward, manager', the term for an official temporarily responsible for a governmental, military or religious function; at col. v.23 τὸν προστάτην 'the steward' is a partner of Ammon. Perhaps such a *locum tenens* (the *archiereus* himself?) is responsible for the *propheteia* and collects its income until an approved candidate is confirmed. At line end Maresch suggests νῦ]ν δὲ καὶ αὐτός.

28. ἀφ]ιξομένου Maresch.

col. v

2. αὐτοῦ or αὐτοὺ[ς.

5. After αὐ[ταῖς Maresch suggests σου]. Ammon now turns to domestic problems, consoling his mother for serious financial losses to the family. If Σα[ραπόδωρος is correctly restored as the subject of ἀνήλωσ[ε], he is responsible for these reverses. A brother at home to whom Ammon sends greetings (vi.18f), he is mentioned again at col. v.29 in connection with the ἀπαιτήσε[ις τ]ῶν φ[όρων] 'collection of the rents' from the eastern desert; yet Ammon refrains from reproof but lauches instead on moral philosophizing and sentimental nostalgia. At end, τινα] or perhaps πολλὰ]; cf. v.12.

6. Among possibilities (e.g. θέλει, μέλει), ἀμέλει seems likely.

7. αὐτὴ presumably modifies τύχη in lacuna; preceding it possibly ἄ[τερ τύχ]η[ς].

7f. Cf. Men. *Sent.* 577 οἷς μὲν δίδωσιν, οἷς δ' ἀφαιρεῖται Τύχη.

8. Perhaps τὰ πατρ[ῷα μὴ ἀπολέσῃ, οὐ] (Maresch); cf. line 12.

14. γένοιτ[ό μοι] or γένοιτ[ο σὲ]; there is not room for both pronouns.

16. ἁυτη pap., the sole occurrence of an accent, as first noted by J. Bingen; by it Ammon assures αὕτη rather than αὐτή. The only frequent adjective with ἐλπίς is χρηστή. Maresch prefers [μεγίσ]ἰτη, citing μέγιστον in the next line.

18. The lacuna after ζητῶ would allow νῦν δ]ὲ or τόδ]ε.

19. ἐπε[ὶ τἀ]λλα αὐτὸς ἔκαμ[νον] εἰς τὸν λάκ[κον ὅτ]ι (Maresch).

21. The antecedent to whom μόνοι (perhaps 'individuals', or 'on their own' [van Minnen]) refers is not clear.

22f. Polycrates, the other of Ammon's 'partners', is another brother to whom he sends greetings at col. vi.23. For προστάτην see note above on col. iv.26. The definite article, which Ammon does not use elsewhere with proper names, indicates a common noun here, 'the steward'.

24. Perhaps τοὺς μὲν πόνους [σ]αυ[τ]ῆς. — Or ὑποστῆ[ναι] (Maresch).

28f. Perhaps π[άρε]χε and ἀπατήσε[ις τ]ῶν φ[όρων] as read by P. van Minnen. Arabia is the district neighboring Panopolis on the east attached to the metropolitan toparchy; cf. *P.Panop.Beatty* 1.328 and note.

35. While Μυρίνωι (a name attested in II-cent. Karanis) is possible, T]αυ-ρίνωι is much likelier, cited at *P.Panop.Beatty* 1.331 as father of a Horion. Tau-rinos may be a relative of Ammon.

col. vi

6. Doubtfully, διὰ τοῦ ναυτι[κο]ῦ *'via* the sailor'.

9. παρηγορήσεται ι might also be read.

10. At the end possibly παραβαλεῖ.

11. At line-end perhaps ἔχ[ειν ἐά]-.

13. Μακαρία here and at line 20 is the Greek name of Ammon's close relative, perhaps one of his grandmothers, who would be identified in official documents only by her Egyptian name. Only his mother Nike / Senpetechensis is known to us by both her names, thanks to the accident of Ammon's interlinear insertion at **13.49**.

20. The surviving traces of ink would conform to Κανέαν but are too slight to warrant confidence. As is the case with Makaria, her Greek name would normally appear in private correspondence, her Egyptian in official documents.

4. HORION II'S PETITION THROUGH AMMON TO THE PREFECT

P.Duke inv. 179r, frr. A–J

A 5.5 x 4.3 cm	F 3.3 x 1.7 cm
B 6.5 x 3.3 cm	G 4.8 x 2.5 cm
C 6.5 x 17.1 cm	H 2.1 x 5.3 cm
D 6.0 x 14.5 cm	I 6.0 x 2.4 cm
E 40.0 x 5.6 cm	J 7.2 x 8.8 cm

+ P.Köln inv. 4536r   8.6 x 14.9 cm

[est. combined w. of frr. 57.5, est. h. 26.5 cm;
est. original w. of papyrus *ca* 84, est. h. *ca* 30 cm]

From Panopolis to Alexandria   Plate XVII   A.D. 348

Through **3** we learn of Ammon's intervention with the high-priest of Alexandria and All Egypt in the attempt to secure for his nephew Horion II appointment to the *propheteia* of the Panopolite nome in succession to his father Horion I, Ammon's elder half-brother now deceased. Although the required fee (εἰσκρι-τικόν) seems to have been paid, it appears that neither Ammon's efforts nor Harpocration's appeal to the emperor have been successful, for the following petition of Horion II apparently to the prefect, composed and written for him by Ammon in his best formal hand, seeks the prefect's authority to overrule the high-priest. Obviously this copy of the petition was not submitted, for reasons that can be only speculated, perhaps because the high-priest complied in the meantime.

Ammon's papers, especially nos. **3, 4, 6** and **13**, provide new information about the offices and functions of the *archiereus* and the *catholicus*, who between them had inherited the duties of the office of the *Idios Logos* in the mid-third century.[1] Originally independent but later becoming subordinate to the *Idios Logos*, by A.D. 348 the office of the high-priest appears to be separate from that of the

---

[1] See M. Stead, "The High Priest of Alexandria and All Egypt," *Proceedings of the XVI Congress* (AmStudPap 23 [1981]) pp.411–18, esp. 412f and references cited there. For the ecclesiastical scope of the Idios Logos and the high-priest's relation to the department prior to the mid-third century see P.R. Swarney, *The Ptolemaic and Roman Idios Logos* (AmStudPap 8 [1970]) esp. pp.83–96; see also D. Hagedorn, "Zum Amt des διοικητής im römischen Ägypten," *YCS* 28 (1985) p.96f.

catholicus, for this complaint against the former is addressed not to the latter but rather directly to the prefect. It seems that, while the *catholicus* inherited the other fiscal functions and responsibilities previously exercised by the *Idios Logos*, those concerned with the temples and their clergy were now the province of the high-priest. Nos. **3** and **4** are the latest surviving attestations of the high-priest in published papyri.

Details of the high-priest's alleged malfeasance and of the remedy sought are lost in the extensive lacunae. The eleven surviving fragments constitute 27.3 per

Text

col. i

(*margin*)

1   [Φλαουίωι Νεστορίωι?   *vacat?*   τῶι διασημοτά]τωι
                  vacat   [*ca ?*   ]   *vacat*   ἐπά[ρχωι Αἰγύπτ]ου
2   [παρὰ Αὐρηλίου Ὡρίωνος Ὡρίωνος δι' Αὐρηλίου Ἄμμωνος
          Πετεαρβεσχί]νιος σχολαστικοῦ [ἀπὸ Πανὸς πόλεως τῆς
          Θηβαίδος.   *ca ?*   ]ιστον ὡς μηδ̣ [ ]̣ [ ]̣τ[   ]ντος
3   [*ca?*   ]
          [*ca ?*   ]α καὶ κ[*ca ?*   ]ν ε-
      [*ca?*   ]τετε
5   [*ca?*   ]̣

- -

[*loss of one or more lines*]

- -

8   [*ca?*   ]ν τῶν μεγίσ[των   *ca ?*   ]
      [   ]ι ἐνδεικνύμενοι [   ]
10 [   ]ς τοῖς ἄλλοις καὶ του [   ]
      [κι]νδυνεύειν τῶν ἀν[   ]
12 [   ] τὴν καταφυγὴν ποιε[   ]
          [*ca ?*   ] μερο[   ]
13 [   ] καὶ παρὰ τοὺς νόμους [ ]
          [   ]εμ[̣ ̣ δε]σπότην

cent of the text by estimated letter-count, quite unevenly distributed. In two wide columns, the better preserved col. ii is *ca* 38.5 cm broad, providing an average of 130 letters per line; the margins measure at top 1.5 cm, at foot 2.5–2.8 cm in col. i and 5.0 in col. ii, the intercolumnar 2.0–2.5 cm. The Cologne fragment of col. ii is adjoined at left by Duke fr. D, at right by fr. H, above by fr. G. The loci of the the widely separated and isolated frr. A, B and C from col. i and frr. G, I and J from col. ii are determined by the lines of an unrelated text on the verso written at right angles much later in Ammon's draft hand.

Translation

col. i

(*margin*)

[1][To Flavius Nestorius(?), *vir perfectissi*]*mus*, Prefect of E[gypt, [2]from Aurelius Horion son of Horion through Aurelius Ammon son of Petearbeschi]nis, Scholasticus [from Panopolis of the Thebaid. ---]ιστον ὡς μηδ [ ] *traces* [ ]ντος

[3–5][*traces*]

[6–7][*assumed loss of two lines*]

[8][*ca?*   ] of the most important [---] [9][-----] (those) showing [---] [10][-----] to the others and (of?) the [---] [11][-----] to risk of the [---] [12][-----] is taking his refuge [with you? ---] portion? [---] [13][-----] contrary to the laws [---] lord

14 [κ]αλούμεθα· ἔστι δ[ὲ   ]
    [   ]μα σοὶ ἐπὶ τὴν
15 [π]αρῆλθεν καὶ [   ]
    [   ]νου διὰ γραμμάτων
16 [   ]ομ[α]ρτυ[   ]
    [   ]ειαν [ ]ηι ἀνὴρ
17 [τοὺς θ]εοὺς θρησκ[   ]
    [   ]ματα [π]ρὸς τοῖς υἱοῖς
18 [   ]νούμενος ε[   ]
    [   ]ων δὲ οὐ [τοὺ]ς ἔχον-
19 [τας   ] · ἐπειδὴ ὁ ἀρ[χιερεὺς?]
    [   ]τειαν γὰρ τὴν
20 [   ] πατρὸς παρ[   ]
    [   ] εις φιλο[τι]μίας
21 [   ]ναι εἰς τοὺς....[   ]
    [τ]ῆς ἀρχιερατικῆς
22 [   ] ι κομίσω καὶ ο [   ]
    [   ]ε καὶ τῆς προσ-
23 [   ]εναι ἠξίωσα καὶ πα[   ]
    [   ] εἶχον κατ᾽ ἐμαυτὸν
24 [ἔ]στι δὲ οὐκ ἄνευ[   ]
    [   ] τούτο[υ τ]οῦ σκῆψιν
25 [   ]μένους καὶ χ[   ]
    [   ] κατο[χὴ]ν τῆς τά-
26 [ξεως   ] τοῦ παιδ[ὸς τὴ]ν φιλοτιμία[ν].[   ]
    [   ] ομε[ν] ἀλλ᾽ ἀπρά-
27 [γμονα   ] [ ] ν ἐξ ἀρχῆς με κελευ[   ]
    [   ]ηδιων πάντα
28 [   ]τον κατὰ τρόπον ἐδίδασκεν [   ]
    [-λ]αβὼν κ[αὶ] ἐπὶ σχολῆς
                         (margin)

_____

16 *supra* ανηρ *spir. asp.* (type 2, Turner) pap.   26 αλλ᾽ pap.

[14]-----] we are called, to wit [---] to you to the [15]-----] (he?) came and [---]
through letters [16]-----] witness [---]..... the man [17]-----] service [to the] gods
[---] toward the sons? [18]-----] being selected? [---] but not those having [19]-----]
since the [high-priest ---].... for the [20][--- from his father ... [---]....
ambition/honor? [21]-----]... to the ...[---] (from?) the high-priest's [22][office ---]
(that) I may obtain ..[---] and of the .... [23]-----].... I requested and ..[---] I had
as regards myself (*or* I held out as far as I could) [24]-----] is not without [guilt?
-----] (of?) this one [offering?] a plea [25]-----] collecting and using? [---]
possession of the [26]office [-----] the honor from the boy [---] but free [27][from
strife? (*or* unsold?) -----].….. from the beginning order me [---] all of the re-
quisites? [28]-----] he duly explained [---] after receiving and at leisure

col. ii

(*margin*)

29 ἀναγνοὺς πάλ[ιν] πρὸς ἐμὲ τὰ βιβλία ἀπέπεμψεν κα[ὶ ο]ὔτε
       ὑπέγραψέν τι οὔτε εἰ[ς τὴν] τάξιν καταθεῖναι ἠξίω[σεν ὡς μ]ὴ
       εἶναι του[ ] ̓ ́ ὀρφαν[*ca 6*] [ ]υμ[ ]ουδ[ ]
30 γάρ ἐστιν ὡς ἀληθῶς ἐπεὶ μηδὲ πράττειν τι τῶν δικαίων πρὸς ἡμᾶς
       ἐγίνωσκεν κα[ὶ] μὴ τοῦτο καθ' ἑαυτὸν ἐλογίσατ[ο ἐκ
       γ]ραμμάτων βασιλικῶν [ ] [τ]οῖς τετυχόσιν
31 καὶ [μ]ὴ σοῦ περὶ πράγματος ἀμφισβήτησίν τινα προσδεχομένου
       καὶ πρὸς κρίσιν εἴτ[ε] μ[ε]τεώρου εἴτε δι' αὐτὸ γενέσθ[ω ὡς]
       μὴ βουλεύεσθαι πρόκει[μαι] ἔ[τ]ι κατα[ ]η με
32 πάλαι ἦν βασιλεὺς ὁ κρίνας καὶ γράμματα [ ] βασιλικὰ
       προύτείνομεν τὰ πᾶσιν πάντα ἀνθρώποι[ς] κρίνοντα μὴ
       [ἀ]δ[ίκω]ς ὑπ' ἀνθρώ[π]ων κρινόμ[εν]οι ἔξω [δικ]αίων
33 ἐκε[ῖ]νοι τῆς ἀ[ρχιπρο]φ[ητ]είας τὴν νομὴν χ [ ]ς υπ[ ] κ[α]ὶ
       ὁ παῖς νῦν ἐπε [ ] [ ] τὴν παράδ[οσ]ιν παρὰ τοῦ πατ[ρὸ]ς
       [πα]ραλαβὼν ὡς [ ]οι ε [ ]χ [ ]κο[ ]ληκ[ ]ονται
34 [*ca 20*   ] βιβλίων [*ca 18*] β[ί]ου ς
       καὶ ἀε[ὶ] θεοῖ[ς] [*ca 9*]ια ω τουτο[ ]ικ[*ca 9*]
       ξα[ ] [*ca ?*   ]
35 [*ca ?*   ] [ ] [   ] [   ]

- -

[*loss of one or more lines*]

- -

38 [   ] ὑπὲρ τοῦ και[*ca ?*   ]
     [   ]α φυλάττοντες [   ]
40 [   ] β [ ]ο ρ ις[   ] αυτ [   ] [ ] [   ]
     [   ] [ ] ς ἀπράγμονα[ ] [*ca 17* ἀ]νειλομ[*ca ?*]
42 [   ]κ ἀφῆκεν τῆς προτά[σεως *ca 10*]ματος τ[ ]
     [ἱε]ρατικῶι ταμείωι τ[*ca 14*   ἀ]δελφιδ[*ca ?*]
44 [   ] κα [ ] ὑπον [*ca 20*   ] πάντα[*ca ?*]
45 [   ]ι οὔτε τὴ[ν] τοῦ πα[τρὸ]ς χώραν ὁ παῖς [*ca 16*]ειν
       ταυτ[*ca 75*   ]

col. ii

²⁹reading the petition he sent it back to me and neither had he endorsed it nor did he think fit to appoint (him) to the office on the grounds that orphans are not [*traces ca 17*].....[.] ³⁰for (he/it?) is in fact [---] since he determined to do no justice toward us and (if?) he had not? reasoned this to himself as a result of the imperial rescript ... to those who have gained(?) ³¹and had, while you were not expecting some dispute about the matter, and ... to a judgement whether of a pending case or ... because of it ...... ³²(It was) the emperor who decided long ago, and we offered to him the imperial rescript, which decides all things for all men, lest being judged unjustly by men, ... ³³those possessing the portion of the *archipropheteia* [*ca 8*], and now the son ..., having received the transmission from his father *ca 35* ³⁴[*ca 20*] petition [*ca 18*] life? that ever to the gods [*ca 10*] *ca 40* [*ca ?*] ³⁵ *traces* ³⁶⁻³⁷

[assumed loss of lines]

³⁸[---] in behalf of the ... [*ca ?*] ³⁹[---] guarding [*ca ?*] ⁴⁰ *traces* ⁴¹[-----] ..... free from strife [*ca 20*] undertook? [*ca ?*] ⁴²[-----].... he ... of the proposal [ca 10]ματος [---] ⁴³[-----] to the priestly treasury [*ca 14*] nephew [*ca ?*] ⁴⁴[-----] *traces* [*ca 20*] all [*ca ?*] ⁴⁵[---] nor the son the place of his father [*ca 16*] *traces* [*ca 75*]

46 [κ]αὶ τῶν νόμων [τῶ]ν ἐκ παλαιοῦ κελ[ευόντων   ca 7   ] ν τοῦ
       πατ[ρὸς   ca 80   ]
47 [̣]σθεισαν τῶι ἱερατ[ικ]ῶι λόγωι προσαγα[γ]εῖν ̣ [ca 10   μα
       ὕστερο[ca ?   ] [̣]ης καθα[̣ ̣ ̣ ̣] θνο [̣] ̣
48 [τ]ῆς πατρῴας τάξε[ως τ]ῶι παιδὶ φυλάττ[ε]σθαι η[ca 11   ] ει
       διὰ του ̣ [ca ?   ]σιν καὶ τὸ εἰσκρ[ιτικὸν] κατὰ τοὺς
49 νόμους καταβαλεῖν, ὁ δὲ δικαιότατος ἡμ[ῶ]ν ἀρχι[ερεὺς ̣ ̣ ̣ ̣ οὐ]
       παράπαν ἐμοὶ ̣ [ca ?   ἀ]ναφορὰν προυτ[είν]ετο ἀλλ᾽
50 [ε]ἰς ἀπειλὰς καὶ τὰ το[ι]αῦτα καθ᾽ ἡμῶν ἐτρ[ά]πη, ἴσω[ς καθ᾽
       ἑα]υτὸν λογιζόμ[ενος ca ?   ] [̣] καὶ πρᾶγμα [ἀνα]μφισβή-
51]τητον εἰς ἀμφισβήτησιν ἄγειν ἐθέλοι τοῖς [ca 14   ]ην ἑαυτὸν
       διδοὺ[ς   ca 70   πέ]-
52 φυκε γίγνεσθαι πάν[τ]ως με εἰς ἔφεσιν α[ca 13   ]μις γάρ ἐστι
       τῶν ἐκ[ca 70   ]
53 διὰ τοῦτο οὐδὲ τὸ παράπ[α]ν ἐμοῦ ἀκούειν η[ca 8   ] ταῦτα τοῦ
       αὐτὸν προκαλ[ca 70   ]
54 [τ]ὰ ἑαυτοῖς πρακτέα ἀλλὰ καὶ πρὸς ἐνιαυτ[ὸν ca 8]αντα
       εντα[ῦθ]ά με κατέσχεν [   ] ̣ [   ]
55 κτισμῶι καὶ χρόνῳ καὶ τριβῆι ἀπαγα[γ]εῖ[ν ἐ]μὲ ἡγούμενος καὶ
       προδώσε[   ]ναι [   ]
56 ἐπὶ τὸ σεμνότατον τ[ο]ῦτο δικαστήριον νῦν κα[ταφε]ύγω ὅπως
       [ἐ]νταῦθα ὅπου οὐδε[ca 12   αὐ]τοκρατορ[̣] ουσ ̣ [   ]
57 δείκνυται κἂν μείζονες ὄντες τύχωσι [ca 7 μ]έσως ἔχει [κ]αὶ εἴ τί
       ἐστι τῶν πα[   ] σθηι κα[ὶ] τῶι πα[   ]
58 διὰ τῆς εὐσεβεστάτης σου ἀποφάσεως κ ̣ [ca 9   πλ]ηρωθῆνα[ι]
       ὅπως καὶ θεοῖς [ὁμολογο]ύμενοι χάριτα[ς   διευτύχει]
59 vacat   Αὐρή[λιος] Ὡρίων Ὡρίωνος
       [ἐπ]ιδέδ[ω]κα δι[ὰ ῎Α]μμωνος θείου Π[ετεαρβεσχίνιος
       σχολαστικοῦ ἀπὸ Πανὸς πόλεως τῆς Θηβαίδος   ]

---

47 ἱερατ[̣ ̣]ωι pap.   49 αλλ᾽ pap.   50 ἴσω[pap.

[46]and of the laws that from of old order [*ca 7*] the father's [*ca 80*]
[47]having been (?) to apply to the priestly account [*ca 10*].. later [*ca ?*]
traces [48]to keep for the son (?) of the paternal office [*ca 12*] through the
[*ca ?*] and to deposit the appointment fee in accordance with the [49]laws. But
our most just *archi[ereus* ... did not] at all [*ca ?*] forward the payment (*or*
petition) to me but [50]turned to threats and such abuse against us, perhaps
reasoning [thus to him]self [*ca ?*] and an [un]disputed matter [51]he would
wish to bring into dispute to the [ca 14] devoting himself [*ca 70*] [52]... me
surely to come to an appeal [*ca 13*]... for ... is ... of the [*ca 70*]
[53]because of this and he did not [want] to hear me at all [*ca 15*] him who
summons (or is summoned) [*ca 70*] [54]what must be done by themselves but
also he kept me there [at *or* away from home] for a year [*ca 70*] [55]thinking
that he had deflected me by contention and delay and wearing me down, and to
betray [*ca 70*] [56]I now take refuge here in this most august court where not
even [*ca 12*] emperor [..].... [*ca 55*] [57]demonstrates even if they happen
to be greater [*ca 9*] is moderate and if there is anything of the fa[thers?] ....
also to the son [*ca 45*] [58]be fulfilled through your most revered decision in
order that (we), acknowledging thanks to both gods [and *ca 10*] may [*ca ?*
Farewell] [59] *vacat* I, Aurelius Horion son of Horion, have submitted (this
petition) through my uncle Ammon [son of Petearbeschinis Scholasticus from
Panopolis of the Thebaid *vacat*]

Notes
col. i

1f. It is possible that fr. A, which bears the middle of lines 1 and 2, may belong not to this papyrus but to another similar petition. The hand, however, appears to be close to that of the rest of this text.

1. If correctly attributed to the summer or autumn of A.D. 348 in the interval between nos. **3** and **5**, the prefect was Flavius Nestorius; see C. Vandersleyen, *Chronologie des préfets d'Égypte de 284 à 395* (Coll. Latomus 4, Brussels 1962) pp.16 (no.28) and 125ff.

2. Restored from line 59, although the presence of the patronymic in either line is doubtful, since the supplement provides a line longer than the 130-letter average line-length of col. ii. Cf. note on line 59.

12. In the first lacuna doubtless ἐπὶ σὲ. Perhaps ποιε[ῖ, the subject probably Ὡρίων (νεώτερος), or possibly ἠπείχθην ... ἐπὶ σὲ] τὴν καταφυγὴν ποιε[ῖσθαι.

13. Possibly] ἐμ[ὸν or] ἐμ[οῦ. There is not room for ἡγ]εμ[όνα.

14. Possibly ἅ]μα σοὶ 'together with you'.

16. Possible are ἀπ]ομαρτυ[ρέω or -[ρομαι, πρ]ομαρτύ[ρομαι,] ὁ μάρτυ[ς and τ]ὸ μαρτύ[ριον, of which the first, 'testify', is likeliest. — There seems to be a *spiritus asper* above ἀνήρ, rather surprisingly.

17. Probably τὴν πρὸς τοὺς θ]εοὺς θρησκ[είαν 'the service to the gods'; cf. *P.Lund* IV 12f.

18. Perhaps ἐπικρι]νούμενος 'being selected, adjudged'. After the second lacuna οὐ[δενὸ]ς ἔχον|[τος would be possible also.

19. Preceding ἐπειδὴ either] ν· or]ς·; possibly προφη]τείαν γὰρ τὴν.

20. Perhaps παρὰ τοῦ] πατρὸς and a form of παραλαμβάνω.

21f. The adjective ἀρχιερατικός has not occurred hitherto in the papyri; here probably τάξεως should be supplied.

22. Either κομίσωμαι or κομίσω καὶ is possible.

23. Or perhaps ἀντ]εῖχον κατ' ἐμαυτὸν 'I held out as far as I could'.

24. ἄνευ or a compound of ἄνευ- such as ἀνεύθυνος. At end the words may be divided]του το[ύτ]ου or] τούτο[υ τ]οῦ with a participle such as προβαλλομένου following σκῆψιν (cf. **6**.15 σκῆψίν τινα προβα[λέσθαι).

25.]μενους και χ[: in documents this sequence has occurred only in the phrase ἀποφερομένους καὶ χρωμένους 'collecting and using', cf. *P.Hamb.* I 30.23; *P.Mich.* III 188.15, X 585.19, XII 635.18f. All these are contracts of loan with right of habitation, providing to the lender the right to collect rents. Perhaps the relevance here, if this is the formula employed, is the right of a priest to enjoy a share of the income of temple property.

26f. At end, ἄπρα|[κτον 'unsuccessful' or ἄπρα|[τον 'unsold' is also possible.

27. At end possibly ἐπιτ]ηδίων (for ἐπιτηδείων) πάντα.

28. Perhaps παραλ]αβών.

col. ii

This column is especially difficult.

29. The subject of the verbs (and modified by the participle) is presumably the *archiereus*. Possibly τὰ βιβλία are the γράμματα τὰ Διοκλητιανοῦ referred to at **3** iv.23–27 and mentioned in the next line, but more likely a petition from Ammon on behalf of Horion II that was denied by the *archiereus*. Near line-end perhaps ὀρφαν[οὺς. Maresch translates οὔτε εἰ[ς τὴν] τάξιν καταθεῖναι ἠξίω[σεν 'he did not deign to deposit the petition in his office'.

30. At line-end apparently τετυχόσιν for standard τετευχόσιν 'for those who have obtained': cf. *P.Cair.Masp.* I 67049.15 τετυχὸς (for τετυχὼς) (Aphrodito, vi cent.). Maresch takes μὴ τοῦτο καθ᾽ ἑαυτὸν ἐλογίσατ[ο to mean 'he did not think that this concerned him'.

31. Although the phrase πρὸς κρίσιν occurs thus far only here among documentary papyri, it is frequent in philosophical, medical and mathematical treatises. — γενέσθ[ω or γενέσθ[αι? — At end, perhaps κατα[νάγκ]η με.

33. After νομὴν perhaps ἔχο[ντ]ες .

39. δι]αφυλάττοντες or παρ]αφυλάττοντες is equally possible.

43. ταμείωι for ταμιείωι, as often in papyri. The ἱερατικὸν ταμεῖον 'priestly treasury' is previously unattested. Presumably it was the fund administered by the high-priest that received fees from applicants to a priesthood and disbursed grants to temple or clergy. Less likely, the phrase may have read ἀρχιε]ρα-

τικῶι ταμείωι, likewise unattested. τ[ὸ εἰσκριτικὸν] would fit the second lacuna; cf. line 48 with note.

48. The εἰσκριτικόν was the investiture fee paid to the government, formerly to the Idios Logos until that office was discontinued in the mid-third century but at this time apparently to the high-priest, by a candidate on succession to a hereditary priesthood. Horion II was therefore obligated to pay this fee if he succeeded to his father's *propheteia*. The fee was presumably paid through the local *strategos*, who would then forward it to the *archiereus*; cf. **3** iii.6.

49. Of the possible supplements to ἀρχι-, -προφήτης is inappropriate to the context; -δικαστής 'chief judge', deputy to the prefect who sometimes presided over the prefectural court, is excluded by the charges in line 50; and -ερεύς, whom δικαιότατος would characterize therefore only in irony.

52. Perhaps δύνα]μις or θέ]μις preceding γάρ ἐστι.

53. At the first lacuna P. van Minnen suggests ἠ[θέλησε.

54. After ἐνιαυτ[ὸν van Minnen suggests ἀπο- or ἐπιδημήσ]αντα.

55. Of the form κτισμός and the compounds containing those syllables, διαπληκτισμός 'disputing' seems likeliest in the context.

59. After θείου van Minnen suggests π[ρὸς πατρὸς, obviating the need for Ammon's patronymic and shortening the over-long line both here and at i.2 above. I have found no precise parallel.

III. THE LAWSUIT BETWEEN AMMON AND THE DELATOR EUGENEIOS, NOS. 5–25

Among the numerous papyri of the Ammon archive an important group pertain to the litigation between Ammon and the *delator* Eugeneios before the court of the *catholicus* Flavius Sisinnius for possession of three female domestic slaves left in Alexandria by Ammon's recently deceased brother Harpocration, a rhetor with the imperial court (*comitatus*).

In no. 3, the letter to his mother in Panopolis, Ammon is eagerly looking forward to Harpocration's imminent return from abroad and mentions (col. iv.10–14) his brother's three female Phoenician slaves left in his care whom he is to bring to Panopolis on his return there; but meantime they are placed with a landlord or innkeeper (Conon) to work for their keep. Presumably it is these slaves who become the subject of contention between Ammon and Eugeneios.

That possession of three slaves should give rise to such momentous litigation might seem surprising. In Egypt, however, slaves were relatively uncommon, progressively so after the first three centuries of Roman rule.[1] "Egypt has never been a slave owning country... The dense population ... has always provided an abundance of laborers for every need... So the slaves mentioned in the papyri are for the most part house-hold attendants... Slaves were mostly house-bred, and few importations from abroad are noted."[2]

Harpocration has died unexpectedly while abroad. A *delator* Eugeneios, introduced as a μεμοράριος (see 6.3 and note), otherwise unknown but

---

[1] Cf. R.S. Bagnall, "Slavery and Society in Late Roman Egypt," in *Law, Politics and Society in the Ancient Mediterranean World*, edd. B. Halpern and D.W. Hobson (Sheffield 1993) 132f, citing earlier editions of nos. 3 and 6. On slavery in Byzantine Egypt see J.F. Fikhman, "Slaves in Byzantine Oxyrhynchus," *Akten des XIII. Int. Papyrologenkongr.* (Münchener Beiträge 66, 1974) 117–26, and *Jb für Wirtschaftsgeschichte 1973/II*, 149–206; I. Biezunska-Malowist, *JJP* 15 (1965) 70, and *L'Esclavage dans l'Égypte gréco-romaine* II (Archiwum Filologiczne 35, 1977) esp. 93ff and for sale prices 165ff. Though evidence is scanty, at mid-IV cent. prices of 913T 2000dr, 1200T, and 18 solidi are attested. For relative evaluation of currency at this period see Bagnall, *Currency and Inflation in Fourth Century Egypt* (BASP Suppl. 5, 1985) 37–41.

2 A.C. Johnson / L.C. West, *Byzantine Egypt: Economic Studies* (Princeton 1949) 132–35 and 149. No female slaves from Phoenicia are listed. Bagnall (*op.cit.* n.1, "Slavery" pp. 220ff) objects, citing paucity of documentation from this period.

doubtless a member of the *comitatus*, learning of Harpocration's death before the news reached Egypt, has rushed to Alexandria to lay claim to the slaves in the belief that Harpocration had died intestate and without a legal heir. The matter is treated in the following texts:

No. **5**: Panopolis, A.D. 348. Ammon's mandate (ἐντολή) to Aurelius Faustinus, citizen and ex-councillor of Panopolis, to notify the prefect of Egypt, Flavius Nestorius, that there is an heir in the person of Aurelius Ammon who is entitled to inherit the slaves of his brother Aurelius Harpocration hitherto considered ownerless.

No. **6**: Alexandria, 9 xii 348. Draft of a certification (διασφαλισμός) by Ammon to the *catholicus* Flavius Sisinnius. Ammon declares his presence in Alexandria, where at the instance of the *delator* Eugeneios he has been summoned to appear before the *catholicus* for adjudication of the dispute about Harpocration's slaves.

Nos. **7–15**: Alexandria, a little later. Numerous fragments of a series of nine drafts of Ammon's petition (διαμαρτυρία) to the *catholicus* asking that all Harpocration's slaves be delivered to him as the lawful heir. The antecedents of the dispute are set forth in detail. No draft is complete. These drafts constitute our best and most profuse example of the composing technique of an ancient practitioner of the New Sophistic: nowhere else are preserved so many drafts of a developing speech.

No. **16**: Alexandria? 348? Four fragments of a text that is probably a petition addressed not to Sisinnius but perhaps to the prefect, Flavius Nestorius. It is possible that fr. A of no. **4** derives from this petition.

No. **17**: Alexandria? 348? A very fragmentary papyrus that seems also to be a petition to the prefect. Possibly nos. **16** and **17** preserve different parts of one and the same petition.

Nos. **18–22**: Further fragments of documents which relate to, or appear to relate to, this case.

Nos. **23–25**: Fragments of which it remains uncertain whether they relate to the case but which were also written by Ammon about the same time.

All these texts were written by the hand of Ammon himself, though in two distinct styles. For final copies of documents that he expected to submit he wrote a more careful upright semi-cursive resembling a chancery hand (as for example nos. **3**, **4** and **5**), which I shall call his 'formal' hand; for drafts apparently intended only for his own eyes he wrote a rough, rapid, often ligatured majuscule sloping to the right (as for example nos. **9** and **10**), which we shall call his 'draft' hand.

Background of the Case

The development of the dispute, in so far as it may be gathered from these texts, was as follows. Ammon's brother, the rhetor Aurelius Harpocration, apparently attached to the imperial court as panegyrist, had some time earlier set out from Alexandria on a speaking tour that took him to distant parts of the Roman Empire. At his departure he left behind to the care of Ammon his three female domestic slaves. In turn Ammon deposited them with Conon,[3] a landlord friend of Harpocration, with the proviso that he hand them over to Harpocration on his return (**13**.21). Whether the contract was one of deposit, loan or lease is not indicated (**7**.18–20 = **12**.19).

Harpocration's journey lasted longer than initially planned, for his return had been delayed time after time. Finally he died while abroad without Ammon's receiving word. Meanwhile Ammon planned a voyage to Alexandria to see about the slaves, who had made themselves independent of Conon. But he postponed the trip for a while until he was alarmed by the report that a *delator* had appeared from abroad (ἔξωθεν, **7**.29 = **9**.17 = **13**.43), Eugeneios, who sought to gain possession of them by fraud or by force (**5**.10f). Eugeneios is called a μεμοράριος, presumably an imperial secretary (see note on **6**.3); he was clearly conversant with juridical procedures, had access to the emperor, and was in position to know of Harpocration's death before news of it could reach Egypt. According to his claim Harpocration had died without heirs and his estate was to be considered *bonum vacans* (ἀδέσποτον). It was a matter that lay in the jurisdiction of the *rationalis* (καθολικός).[4] Since the office of the *rationalis* had at its disposal insufficient staff to

---

[3] See below nn. on **7**.15–18 and **13**.16–19. It is probable that Conon is the σταθμοῦχος mentioned in Ammon's letter to his mother (**3**.iv.13).

[4] According to the traditional view (so A.H.M. Jones, *The Later Roman Empire 284– 604* I [Oxford 1964] 412f), in Egypt there were two *rationales* (καθολικοί) corresponding to the two departments of the central administration, *fiscus* and *res privata*, each headed by a *comes*. One καθολικός was thought to be a *rationalis summarum* in charge of the *fiscus* (ταμιεῖον), the other a *rationalis rei privatae* (see J. Lallemand, *L'Administration civile de l'Égypte* [Brussels 1964] 80f, 84ff). The former would be the successor of the διοικητής (D. Hagedorn, "Zum Amt des διοικητής im römischen Ägypten," *Yale Classical Studies* 28 [1985] 197), the latter the successor of the ἐπίτροπος τοῦ ἰδίου λόγου, who had authority over ἀδέσποτα in behalf of the *res privata*. If this hypothesis were correct, the

track by itself all instances of *bona caduca* and *bona vacantia* that were due to it, the help of informers was gladly accepted. Sometimes the *bona* to which a *delator* had pointed were not incorporated into the treasury but were granted to the *delator* himself.[5] Such is the case presented here. Eugeneios had applied to the emperor (doubtless Constantius II) through petition and the emperor had answered by rescript that the slaves should be granted to him if no one else entered a protest or claimed ownership of them (**8**.3f, **9**.21f, **13**. 47f, **15**.6f).

When Eugeneios arrived in Alexandria, he succeeded in finding the slaves, taking possession of them and delivering them to the office of the *catholicus*. Soon, however, he must have learned that Harpocration had left behind as legal heir a brother who he feared would advance a claim to the slaves. He then set out for the Thebaid to seek this brother. From no. **5** we know that Ammon, who had been detained in the Thebaid because of obligations, had the intention of sending to Alexandria a citizen of Panopolis, Aurelius Faustinus, who would declare before the prefect that an heir to the slaves alleged to be ownerless would be present in the person of Aurelius Ammon. This journey of Faustinus was apparently not carried out, since Eugeneios had anticipated this plan by his arrival in Panopolis, bringing a summons for Ammon to appear before the *catholicus* in Alexandria (**7**.37f = **9**.27–29 = **13**.51–53). But because Ammon actually intended to take possession of his brother's estate, the emperor's rescript had thus become moot.

Eugeneios therefore then put forward his claim to the slaves with a new argument. Having got possession of unclaimed property (ἀδέσποτα), by

---

καθολικός of our texts would presumably be a *rationalis rei privatae*, to be distinguished also from a *magister rei privatae* (Lallemand pp.86f, 260), a subordinate sometimes promoted to *rationalis*. Our texts, however, like all other papyri, mention only a single καθολικός without differentiating or specifying his function; the plural form of the word seems not to occur. Latin official fiscal terms continued in flux throughout the IV century onward so that their Greek equivalents may not be precisely defined (see R. Delmaire, *Largesses sacrées et res privata* [Collection de l'École Française de Rome 121, 1989] 3–23). Delmaire claims (p.13) that the distinction between the *fiscus* and the *res privata* disappeared after A.D. 330 and that confiscated property was absorbed by the *res privata* functioning as a component of the *fiscus*; see also Delmaire, "Le personnel de l'administration financière en Egypte sous le Bas-Empire romain (IV–VIe siècles)," *CRIPEL* 10 (1988) pp.113f, where Sisinnius is listed as no. 23 (p.123), as attested by an earlier edition of our text no. **6**. Thus at the time of Ammon's suit there was only one *rationalis* (καθολικός) in Egypt, the high official second in rank only to the prefect.

    [5] Jones (*op.cit.* n.4) I 422.

reason of his thus attained δεσποτεία he had gained a claim to it. Moreover, he had incurred expenses which had to be taken into account. Since his initial effort did not succeed, at this point he turned to a second scheme, namely arbitration conducted in Panopolis among certain 'friends' known to both parties, some of these friends being relatives of Ammon. Apparently the friends considered Eugeneios' arguments sufficiently weighty (or his presence so intimidating) that they and the principals agreed to a compromise. Ammon and Eugeneios thus concluded an agreement (**6**.7) providing for an equal division of the slaves (**13**.62f, **16b**.2–4). How three might be so divided is not explained.[6]

Ammon apparently thought that the affair had been settled with the concluding of this agreement, for when despite it he received summons from the *catholicus* to appear before his court, Ammon was greatly surprised (**6**.8). He proceeded to Alexandria and arrived there on 11 Choiak (7 xii 348) just before the expiration of the twenty-day period set for him. Two days after arriving he filed with the *catholicus* an affidavit (no. **6**) in which he declared that he had arrived on time and was presenting this διασφαλισμός because he had thus far been unable to find Eugeneios. In case Eugeneios were to allow the deadline to lapse without appearing, Ammon wished to forestall the possibility that his adversary might attempt some subterfuge. This document was to have been submitted by a public recorder to the *catholicus*. Whether a copy of it was actually submitted or such a step became superfluous because of Eugeneios' appearance we do not know.

Ammon must in any case have met with Eugeneios shortly after drawing up this document. What happened at their meeting is unknown since at this point a gap intervenes between the end of draft **13** and the beginning of draft **10a** (= **7**.63–66). After this gap we are informed for the first time of still unopened wills of Harpocration, which introduced a completely new situation. A first mention of these wills must have occurred in the gap.[7] Ammon himself apparently learned of them for the first time in the brief interval after

---

[6] In **13**.69f and perhaps in **15**.1, three slaves are mentioned. Since the agreement is for an equal division, it would seem to follow that the slaves were of an even number (four or six). But see above p. 22.

[7] At **7**.66 (= **10a**.13f) the mention of wills (διαθηκῶν) is explicit, but it is not clear why more than one will has been produced. For the possibility of the coexistence of several wills in the law of the papyri, see H. Kreller, *Erbrechtliche Untersuchungen auf Grund der graeco-aegyptischen Papyrusurkunden* (Leipzig/Berlin 1919) 391f.

drawing up his first address to the *catholicus* (**6**) and in the course of the week (or soon after) while he was drafting the second (nos. **7–15**).

Ammon applied himself now to the task of preparing a petition to the *catholicus* in which he set forth in detail the prior history of the dispute. Since the agreement of partition had evidently come to nothing and in fact Ammon was not entitled to agree to its terms after disclosure of the wills, he now advanced his claim to all the slaves in the confidence that the wills would name him as heir. Until the wills should be opened, he demanded as a first measure that the slaves be released from custody and turned over to him, apparently asking Eugeneios to name a citizen of either Alexandria or the Thebaid as his surety until the wills were opened and the matter be resolved conclusively.

Thus far the sequence of outward events.

The Legal Situation

At the time of this litigation Egypt was once again (A.D. 326–357) divided into two provinces, the 'Thebaid', Upper Egypt as far north as Hermoupolis and Antinoopolis, and 'Egypt', northward from there to the Delta. Though perceived by Ammon and his contemporaries as two distinct countries, both were governed from Alexandria at the imperial level by a single prefect and his next-in-command, the *catholicus*.

The emperor's rescript determined that Eugeneios should get the slaves εἰ μή τις τούτων ἀντιποιοῖτο μηδὲ φανείη τις τὴν τούτων δεσποτείαν ἐκδικῶν (**8**.3f = **9**.21f = **13**.47f = **15**.6f). This was the question of fact that the *catholicus* in Alexandria had to decide. It was to him that Eugeneios evidently had delivered the rescript,[8] and to him also he had handed over the slaves for safekeeping when he had found them (**9**.32f = **10a**.21).

Accordingly Eugeneios brings to Panopolis a summons issued by the *catholicus*. But when on arriving there he learns the facts of the case and realizes that the rescript alone is no longer effective, he changes his argument (writes Ammon) and insists on the question of δεσποτεία (**13**.54–56). Since the slaves were unhindered, they have run away and become ὡς ἐν ἐρημίαι ἀδέσποτα (**7**.44 = **13**.60). In Roman law a *servus sine domino* is *res nullius*, a property which belongs to no one. Whoever takes possession

---

[8] For further discussion see note on **9**.20 *infra*.

of it becomes its owner; assumed personal property in this case is possible.[9]
Evidently it is this legal position that Eugeneios adopts. Moreover he ad-
duces in support yet a second argument, that in searching for the slaves and
in caring for them he has incurred expenses that must be taken into account.
He is apparently not able, however, to carry through this extreme position.
He is therefore ready for a compromise offered by a partition agreement. One
suspects that he cannot easily prove that the slaves have become guilty of
δρασμός,[10] and besides in Roman law the ownership of slaves after their
flight is not so quickly forfeited. Originally in Roman law the actually exercised control of property, in addition to the intent to possess, was required
for continuance of possession. Ownership was therefore forfeited if effective
control ceased. In certain cases such as with runaway slaves, however, the
classical doctrine then prevailed, to allow possession to continue in spite of
cessation of effective control.[11] That the arguments of Eugeneios carried
some weight is shown by the fact that Ammon's friends had argued for a
compromise and Ammon had accepted.

Since the division agreement is not preserved and is cited only briefly in
our texts, we do not know how Ammon established his right to decision
concerning the slaves. Initially he probably held out for intestate inheritance
and up to this time had no knowledge of one or more unopened wills of Harpocration, a supposition supported by several indications. It would be the
simplest explanation for Ammon's surprise at being summoned before the
catholicus and for the fact that by the time he began formulating the drafts he
no longer felt bound by the division agreement. As recounted above, the
wills appear to be mentioned for the first time in the lacuna between the end
of **13** and the beginning of **10a** (= 7.63–66); also in support is the fact that

---

[9] On δεσποτεία see R. Taubenschlag, *The Law of Greco-Roman Egypt in the Light
of the Papyri*[2] (Warsaw 1955) pp.230ff and 249ff. On the acquisition of ownerless property
see M. Kaser, *Das römische Privatrecht* (Hb d. Altertumswissenschaft 10.3.3, Munich
1955) I sec.102 I.1 (p.358) and II sec.244 I.1 (p.207).

[10] Ammon himself never speaks of δρασμός in this connection; the slaves had merely
withdrawn κ]αθ' ἑαυτοὺς ζῶντες ἄνετοι καὶ ὥσπερ ἀπροστάτη[τοι (9.11f).

[11] On the question whether ownership of runaway slaves was retained or forfeited, see
Kaser I (*op.cit.* n.8) p.334 n.27; see also G. Nicosia, *L'acquisto del possesso mediante i
'potestati subiecti'* (Milan 1960). Cf. also H. Bellen, *Studien zur Sklavenflucht im
römischen Kaiserreich* (Wiesbaden 1971) 41–43 [= Forschungen zur antiken Sklaverei vol.
IV]. On mention of *servi fugitivi* in the papyri see P. Meyer in *Zeitschr. für vergleichende
Rechtswissenschaft* 39 (1921) 223 and *Sav.Z.* 46 (1926) 313; further Taubenschlag, *Law*[2]
p.83.

Ammon learned of them only after drafting no. **6**. In no. **5** he had in any case presented himself without reference to a will as consanguineous brother of the deceased and for this reason νόμιμος κληρονόμος, therefore heir despite absence of a will.

The evidence shows that Eugeneios too initially knew nothing of the existence of any wills. In his petition to the emperor he asked that the slaves be awarded to him ὡς ὄντα νῦν ἀδέσποτα καὶ μὴ ἐπὶ κληρονόμοις ἐκείνου τελευτήσαντος (**13**.44f = **5**.12f; cf. also **7**.32f and **9**.18f). That he might have sought to deceive the emperor Ammon does not impute to him; on the contrary he says that Eugeneios first discovered in Alexandria that Harpocration had relatives in Panopolis.

Nor do we learn at what point nor from what source the *catholicus* received information that the wills existed. In any case Ammon had reckoned that with the settlement of the division agreement the dispute would be resolved. That the *catholicus'* office intervened suggests that those officials may not have been willing to allow a fait–accompli to proceed on the basis of an agreed division and perhaps wished to verify whether Ammon was actually entitled to make any determination in regard to the slaves. Possibly too the summons was occasioned by discovery of the wills.

If Ammon had had knowledge of the wills at the time when he acceded to the partition agreement in Panopolis, he would have been able to dispose of the property only with the proviso that he should prove to be heir in fact after the wills were opened. At **7**.64 the aforementioned lacuna of unknown length, however, we read that Ammon is angry that some interloper could lay claim to his property, and after a further lacuna, πα]ρῆλθεν δὲ (Eugeneios is doubtless to be supplied) ` ´ ημ[ .... ἡ]μῖν .. [τοῦτο] καὶ ἀσφαλῶς `ἀναγκαίως´ τῶι γραμματείωι προσθεῖναι αὐτὸ δὴ τοῦτο τό· εἰ μὴ διέθετο ἐκεῖνος μη[δὲ]ν ἄλλο ἢ π[(cf. note on **7**.64). If γραμματεῖον refers to the agreement concluded in Panopolis, it means that Eugeneios subsequently in Alexandria demanded just such a proviso to the agreement. That too shows that Ammon first learned of the wills in Alexandria, and Eugeneios pressed him to adapt the agreement to the new situation. Ammon was not prepared for this. On the strength of this new situation he would have nothing more to do with an agreement resting on false grounds and therefore about to prove invalid.

Since Ammon seems initially to have had no notion of the wills and they were not yet opened, they must have been drawn up either outside Egypt or less likely in Alexandria.[12] If abroad, the witnesses whose presence would be required at the opening would have been difficult to assemble, and bringing them to Alexandria would have entailed delay. The only surprise is that there seems to have been more than one will (see note on **7**.66).

Delator proceedings have a long tradition. Like the *catholicus*, during the Roman period the ἐπίτροπος τοῦ ἰδίου λόγου often had to decide similar cases concerning informers. The edict of Tiberius Julius Alexander (A.D. 40–45) treats of the abuses of sycophants in connection with this department.[13] A lawsuit instigated by a sycophant and taking place before the Idios Logos which concerned usurpation of ἀδέσποτα is the so-called Nestnephis case, of which are preserved sixteen documents from the period A.D. 11–17.[14]

---

[12] A clear illustration of the opening of a will (λύσις διαθήκης), which at this time took place before the λογιστής (*curator civitatis*), is provided by *P.Oxy.* LIV 3758.134–55 (A.D. 325). Cf. also *P.Diog.* 10 pp.92ff and n.5; also *P.Köln* II 100.35–40; and *P.Oxy.* LIV 3741.5–7 n. and 39f. See further, Kreller (*op.cit.* n.6) 396–406; and O.E. Tellegen-Couperus, *Testamentary Succession in the Constitutions of Diocletian* (Zutphen 1982) 49–52.

[13] On this see G. Chalon, *L'édit de Tiberius Julius Alexander* (Olten/Lausanne 1964) 197–205; N. Lewis, "On Legal Proceedings under the Idios Logos: κατήγοροι and συκοφάνται," *JJP* 9–10 (1955–56) 117–25, repr. in *On Government and Law in Roman Egypt* (Am.Stud.Pap. 33 [1995] 56–64); and P.R. Swarney, *The Ptolemaic and Roman Idios Logos* (Toronto 1970) 61–64. On the conduct of *delatores* in the papyri, see R. Taubenschlag, "Il delatore e la sua responsabilita nel diritto dei papiri," *Studi Arangio-Ruiz* I (Naples 1952) 501–07 (= *Op.min.* II 729–36).

[14] Swarney (*op.cit.* n.12) 40ff; to the sixteen documents listed and analyzed add now eleven more, *CPR* XV 1–11 from the Satabous archive, 3 B.C.– A.D. 15. For further examples from papyri of the cooperation of *delatores* and the office of the Idios Logos see Chalon (*op.cit.* n.12) 198 n.4. Perhaps not a *delator* but rather a regular κατήγορος working in the the office of the Idios Logos is mentioned in *P.Oxy.* XLVI 3274 (*ca* A.D. 99–117), on which see N. Lewis, *BASP* 23 (1986) 127–30; this papyrus mentions the μήνυσις of a κατήγορος on the basis of which the Idios Logos intervened in the case of an inheritance. *Mitt. Chr.* 372 col. vi (A.D. 136) concerns a case before the Idios Logos that superficially resembles our case. Here a question of legal restraint on the possession of seven slaves is decided. The slaves are part of a deceased soldier's estate which the Idios Logos adjudged *bonum vacans*; the widow's claim was denied because according to military law the soldier's marriage was not valid.

A. PRELIMINARY DOCUMENTS, NOS. **5** AND **6**

5. DEPUTATION (ἐντολή)[1]

P.Köln inv. 4532r	20.3 x 20.2 cm.	Panopolis, A.D. 348
+ P.Duke inv. 19r	Plate IV	

Aurelius Ammon appoints Aurelius Faustinus to inform the prefect of Egypt, Flavius Nestorius, that in himself an heir is at hand who is entitled to inherit his deceased brother Harpocration's slaves, hitherto considered ownerless. Ammon declares further that it has come to his ears that someone is seeking to appropriate these slaves for himself as ownerless property. The name Eugeneios is not mentioned. Ammon himself has not come to Alexandria because he is detained in Panopolis on account of weighty business, especially the sowing. At no. **13**.29f τῶν δημοσίων μου τελεσμάτων δι-άλ[υσ]ις is cited as reason for hindrance.

Faustinus' journey was apparently not carried out since it is not mentioned in any of the drafts of the petition. Doubtless this plan was allowed to lapse because of the arrival of Eugeneios, which created a new situation. Since Ammon mentions that he is concerned about the sowing, the document may have been written in October or November.[2]

The papyrus is carefully written in Ammon's formal hand. He employs a high point to mark sentence-end (lines 9, 13, 21). Apparently also a low point is used in line 8 to mark the end of a subordinate clause (see note *ad loc.*). As in other documents that Ammon actually sent or intended to send, he meticulously distinguishes final -αι of the first-declension dative singular from all other occurrences by marking the dative ending -α͞ι as in line 11; thus the dative singular cannot be mistaken for the nominative plural. On the

---

[1] On deputizing a representative see L. Wenger, *Die Stellvertretung im Rechte der Papyri* (Leipzig 1906); O. Montevecchi, *La papirologia*[2] (Milan 1988) p. 233; J. Herrmann, "Interpretation von Vollmachtsurkunden," *Akten XIII Int. Papyrologenkongress* (Munich 1974) pp. 159–67 (= *Kl. Schr. zur Rechtsgeschichte* [Munich 1990] pp. 240–48). Examples of IV-cent. deputations are *P.Oxy.* XLVIII 3389, A.D. 343; *P.Lips.* 38.i.4–6 (=Mitt.*Chr.* 97 and Meyer, *Jur.Pap.* 91, A.D. 390); P.Lond. inv. 2222 at *Pap.Flor.* 19 (1990) p.507, A.D. 319; *P.Matr.* 5, A.D. 336/7; and *SB* XVI 12692.6–15, A.D. 399.

[2] On the time of sowing in Upper Egypt see M. Schnebel, *Die Landwirtschaft in hellenistischen Ägypten* (Munich 1925) 137ff.

verso in Ammon's draft hand is no. **12**, which is continued by two broken vertical lines in the upper left margin of the recto.

From the papyrus is missing at its foot about one-fifth of its height (see introduction to **12**) as a result of a crude, apparently modern cut, so that the remainder may have found its way into another collection. The text, almost complete, has lost perhaps only one or two lines and probably a generous margin at the foot. The Duke segment, approximately 6 cm in height and bearing lines 17–23, when acquired was wrapped in a strip of coarse linen; a larger adjoining piece at Duke doubtless originally encased the Cologne segment.

Text
(*margin*)

Αὐρήλιος Ἄμμων Πετεαρβεσχίνιος σχολαστικὸς ἀπὸ Πανὸς
          πόλε[ως]
τῆς Θηβαίδος *vacat* Αὐρηλίωι Φαυστίνωι πολίτηι καὶ φίλωι ἄρ-
          ξαντι
βουλευτῆι τῆς αὐτῆς πόλεως χαίρειν. *vacat* ἐπειδὴ ἐγὼ τέως
          ἀσχο-
4   λούμενος τυγχάνω, πρᾶγμα νῦν σπουδαιότατον μετὰ χεῖρας
    ἔχων καὶ τὸν τῆς γεωργίας ἅμα καιρὸν ἐπέχοντά με στέλλε-
    σθαι πρὸς ἀποδημίαν, βλέπων ἐν τῶι παρόντι, ὅπως μὴ ἄσπο-
    ρος ἡ ἡμετέρα γῆ γενομένη πρὸς τὰς δημοσίας με εἰσφορὰς
8   ἐνεδρεύσηι, ἐντέλλομαί σοι κατὰ ταύτην μου τὴν ἔγγρ[α]φον
    ἐντολὴν τὴν χώραν μου τέως πληρῶσαι. ἀκήκοα γάρ τινα
    ἐξαίφνης ἔξωθεν ἐπιστάντα βιαίωι τρόπωι ἢ κατὰ παραλογι-
    σμὸν ἐπιχειρεῖν ἁρπάσαι τὰ [ἐ]ν Ἀλεξανδρείαι ἀνδράποδα τοῦ
12 ἐμοῦ ἀδελφοῦ Ἀρποκρατίων[ο]ς, ὡς ὄντα νῦν ἀδέσποτα καὶ ὡς
    μὴ ἐπὶ κληρονόμοις ἐκείν[ο]υ τελευτήσαντος. ἐντέλλομαι
    οὖν σοι τὸν κύριόν μου τὸν δ[ι]ασημότατον ἔπαρχον τῆς
    Αἰγύπτου Φλάουιον Νεστόρ[ιο]ν περὶ τούτου διδάξαι, ὡς
          ἀδελφὸς
16 ὑ[πάρ]χει τοῦ ἀπελθόντος ἐκ[εί]νου Ἀρποκρατίωνος ὁμο-
          πάτρι-
    ός τε καὶ ὁμομήτριος νόμι[μ]ος ἐκείνου κληρονόμος Ἄμμων
    τοὔνομα, ὃς καὶ τῶν κατὰ Θη[η]βαίδα ὀλίγων αὐτοῦ
          πραγμά[τω]ν
    καὶ ταῦτα χερσωθέντων τὰ[ς] ὀχλήσεις φέρει καὶ κατ' ἀνά[γ]-
          κην
20 τῶν νόμων αὐτὸν εἰς τὴν τούτων φροντίδα συνελαυνόν-
    των διὰ τὰ τελέσματα τὰ δημ[ό]σια· ταύτην δέ σοι τὴν ἐντολὴν
    ὑπ' ἐμοῦ ἰδίο[ι]ς γράμμασι γρα[φε]ῖσαν ἐπιδίδωμι κυρίαν
          οὖ[σα]ν
    καὶ βεβα[ίαν   *ca 14*   ] ις ὑπερ[   ]
    -

2 Θηβαῖδος pap. 8 ενεδρευσηι. pap. 9 πληρωσαι· pap. 11 αλεξανδρειαι pap.
13 τελευτησαντος· pap. 18 θ[ ]βαϊδα pap. 20 δημ[ ]σια· pap.

Translation

Aurelius Ammon, son of Petearbeschinis, advocate, from Panopolis of the Thebaid, to Aurelius Faustinus, fellow-citizen and friend, ex-magistrate, councillor of the same city, greetings. Since just now I happen to be engaged, having in hand business now most urgent together with the season of farming that keeps me from setting out on a journey, concerned at present that our land if it is not sown may not embarrass me with respect to the public levies, I deputize you by this my written authorization to fill my place during this time. For I have heard that someone coming forward suddenly from abroad is attempting forcibly and fraudulently to seize my brother Harpocration's slaves in Alexandria on the grounds that they are now ownerless and that he has died without heirs. I appoint you therefore to inform my lord the prefect of Egypt, Flavius Nestorius, *vir perfectissimus*, about this, that there exists a full brother of the said deceased Harpocration as his lawful heir, Ammon by name, who bears the travails of his few possessions in the Thebaid which are, moreover, uninundated, and by force of the laws that compel him to the care of them on account of the public taxes. This deputation written by me in my own hand I convey to you as authoritative and binding [   ] in behalf of (?) [

2–3. On ἄρξας βουλευτής see F. Oertel, *Die Liturgie* (Leipzig 1917) 315 with n.4; A.K. Bowman, *The Town Councils of Roman Egypt* (Toronto 1971) 29; H. Geremek, "Les βουλευόμενοι égyptiens sont-ils identique aux βουλευταί?" *Anagennesis* 1 (1981) 231ff. The complimentary πολίτηι 'fellow-citizen' and φίλωι are added not to please Faustinus but to commend him to the eye of the prefect to whom the ἐντολή would be shown.

3. In the late period τέως undergoes an extension of meaning from purely temporal to modal: 'γε, quidem, certe' (D. Tabachovitz, *Études sur le grec de la Basse Époque* [Uppsala/Leipzig 1943] 70ff). Cf. also the use of τέως at line 9 and in **3** *passim*.

4. The phrase μετὰ χεῖρας, although not cited by LSJ, is the equivalent of ἐν χερσί and κατὰ χεῖρας as exemplified by nine III/IV-cent. occurrences (*P.Cair.Goodsp.* 15.19, *P.Lond.* V 1650.r.1, *P.Oxy.* VI 901.10 [= LIV 3771] and 934.r.8, XXXIII 2668.14, XLIII 3126.r.2.11, *PSI* IX 1081.r.8, *SB* VIII 9875.14 and XVI 12693.3.41).

8. After ἐνεδρεύσηι occurs a point below the line. If it is not an accidental inkspot (as e.g. below ἡμετέρα in line 7), it is here a low point marking the end of a dependent clause.

9. τὴν χώραν μου ... πληρῶσαι: on the various phrases used for designating deputation, see E. von Druffel, *Papyrologische Studien zum byzantinischen Urkundenwesen* (Munich 1915) 34f.

12f. This phrase is adopted again at **13**.44f; cf. also **7**.32f and **9**.18f.

14f. Here and at *P.Vindob.* inv. L 132.3 and 10 (P.J. Sijpesteijn / K.A. Worp, *Tyche* 1 [1986] 189) Flavius Nestorius has the rank-designation διασημότατος (*perfectissimus*), while Flavius Philagrius before him was entitled λαμπρότατος (*clarissimus*) (*ibid.* p.193 and Lallemand, *op.cit.* n.6, 61). On Flavius Nestorius see Cl. Vandersleyen, *Chronologie des préfets d'Égypte de 284 à 395* (Brussels 1962) 16 no. 28, Lallemand 244 no. 20, and Jones/Martindale/Morris, *Prosopography of the Later Roman Empire* I (Cambridge 1971) pp.625f.

16. For ἀπέρχεσθαι in the meaning 'die' cf. e.g. *P.Oxy.* LIV 3758.140 and 189 [εἰ] τοῦ βίου ἀπέλθοι, and the examples in *WB* I.

18ff. Understood is "who cannot come in person because" *vel sim.*

19. καὶ ταῦτα χερσωθέντων 'and moreover lie waste': on this usage see LSJ *s.v.* οὗτος VIII 2a καὶ ταῦτα, adv., 'and *that*, particularly'.

23. Possibly βεβα[ίαν ἐπὶ πᾶσι τοῖς προκειμέν]οις as at *P.Oxy.* XLVIII 3389.19, but what followed departs from that parallel.

6. AMMON'S CERTIFICATION TO THE *CATHOLICUS*

P.Köln inv. 4533r   30.5 x 26.5cm   Alexandria, 9 xii 348
[= *SB* XIV 11929, P.Duke inv. 1278]   Plate XVIII

Despite the contract which has been negotiated between Ammon and Eugeneios in Panopolis and which provided for a division of the slaves, Ammon has received a summons to appear before the court of the *catholicus* Flavius Sisinnius, named here for the first time in the papyri. He arrives in Alexandria just before the expiration of the appointed twenty-day interval (beginning 27 Hathyr = 23 xi 348) on 11 Choiak (7 xii 348) and for two days searches in vain to make contact with Eugeneios. In order to establish that Eugeneios can offer no pretext at the expiration of the interval, Ammon draws up this document for presentation to the *catholicus* through a public notary (ταβουλάριος). On such notifications for the purpose of protecting one's rights see Mitt. *Grundz.* pp.33f and Meyer, *Jur.Pap.* p.314. A parallel to our text is *P.Ant.* II 88 (probably A.D. 221)[1] and the affidavit addressed to the Idios Logos, Mitt. *Chr.* 68 (A.D. 14), in which the parties likewise charged in an informer case (the Nestnephis case) declare their presence at the *conventus* in Alexandria. On unexcused failure to appear at a court-appointed date see A. Steinwenter, *Studien zum römischen Versäumnisverfahren* (Munich 1914) pp.73–91. On assessment of a fine for unexcused absence cf. *P. Flor.* I 6.24.

Although written in Ammon's formal hand as if for presentation (consistently observing his idiosyncratic macron to distinguish dat.sing.fem. as in no. **5**), infelicities and errors noted in lines 6, 7f and 17 explain why this copy was not submitted and so remains a draft; its verso and all four margins were then reused for a draft of another document, **13**. Whether a formal copy of **6** was actually presented, or became moot because of the subsequent discovery of Eugeneios, remains unknown.

The papyrus was first edited by G.M. Browne[2] and his text was reprinted as *SB* XIV 11929.

---

[1] On this papyrus see J. Bingen, *Essays in Honor of C. Bradford Welles* (Am.Stud.Pap. I [New Haven 1966]) 231–34.

[2] Browne, "Harpocration Panegyrista," *op.cit. supra* p. x.

Text

(margin)

Φλαυίωι Σισι[ννί]ωι   τῶι διασημοτάτωι καθολικῶι

παρὰ Αὐρηλίο[υ "Αμμων]ος Πετεαρβεσχίνι[ο]ς σχολαστικοῦ
       ἀπὸ Πανὸς πόλεως

τῆς Θηβαίδο[ς. ἐ]πειδὴ Εὐγένειος μεμ[ορ]άριος καὶ ἐγὼ ὁ
       "Αμ[μ]ων, φίλων με-

4 ταξὺ ἡμῶν γ[εν]ομένων ἐπὶ τῆς Πανοπ[ολ]ιτῶν πόλεως Πα[ν]ί-
       σκ[ο]υ ἀπὸ δικαιο[δ]ότου

   καὶ Ἀπόλλωνο[ς π]οιητοῦ καὶ ἄλλου Ὡρίωνο[ς], ὁμολογίαν
       ἔγγραφον κοινὴν πεπ[οι]ή-

   μεθα περὶ ἀνδ[ρ]απόδων ἐν Ἀλεξανδρείαῑ νῦν ὄντων [τ]ῆι
       λαμπρᾱῑ ταύτηι πόλει

   ὑπὸ Ἀρποκρατίω[ν]ος καταλελ[ε]ιμμένων το̣ῦ ἀδελφοῦ τοῦ
       [ἐ]μοῦ ἐν δισ[σ]ῆι ὁμολογ[ί]αῑ

8 ταύτηι, οὐκ οἶδ[α ἀν]θ᾽ ὅτου ὑπήχθην προθεσ[μί]αν ὁρισθεῖ-
       [σα]ν τοιαύτη[ν] κατα̣δέξασθαι

   ὥστε εἴσω ἡμ[ερ]ῶν εἴκοσι ἀπὸ ἑβδόμης καὶ ε[ἰ]κάδος Ἀθὺρ
       [τοῦ] παρελθόν[τ]ος μηνὸς εἰς

   τὴν Ἀλεξάνδρ[ειά]ν με παραγενέσθαι, ὅπω[ς] πέρας ἐπιτεθῆι τῶι
       πρά[γμα]τι. ἐλθ̣ὼ̣ν δὲ̣

   νῦν ἐνταῦθα π[ρ]ὸ̣ ἄλλων δύο ἡμερῶν τῶι προειρημένωι
       Εὐγενείωι οὐ συνῆλ[θ]ον

12 οὐδὲ εὑρεῖν αὐτ[ὸ]ν δεδύνημαι, διὰ τοῦτο σήμερον δημοσίαῑ
       μαρτύρομαι, ἥτ̣ι̣[ς] ἐστὶ

   Χοιὰκ τρισκαι[δ]εκάτη, πρὸ ἄλλων ἡμερῶν τεσσάρω`ν´ τῆς
       π[ροθεσμίας π]α̣ρ̣α̣γ̣ε̣ν̣[ό]μενος,

   καὶ ἀξιῶν τοῦτόν μου τὸν δι[α]σφαλισμὸν κατακεῖσθαι ἐν
       [ἀσφαλεῖ ἕως ἂν ἐκεῖ]νος

   [π]αραγένηται πρὸς τὸ μὴ ἐξεῖναι αὐτῶι σκῆψίν τινα προβα[λέ-
       σθαι, τὰ δὲ ὑπ᾽ ἐμο]ῦ

16 π̣ρ̣οτεθέντα ἀξιῶ ἐπὶ τὸ σὸν μεγαλεῖον, δέσποτα, ἀνενεχθῆν[αι
       διὰ τοῦ δημοσίο]υ

   τ̣α̣βουλαρίου κατὰ τὴν σήμερον ἡμέραν {κατὰ τὴν σήμε[ρον
       ἡμέραν]}.

Translation

To Flavius Sisinnius, *rationalis*, *vir perfectissimus*, from Aurelius [Ammon] son of Petearbeschinis, advocate from Panopolis of the Thebaid. Whereas Eugeneios, imperial secretary (*memorarius*), and I, Ammon, (friends having come between us in Panopolis — Paniskos, former *juridicus*, and Apollon the poet and another, Horion) have made a written agreement in common concerning slaves now in this splendid city Alexandria left behind by my brother Harpocration, in this agreement in duplicate, for some unknown reason I was summoned to accept a fixed time such that within twenty days from the 27th of the preceding month Hathyr I was to be present in Alexandria in order that a final decision be imposed in the matter. But now after arriving here two days ago I did not meet the aforesaid Eugeneios and I have not been able to find him. For this reason I bear witness publicly today, which is Choiak 13th, having arrived four days earlier than the appointed time (expires) and asking that this my certification be deposited in security until that person arrives, in order that it may not be possible for him to proffer an excuse. I ask that the facts set forth by me be referred to your greatness, my lord, through the public notary on this day.

ὑπατείας Φλαυίου Φιλίππου τοῦ λαμπροτάτου ἐπάρχου τοῦ
[ἱεροῦ πραιτωρίου κ]αὶ
Φλαυίου Σαλιᾶ τοῦ λαμπροτάτου μαγίστρου ἱππέων Χο[ιὰκ ιγ.]
20   Αὐρήλιος Ἄμμων προὔθηκα ὡς πρόκειται.
(margin)

---

3 θηβαϊδος pap.   7 λαμπραι pap.   passim -αι pap.

Notes

1. On Flavius Sisinnius see note on **12**.1–8. διασημότατος, *perfectissimus*, is the proper rank designation for the *rationalis* (see Lallemand, *op.cit. supra* p. 53 n.4, 83).

2. Compare ἀπὸ Πανὸς πόλεως with line 4 ἐπὶ τῆς Πανοπ[ολ]ιτῶν πόλεως. The former is a purely topographical designation, which as a rule appears without the article; the latter is the 'official' nomenclature, with which the article normally stands (D. Hagedorn, *ZPE* 12 [1973] 277–92).

3. μεμ[ορ]άριος, at **7**.29 μεμοράριο[ς: cf. *Corp.Gloss.Lat.* II 467.8 s.v. ὑπομνηματογράφος : *actuarius, memoralius*, by dissimilation from *memorarius* as suggested by W. Heraeus at *TLL* s.v. Epiphan. *Haer.* 71.1 p.250. 26 Holl has μεμοραδίοις, where the Migne editor (*PG* 42 376c) considers μεμοραρίοις. Cf. also μεμοριάλιος, Lat. *memorialius*. On the *memoriales* cf. *Codex Theod.* VI 35,2. The word μεμοράριος itself appears to indicate a member of the *officium memoriae*, foremost of the three palatine civil secretariats (cf. p.2, n.2). Eugeneios was no doubt therefore an important official at court who would have had direct access to the emperor, perhaps too a member of the imperial *schola notariorum* with the rank of *tribunus et notarius*. For a recent discussion of the functions of this rank and its advancement in the early IV century see H.C. Teitler, *Notarii and Exceptores* (Amsterdam 1985) 54–68 and notes thereto, although the term *memorarius* is not cited, nor has it occurred elsewhere in the papyri. A military *exceptor* at Oxyrhynchus in A.D. 295 is named Εὐγένιος (*P.Oxy.* I 43.2.26). Perhaps equivalent is the term *adiutor memoriae* (= βοηθὸς τῆς μνήμης τοῦ Αὐτοκράτορος), for which see J.R. Rea *et al.*, "A Ration-warrant for an '*adiutor memoriae*'," *YCS* 28 (1985) p.104 n. on line 4 and p.110 (a bilingual papyrus from Caesarea dated A.D. 293).

In the consulship of Flavius Philippus the *clarissimus* prefect of the Sacred Praetorium and Flavius Salia the *clarissimus magister equitum*, Choiak 13.

I, Aurelius Ammon, have set forth (this affidavit) as above.

3f. φίλων μεταξὺ ἡμῶν γ[εν]ομένων : cf. *PSI* XII 1256.8 (iii cent.) φίλοι μεταξὺ γενόμενοι, *P.Haun.* III 57.10 (v cent.) φίλοι μεταξὺ γενάμενοι ... εἰς διάλυσιν ἤγαγον. On mediation, see T. Gagos / P. van Minnen, *Settling a Dispute: Toward a Legal Anthropology of Late Antique Egypt* (Ann Arbor 1994), esp. pp.30–46.

4f. Cf. **7**.42ff and **13**.55f. Paniskos is a name very common in the Thebaid, especially Panopolis; this Paniskos, presumably a former δικαιο-δότης (*iuridicus*) or at least a subordinate in that office (cf. **13**.55 and n.), was a Panopolite who had been a member of the higher administration in Alexandria and therefore probably known to both Eugeneios and Ammon. Cf. H. Kupiszewski, "The Juridicus Alexandreae," *JJP* 7–8 (1953–54) 187–204; H.J. Mason, *Greek Terms for Roman Institutions* (Am.Stud.Pap. 13, 1974) 23 *s.v.* ἀπό 2; and N. Lewis, *AJP* 81 (1960) pp.186f (= Am.Stud. Pap. 33 [1995] pp.73f.

5. On the personal name Ἀπόλλων see note on **7**.42. At **7**.44f = **13**.56 Ammon calls Apollon ἀδελφιδοῦς ὁ ἐμός. From nos. **3** and **4** we learned that Ammon's deceased half-brother Horion, *archiprophetes* of the Panopolite nome, had a son Horion 'the Younger' who was expected to succeed his father. By the phrase ἄλλου Ὡρίωνος Ammon means 'another person, Horion', i.e. another nephew. Although Ammon chooses to call them φί-λων, one is his nephew and another probably so. The ὁμολογίαν ἔγγρα-φον κοινὴν was a διάλυσις, the compromise agreed upon through media-tion.

6. λαμπρᾶι ταυτηι seems to be the reading here, therefore not the expected λαμπροτάτηι, but it may be a lapse for the latter and a reason why this copy was not presented. When Ammon arrived in Alexandria the slaves had been in custody at the office of the *catholicus* (cf. **13**.69f) but eventually

escaped (cf. **13**.69f). When writing **6** Ammon apparently didn't yet know about their escape.

7f. The phrase ἐν δισ[σ]ῆι ὁμολογ[ί]αῑ ταύτηι ought to refer back to ὁ]μολογίαν ἔγγραφον at line 5, though one would expect δισσὴν γραφεῖσαν, although far removed from its referent. It is conceivable, albeit unlikely, that it should be taken with the following ὑπήχθην κτλ.

8. On summons see E. Seidl, *Rechtsgeschichte Ägyptens als römischer Provinz* (Sankt Augustin 1973) 116ff.

9. For summons to appear at court within a 20-day period, cf. *P.Giss.* 34.6 (= Mitt. *Chr.* 75); for other fixed periods of 20 days, *P.Berl.Leihg.* II 46.A.1.7, *P.Hib.* II 197.1.8, and Mitt. *Chr.* 88.3.9. Other προθεσμίαι were sometimes prescribed, especially of 10 or 30 days. Twenty days for a summons from Panopolis to Alexandria seems rather tight.

10. Cf. *P.Giss.* 25.7 δεόμενος αὐτοῦ, ὅπως πέρας ἐπιθῇ τῷ πράγματι. — ἐλθὼν δὲ : ἀλλ' ἐπεὶ Browne.

11. Cf. no. **18a**.1.

12. Cf. no. **5**.24.

13. π]αραγεν[ό]μενος : of the presumed six letters between lacunae only the tops are preserved and so are very doubtful, but thereafter -μενο- seems quite clear; μαρτύρομαι with participle is a classical usage. Browne read παρα]γενέσθαι before our realignment of the fragment bearing the right margin. If Ammon had departed from Panopolis the day after receiving his summons and arrived in Alexandria four days before the end of the twenty-day προθεσμία, his voyage downriver would have taken fifteen days. Comparative estimated times for travel upriver, manifestly slower, are inferred by D.W. Rathbone in "Dates of Recognition in Egypt," *ZPE* 62 (1986) 102f; time from Alexandria to Panopolis in the III century he calculates to require 25–30 days.

14. δι[α]σφαλισμὸν 'certification, affidavit' (not in LSJ): the noun occurs elsewhere only at *P.Rain.Cent.* 84.5 (Arsinoe, A.D. 315); its rare parent verb is found at *P.Oxy.* XVII 2104.17 and XXII 2343.10 (as revised at *SB* XVIII 13932).

15f. προβα[λέσθαι, τὰ δὲ ὑπ' ἐμο]ῦ | προτεθέντα : προβα[λέσθαι πρὸς τὰ ὑπ' ἐμο]ῦ | [π]ροτεθέντα, Browne.

17. The careless repetition of the phrase κατὰ τὴν σήμερον ἡμέραν is another reason why this copy was not presented; see nn. on lines 6 and 7f above.

18f. On the dating see R.S. Bagnall / K.A. Worp, *The Chronological Systems of Byzantine Egypt* (Stud.Amst. VIII, Zutphen 1978) 112.

B. AMMON'S PETITION TO THE CATHOLICUS (διαμαρτυρία)

7	P.Duke inv. 189r	Alexandria, between 9 and 13 xii 348
8	P.Duke inv. 187r	
9	P.Duke inv. 18v (on the verso of **10a–b**)	
10a, 10b	P.Duke inv. 18r	
11	P.Duke inv. 189v (on the verso of **7**)	
12	P.Köln inv. 4532v + P.Duke inv. 19v (on the verso of **5**)	
13	P.Köln inv. 4533v + r (on the verso and the recto margins of **6**)	
14	P.Duke inv. 188r	
15	P.Duke inv. 217r + P.Köln inv. 4547r	

This petition, of which a considerable number of fragmentary drafts are preserved (**7–15**) although none is complete, has the form of a petition addressed to the *catholicus* and toward the end (**10a**.9ff) comes to a close with a request for the return of the slaves then held in the office of the *catholicus*. At the same time it is also a *protestatio*, designating itself properly as a διαμαρτυρία (see note on **13**.11). Its purpose is set forth at **10a**.9–14 (= **7**. 65f). By it Ammon seeks to counteract and thwart the ἀπάτη (**10a**.11 = **7**. 65), evidently of Eugeneios, in order that no prejudice (πρόκριμα, **10a**. 14 = **7**.66) may be caused. The petition may thus be classed as a *protestatio* of a legal-evidentiary character.

The drafts were written after no. **6** but surely before the expiration of the twenty-day period referred to at **6**.9, therefore between 9th and 13th December 348.

The Sequence of the Drafts

The outline and content of the several drafts of the petition vary in three principal respects: first, there is a progression of rhetorical embellishments and *sententiae*; second, Ammon is inconsistent in his accounts of his role in receiving the slaves initially from his brother and depositing them with Konon, perhaps because of embarrassment at his own neglect; and third, the developing situation regarding the discovery of Harpocration's wills. Each of these criteria is severely hampered by coinciding lacunae and the fragmentary state of most of the drafts. Only two are written in Ammon's formal hand, **7** (which he discontinued after two columns and used its margins to

interpolate and continue the text in his draft hand) and the extremely fragmentary and less carefully written **14**. All the others are written in the draft
hand.

A postulation of the sequence in which the drafts were composed is aided
by the circumstance that papyri are normally written first on the recto and
only then on the verso.[1] Thus it seems clear at the outset that **7** (P.Duke inv.
189r) must have been written before **11** (P.Duke inv. 189v), although **9**
(P.Duke inv. 18v) was irregularly written before **10** (P.Duke inv. 18r), as
explained in the introduction to **9**; in **9** the wills of Harpocration are not yet
mentioned but are mentioned in **10a**. In **8** are phrases expanded from **7** but
briefer than their versions in **9**, **13** and **15**. That **10** is later than **7** is shown
by the incorporation at **10a**.7–14 of a passage that had been formulated on
the margin of **7** (lines 63–66), although the margins of **7** were obviously
written after the body of **7** and possibly after paragraphs drafted initially in **9**
and **10**. The relative order may therefore be **7–8–9–10** but is not certain.

It seems evident that the more expanded drafts **12** and **13** were written
after the shorter **7**, **8**, **9** and **10**. As the most fully elaborated drafts, they
were presumably written later. It seems to be characteristic of Ammon to am-
plify, hardly ever to contract his prose, which he particularly likes to orna-
ment by inserting moralizing, quasi-philosophical *sententiae*. Since **13** is the
most comprehensive of the surviving drafts and has incorporated something
from each of the others, it would appear to be the latest of the series. Moreover it is the only draft that frequently employs abbreviation and suspension,
as though passages adopted from earlier drafts (even the eloquent preamble
developed in **12**) are already familiar. It might be argued that certain rhetorical flourishes like the clause at **13**.9ff are somewhat awkward in a petition
and consequently have been suppressed in **12**; but it is unlikely that Ammon,
well versed in late Roman rhetoric, would have appreciated our own sense of
restraint. Small blemishes like the unneeded ἑστάναι at line **13**.8 (but not at
12.8) would doubtless have been corrected in a final fair copy.

The position of **11** is puzzling. Obviously later than **7** on the verso of
which it stands, its overlap with **12** is slight (**12**.18 = **11a**.4), and **11a**.4
seems to stand closer to **7**.19f than the corresponding passage in **12**. It is

---

[1] U. Wilcken, "Recto oder Verso?," *Hermes* 22 (1887) 487–92; E.G. Turner, "The
Terms Recto and Verso: the Anatomy of the Papyrus Roll," *Actes du XVe Congrès* (Pap.
Brux. 16.1, Brussels 1978) sec. 3.2–4.

likely therefore to have stood between **7** and **12**. Because of its poor preservation and apparent disorganization, however, it is difficult to determine its place in the sequence of drafts. **14** and **15** cannot be placed in the sequence with any confidence.

To attempt to construct a single combined text of these changing and disparate drafts would be misleading and indeed useless; but to illustrate our interpretation of these nine drafts, following **15** we offer a translation of them as hypothetically combined. Indeed a final fair copy of the complete petition may never have been written or delivered, for altered circumstances may well have obviated the need for it: possibly Eugeneios may have abandoned his attempts, or the case may have become moot for other reasons.

7

P.Duke inv. 189r   *ca* 43.6 x 26.8 cm   Plate XIX
(formal hand 1–44, draft hand 45–71)

The recto of this large but very fragmentary papyrus bears two columns of what is apparently Ammon's initial effort, written in his formal hand, to compose his principal petition to the *catholicus* Sisinnius. The lines of each column average 62 to 64 letters. Since the two columns failed to suffice for all he wished to say, he filled the intercolumnar space with an insertion keyed apparently to col. ii.42, then continued with addenda (all in his draft hand) in the outer margins. Even these did not suffice, and he proceeded to compose further elaborations and revisions on separate sheets and the versos of other documents.

On the verso is **11**.

Text

col. i

(*margin*)

1   [Φλαυίωι Σισιννίωι   *vacat*   ] τῶι διασημ[οτάτωι]
      καθολικῶι

2   [παρὰ Αὐρηλίου Ἄμμωνος Πετεαρβεσχίνιος] σχολαστικο[ῦ
      ἀπὸ Παν]ὸς πόλεως τῆς

3   Θ[ηβαίδος. ἡσυχίαν τοῖς ἐν φιλοσο]φίαι καὶ λό[γοις ἀνηγ]μένοις
      πρέπ[ει]ν

4   κα[ὶ αὐτὸς ἐπιστάμενος   *ca 11*   ]μετερα δια[*ca 16*   πρ]ο-

5   [αχθεὶς ἐπὶ ταύτην τὴν διαμαρτυρίαν· εἰ] μὲν γὰρ ἐξῆ[ν τοῖς   *ca 9*
      ηρη]μέ-

6   [νοις κατὰ τὸ τῆς φύσε]ως αὐθ[αίρετον μέχ]ρι τέλου[ς ἀπολαύ-
      ειν τῆς   *ca 7*   ]

7   [*ca 18*   ]ων ὑπ[*ca 8*   ἀπειλ]εῖ δὲ φθόν[ος ἀεὶ τοῖς καλοῖς]

8   [*ca 15*   πρὸ]ς ταῦτα [ἀ]ναγκασθέντ[*ca 18*   ]ν

9   [*ca 18*   ]τοις ἀδι[κ   *ca 8*   ἡ] λῆξις [κ]ηδεμ[όνα   ]
                   `ἐμὸς`

10 [*ca 18*   ] κατεμ[*ca 9*   ]..[.] α[.]οκρα[*ca 10*   ].ου.

11 [ca 18   ]ντων [*ca 11*   ἀπ]οδημίαν [*ca 13*   ]ων
12 [*ca 18*   ] [ ] [*ca 12*   ] εντ[   ]
13 [*ca 17*   ] τε[ ] [   ]

- -

[*loss of probably one line*]

- -

14 [   ] τότε [*ca 18*   ] [   ]
15 [ ] παρ' ἐ[μοὶ   *ca 9*   ] ἐνετείλατό μοι ἀ[ναγαγεῖν εἰς
        Θη]βαίδα [   ]
16 μενος δέ [τιν' ἐκ τῶν ἀνδ]ραπόδων τούτω[ν   *ca 19*   ] κἀμο[ὶ
        ἕ]πεσθ[αι εἰς Θηβαίδα]
17 ἀνήγαγ[ον κ]ατὰ [τὰς τοῦ] ἀδελφοῦ ἐντολὰς [*ca 15*   ]ς
        ἐβουλήθη π[ρὸ τῆς τοῦ ἀδελ]-
18 φοῦ παρο[υσία]ς οὐκέτι ἀκολ[ο]υθεῖν ἀναγκάσαι, ἀλλὰ [παρὰ
        τῶι αὐτῶι] Κόνωνι κατέλ[ε]ιπ[ον ὁμο]-
19 λογίαν πα[ρ' α]ὐτοῦ δεξάμενος, ὅπως ἐπανελθ[όντι ἐκείνω]ι
        ἀποκαταστήση[ι τὰ ἀν]-
20 δράποδα, προσεδ[ό]κων γὰ[ρ] τὴν ἐκείνου ἐπ[άνοδον μετὰ
        βραχύν] τινα γενήσε[σθαι χρό]-
21 νον. ἀεὶ δὲ τοῦ ἀνδρὸς τὴν ἄφιξιν πρὸ ὀφθαλ[μῶν   *ca 16*   ]
        εν[   ]χος [   ]

22 βανον ει η[ ]α   αὐτοῦ [τὴ]ν ἐπάνοδον [*ca 30*   ]
        [ ]
23 ἐπὶ τὰ ἀνδράποδα αὐτὸς ε [ ], φήμης δὲ πρ[ώην διαδοθείσης ὡς
        εἴη τελευτήσας]
24 ἐκεῖνος, πρὸ χρόνου γὰρ βραχ[έο]ς τοῦτο ἀκήκοα, [οὐ γὰρ
        ταχέως εἰς ἀκοὴν τῶν οἰκείων ἀφι]-
25 κνεῖται ὁ περὶ τοῦ θανάτου τῶν ἐπὶ ξένης λόγο[ς διὰ τὸ μηδένα
        βούλεσθαι μετὰ τοιαύτης]
26 ἀγγελίας προσιέναι τοῖς τῶι τετελευτηκότι κα[τ' ἀγχιστείαν δια-
        φέρουσι. παρεσκευαζόμην]
27 μὲν ἐ[πὶ τ]ῆι ἀκοῆι [τ]αύτηι δεῦρο καταπλεῦσαι, π[*ca 20*
        διὰ τὰ ἀνδράποδα]
28 ἡμῶν τὰ ἐνταυθοῖ διατρίβο[ν]τα. ἕως δὲ ταύτη[ν ἐν χερσὶν εἶχον
        τὴν φροντίδα, ἐξαί]-
29 φνης ἔξωθεν ἐπιστὰς Εὐ[γε]νειος μεμοράριο[ς   ]

30 κατασχεῖν ἠξίου καὶ ὑπ' [α]ὐτοῦ μὴ δι' ἀγχι[στείαν   ]
31 β ετ ε καὶ μὴ τὴν τού[τ]ων διάπρασιν [ca 20   τὰ ἀνδράποδα]
                          (margin)
col. ii

                          (margin)
32 τοῦ ἀδελφοῦ μου ὡς μὴ ἐπὶ κληρονόμοις ἐκείνου τελευτ[ήσαντος
                καὶ ὡς νῦν ὄντα]
33 ἀδέσποτα ἐξ αἰτήσεως ἐσχηκέναι παρὰ τῆς ἐνθέου τύ[χης τῶν
                καλλινίκων]
34 δεσποτῶν ἡμῶν. ἐν Ἀλεξανδρείαι δὲ γενόμενος οὗτος κ[αὶ γνοὺς
                ἐκεῖνον τὸν]
35 Ἀρποκρατίωνα κλη[ρον]όμον ἔχειν ἀδελφὸν ὁμοπάτρι[όν τε καὶ
                ὁμομήτριον, ἐμὲ δὴ]
36 τὸν Ἄμμωνα, παρ[αυτίκ]α εἰς Θηβαίδα ἀνέδραμεν ἴ[σως τοῦτο
                πυθάνεσθαι βου]-
37 λ[ό]μενος, ἔλεγε[ν δὲ γ]ράμματα ἔχειν παρὰ τῆς σῆ[ς   ca 10
                π α ρ α]-
38 καλοῦντά με εἰς [τὴν Ἀλεξα]νδρέων πόλιν, τὸν πρὸ τ[ῆς τούτου
                ἀφίξεως προπαρεσκευασμένον]
39 δεῦρο καταπλε[ῦσαι διὰ ταῦ]τα τὰ ἀνδράποδα. ἀφικόμεν[ος δὲ
                εἰς τὴν πατρίδα τὴν ἐμὴν]
40 καὶ γνοὺς τοῦ π[ράγματος] τὴν ἀκρίβειαν καὶ ὡς το[ῦ πρώτου
                ἐπιχειρήματος ἀποτυχών],
41 λοιπὸν εἰς ἄλλο τ[ι ἐτράπη] καὶ περὶ τοῦτο ἐστρέφετο. φ[ίλους
                γὰρ ἀξιώσας μεταξὺ]
42 γενέσθαι (ancora, insertion from intercolumnar margin) καὶ Ἀπόλλων
    ὁ ποιητὴς
44 ὁ ἀδελφιδοῦς
    ὁ ἐμὸς, ὃν
    καὶ ἡ σή,
    ὦ δέσποτα,
48 περὶ τοὺς λό-
    [γο]υς ἀρετή
    τε καὶ φιλη-
    κοΐα γινώ-
52 σκει τὴν

παρὰ σοῦ,
τοῦ ἐμοῦ
δεσπότου,
56 ἐν Θηβαίδι
εὐτυχή-
[σα]ντα ἀκρόα-
[σ]ιν, [vacat?]
- - - - - - - -

60 (from 42) καὶ [*ca 10*   ]α τινα καὶ καμάτους επ[*ca 10*   , ἕως
                 ἂν συλλάβηι καὶ]
61 [σ]υναγάγηι τὰ [ἀνδράποδα] ταῦτα τῆι δ [..... ἐσκορπισμένα καὶ
                 δρασμὸν πλημμε]-
62 [λ]ήσαντα κα[ὶ ὡς ἐν ἐρημίαι ἀδ]έσποτ[α   ]
                 [*ca 20 lines lost*]

(addendum in the upper margin)
63 [*ca 45 ?*]μαι τέλει τοῦ πρ[άγματ]ος καὶ σχεδὸν οὐδὲ ἐμαυτοῦ
                 εἶναι ἐδόκουν ὁρῶν τοὺς βουλομένους οὕτως
                 ἄγοντας καὶ φέροντας τὰ ἡμέτερα ὡ[ς]
                                       ʽἀναγκαίωςʼ
64 [πα]ρῆλθεν δὲ ημ[.....]μιν [τοῦτο] καὶ ἀσφαλῶς τῶι
                 γραμματείωι προσθεῖναι αὐτὸ δὴ τοῦτο τό· εἰ μὴ
                 διέθετο ἐκει .... η[ ] ἀλλ π[   ]
65 [τῆ]ς σῆς, ὦ δέσποτα, π[ρὸς τοὺ]ς νόμους ἀκριβείας, εἴπερ
                 ἀνάγκη με τὴν ἀπάτην φέρειν κἂν διόρθωσιν τοῦ
                 σφάλματος ἐπὶ ὑπομνημ(ατισμῶν) δόσθαι .. [   ]
66 [   ] ἐπάναγκες κα[ὶ τοῦτο]ν πεισθῆσεσθαι τοῖς διὰ τῶν
                 διαθηκῶν δεχθησομένοις καὶ μη⟦δενὶ⟧ πρόκριμα
                 εἶναι· εἰ τοῦτο φαίνεταί σοι ἀγαθ[όν   ]
- -

(Addendum in the left margin of col. i, across the fibers)

67 [*ca?*   ]̤ εικ   *traces*
68 [   ]̤ υτο ̤ τουδια   *traces*
69 [   ]̤ σ ̤   πρὸς αὐτὸν̤ *traces*
70 [   ]̤ ο Ἀλεξανδρείας καὶ του̤ *traces*
71 [   ]̤   *traces*

(*margin*)

---

3 φιλοσο]φιαῖ pap. 18 *spir.asp.* (type 2 Turner) over α̣ pap. 34 αλεξανδρειαῖ pap.
36 ϊ[pap. 50f φιληΙκοια pap. 66 ειναι· pap.

Notes

1. After Σισιννίωι a free space as at no. **6**.1, which supports the restoration here. Cf. **14a**.1.

2. Perhaps [παρὰ Αὐρ(ηλίου) κτλ.

3. After ἡσυχίαν **13**.9 inserts τοίνυν ἀπράγμονα. Here the average line-length would allow τοίνυν but not ἀπράγμονα.

4, where not lacunose, differs from **13**.10.

5–7. For the restoration see **13**.11f with notes.

8. Or [̤ κατα]ναγκασθέντ̣[.

9. For the latter half-line cf. **12**.4 and **13**.4.

10. Perhaps] κατ' ἐμ[οῦ ---]; thereafter the space and traces would conform to] τις̣ Ἀ[ρπ]ο̣κρα[τίων περὶ λο]γους̣. Cf. **9**.1, **12**.10 and **13**.16f.

11. Possibly ἀπ]οδημίαν ὑπ[ερόριον ; cf. **12**.11 and **13**.17. At end perhaps ἀποδημ]ῶν (cf. **13**.18), omitting some words preceding in **12** and **13**.

12. Possibly] ἐντ[εῦθεν (as at **13**.18) or ἐνταυθοῖ (cf. **12**.12f, **13**. 19).

14f. Perhaps κατέ]Ιλε[ι]π[ε]ν̣ ἀνδ[ράποδα ̤ ̤ ̤]̣ ; cf. **9**.3, **12**.12 and **13**.19. Instead of ἐνετείλατο **12**.13 has ἐντειλάμενος.

15–18. These lines are paralleled by **12**.16–19, but in both instances lacunae impede a clear understanding. The lacunae of **11a**.1–4 may have provided something similar, and the illegible remains of **13**.20 probably held a shorter version of this passage; **9** omits it altogether. At the first lacuna of line 16 the parallel place at **12**.16 is so smeared and over-written as not to be legible, so that the subsequent lacunae are difficult to hypothesize. Since the wider context reveals that Ammon did not take the slaves upriver to Panopolis when he returned there, ἀνήγαγ[ον at line 17 (ἀνήγαγον **12**.17) must somehow be negatived, perhaps by ἄν, e.g. --- ἐντολὰς [ἄν·; van Minnen suggests possibly ἂν ἤγαγον. In **7**.16 the letter preceding the *alpha* of] κ̣ἀμο[ὶ could also be *gamma* or *tau*. At issue is a fear that the slaves might run away. On the aggravating problem of slave flight in the fourth century see H. Bellen, *Studien zur Sklavenflucht im römischen Kaiserreich* (Wiesbaden 1971) 122–24.

16. For the first supplement see **12**.16 and note. In the second lacuna perhaps τούτω[ν αὐτῶι ὑπηρετεῖσθαι], for which cf. **12**.17 and **11a**.15 with note.

17f. This probable restoration is not closely paralleled in the other drafts, but cf. **11a**.4 and **12**.18f.

18. The broken strokes we read as *theta* in -θειν might be taken for *delta* (meaningless here) or an irregular *beta* (as in λα̣βεῖν)

18–19. Cf. **11a**.5 and **12**.19–20; after ἀποκαταστήσηι **12** has a longer phrase. What content the contract had Ammon does not say. The contract might have been one of custody or loan or lease. In lease agreements the liability of risk is imposed on the lessee, but in custody and loan agreements it was customary that the risk was assumed by the owner (see Bellen, *op.cit.* p.40). Ammon does not mention a loss claim against Konon. If at no. **17**.2 διαμισθῶν refers to this agreement, it would have been a lease. On custody agreements see K. Kastner, *Die zivilrechtliche Verwahrung des gräko-ägyptischen Obligationsrechts im Lichte der Papyri (παραθήκη)* (diss. Erlangen 1962); J. Herrmann, "Verfügungsermächtigungen als Gestaltungselemente verschiedener griechischer Geschäftstypen," in *Symposion 1971* (Köln/Wien 1975) 326f (= *Kleine Schriften zu Rechtsgeschichte* [Munich 1990] 64f); H.T. Klami, "Depositum und Parakatatheke," in H.-P. Benöhr, K. Hackl, R. Knütel, A. Wacke, edd. *Iuris professio: Festgabe für M. Kaser* (Wien/Köln/Graz 1986) 89–100. On loan agreements in the law of the papyri see R. Taubenschlag, *Aegyptus* 13 (1933) 238–40 (= *Op.min.* II 527–29).

20f. Cf. **9**.4f, **11a**.6, **12**.21 and **13**.21f with notes. Where all others have προσεδόκων **9**.4 has προσεδόκα in different word order.

21f. Perhaps πρὸ ὀφθαλ[μῶν ἔχων ---] ἔν[αγ]χος (or ἔν[ο]χος) [προυλάμ]ι̣βανον ε̣ἰς Θη[β]α̣ί̣δ̣α̣ αὐτοῦ [τὴ]ν ἐπάνοδον "I was just then anticipating his arrival in the Thebaid." The possibly parallel text at **12**.

22 has lost too much ink to be legible. Perhaps the long lacuna of line 22 contained γραμμάτων as at **12**.23. **11a**.7 and **13**.22f have a quite different *sententia*, while **9** has neither.

23. Here begins the account of Harpocration's death: cf. **9**.12f, **11c**.3, **12**.27 and **13**.36f with notes. All begin φήμης except **13**, which cites Aurelius Aëtios as source of the news. After φήμης, **7** and **12** read δὲ, **11c**.3 and apparently **9** have τοίνυν. For the genitive absolute φήμης with participle, see note on **11c**.3. The lacuna here allows no room for περὶ αὐτοῦ.

24. πρὸ χρόνου --- βραχ[έο]ς : at **9**.13 and **13**.37 the word order is reversed to become more emphatic; **11c** and **12** are in lacuna.

24–26. Overlapping parts of **11c**.4–6 and **13**.38f provide the complete *sententia*, of which **9** omits the latter half; see note on **13**.38f.

27. παρεσκευαζόμην] --- καταπλεῦσαι : cf. **9**.15, **11c**.6f and **13**.39f. Next Ammon cites his reasons for planning a journey to Alexandria; cf. **9**.16 in curtailed form, fully at **13**.40f and apparently at **11c**.7f. The lacuna here has space enough only for π[ρῶτον δι᾽ ἐκεῖνον, ἔπειτα διὰ τὰ ἀνδράποδα] *vel sim.*, suggesting a sequence **9–7–11–13**.

28. For ἡμῶν cf. ᾽ἡμ[ῶν]᾽ at **11c**.8 but αὐτοῦ at **13**.40. The ensuing clause is restored from **11c**.9 and **13**.41; **9**.16 differs.

29. ἔξωθεν evidently means 'from outside Egypt'; cf. **13**.17f = **12**.11 ἀποδημ[ίαν ὑ]περόριον ἔξω τῆς Αἰγύπτου. On μεμοράριος see note on **6**.3; this designation doesn't occur in preserved parts of the other drafts; cf. **9**.17 and **13**.42.

30f. These lines appear only here in the archive, unless they are partly echoed at **11c**.10. διάπρασιν occurs only here, apparently alluding to a hypothetical sale (or lease?) of the slaves.

32. The phrases ὡς μὴ ἐπὶ κληρονόμοις ἐκείνου τελευτ[ήσαντος and ὡς νῦν ὄντα] ἀδέσποτα are transposed at **8**.1, **9**.18f and **13**.43f; they are not preserved in the other drafts.

33f. ἐξ αἰτήσεως --- δεσποτῶν ἡμῶν : so also **8**.1f, **9**.19f, **13**.44f and **15**.4f; **11c**.19 is illegible and lacunose. Where other drafts offer παρὰ τῆς θειότητος, **7** has παρὰ τῆς ἐνθέου τυ[, for which cf. *P.Panop.Beatty* 2.11. 299 (A.D. 300) ἔνθεος τύχη τῶν δεσποτῶν ἡμῶν. From here **7**.34, skipping the text of **8**.2–6, **9**.20–23, **13**.45–47 and **15**.5–7, goes directly to Eugeneios' discovery in Alexandria that Harpocration has a legal heir, Ammon.

34ff. ἐν ᾿Αλεξανδρείαῑ --- ῎Αμμωνα : cf. **9**.24f, **13**.48f and **15**.7f; **7**'s (and probably **15**'s) οὗτος becomes ἐκεῖνος in **13**; either might fit the lacuna in **9**.

36. For the restoration cf. **9**.27 and **13**.50.

37f. ἔλεγε --- πόλιν : cf. **9**.27f and **13**.50f; the following phrase in **9** and **13** is omitted here.

38f. τὸν πρὸ --- ἀνδράποδα : cf. **9**.29, **12**.34 and **13**.52f. Instead of διὰ ταῦ]τα τὰ ἀνδράποδα **13** substitutes δι᾿ αὐτὸ τοῦτο. From this point **9** skips the remaining text of **7** and **13**.

39f. ἀφικόμενος --- ἀποτυχών] : supplements drawn from **13**.53f; cf. also **15**.9.

41f. λοιπὸν --- ἐστρέφετο : cf. **13**.54f and **15**.10; περὶ τοῦτο becomes περὶ τὴν δεσπο]τείαν at **13**.54. φ[ίλους ---]ǀ γενέσθαι is supplemented from **13**.55, on which see note about compromise. Immediately hereafter is to be inserted the addendum from the intercolumnar margin, lines 42–59.

42–59. An *ancora* marks the start of the intercolumnar addendum, probably answered by a similar symbol in a lost margin beside its intended point of insertion, perhaps at the end of line 41; cf. **13**.55–57. A similar *ancora* is found at no. **19b**.5. On the *ancora* (which occurs in both the left and right margins) see K. McNamee, *Sigla and Select Marginalia in Greek Literary Papyri* (Pap.Brux. 26, Brussels 1992) 11–13 and Table 2.A; E.G. Turner and P.J. Parsons, *Greek Manuscripts of the Ancient World*[2] (Oxford 1987) 16. The personal name ᾿Απόλλων seems not to have been rare in Panopolis: cf. *P.Panop.* Index IV and *P.Berl.Bork.* Index I.

The insertion, here couched in the nominative, appears to be an afterthought that Ammon hopes may ingratiate himself further with the *catholicus*. He incorporates it in the subsequent draft **13** syntactically in the accusative, where he begins the list Πανίσκον τὸν ἀπὸ δικ[αιοδότου.

50f. Cf. **13**.56. For φιληκοΐα as an honorific term of address cf. Joh. Chrys. *Rom.mart.* 2 (*PG* 50, 614.46) πρὸς τὴν ὑμετέραν φιληκοΐαν βοῶν.

54f. At **13**.57 τοῦ ἐμοῦ δεσπότου becomes simply κύριε.

60. Perhaps καὶ [ἀναλώματ]ά̣ τινα, cf. **13**.57f.

61. Perhaps τῆι δε[σποτείαι ἐσκορπισμένα, cf. **13**.58f.

63. Perhaps (following **10a**.6) ἐκπέπληγ]μαι τέλει τοῦ πρ[άγματ]ος. ἐμαυτοῦ is presumably a variant revised to ἐμαυτῶι at **10a**.7, where δοκ[ῶ]ν replaces ἐδόκουν, then a lacuna *ca* 15 letters longer than the text of **7**. τὰ ἡμέτερα *sc.* ἀνδράποδα, thereafter ὡ[ς] | [ἐπαν- as at **10a**.8 and note.

64. With   [τοῦτο] καὶ ἀσφαλῶς ΄ἀναγκαίως΄ κτλ cf. **10a**.9. Perhaps εἰ μὴ διέθετο (made a will) ἐκεῖνος (Harpocration) μη[δὲ]ν ἄλλο ἢ π[. For the sequence -αι αὐτὸ δη cf. **10a**.3.

65. ἀξιῶν --- ἀκριβείας is repeated at **10a**.9–10. On ἀκρίβεια *subtilitas* as a form of address see H. Zilliacus, "Anredeformen," *RAC* Suppl. I Sp.485. *Subtilitas* is the form of address used for the *comes rerum privatarum* at *Cod.Theod.* X 10.7. τὴν ἀπάτην --- σφάλματος : cf. **10a**.10–11, where the lacuna is *ca* 13 letters longer than **7**'s version. Between τοῦ and σφάλματος **10a** inserts γενομένου.

For κἄν 'at least' cf. A.N. Jannaris, *An Historical Greek Grammar* (London 1897) p.165 sec.598, and for further examples *P.Oxy.* LVI 3860.39f and P.Naqlun I 12.7.   Here, κἄν διόρθωσιν τοῦ σφάλματος ἐπὶ ὑπομνημ(ατισμῶν) δόσθαι "and at least make a correction of the (fraudulent) error in the proceedings (of the court)." On the phrasing cf. *PSI* X 1039.36 προσφορὰν δέδωκεν ἐπὶ ὑπομνηματισ(μῶν). Thereafter possibly ἀρξ or αρα.

65f. The ὑπομνηματισμοί are presumably the court records of the claims presented by the litigants.   What exactly is meant by ἀπάτη is not clear. Possibly this accusation refers to something said in the lacuna between **13**.70 and **10a**.1 so that it might relate to the sudden emergence of Harpocration's wills; cf. also **10b**. On cases of fraudulent error in contract agreements see R. Taubenschlag, "Die Geschäftsmängel im Rechte der Papyri," *Op.min.* II 200–03; also K. Wiese, *Irrtum und Unkenntnis im Recht der griechischen und lateinischen Papyrusurkunden* (diss. Köln 1971) 76ff, 127ff.

66. διαθηκῶν : Harpocration accordingly had left more than one will. In the law of the papyri, contrary to Roman law, the coexistence of several wills was possible; see Kreller (*op.cit.* n.7 *supra* p.63) 390–92. At **10a**.14 πρόκριμα εἶναι is transposed, and after φαίνεται **10a** reads παραλελιμ[. Here, after φαίνεταί σοι, traces of a letter, then *gamma*, a clear *alpha* and traces of a tall letter seem to conform to αγαθ[, though doubtful σοι might be read as καὶ, followed by τα [, in any case not the the reading of **10a**.14.

The addendum in the top margin ends; perhaps it was written after **10a** unlike the body of **7**.

67ff. The virtually illegible addendum written in the left margin perpendicularly to the rest of the text of **7** seems not to be paralleled in any other draft.

68. Possibly ἐμαυτοῦ δι' Ἀρποκρ   and further traces.

70. The genitive Ἀλεξανδρείας occurs nowhere else in the petition.

8

P.Duke inv. 187r   *ca* 15 x 3.1 cm   Plate V
(in Ammon's draft hand)

Two small disconnected fragments bearing six consecutive lines, the left having a preserved narrow left margin, a lacuna of about 13 to 15 letters between the left and right fragments, the right extending to within 3 or 4 letters of the lost right margin. Between lines 2 and 3 on the right and lines 3 and 4, 5 and 6 on the left are interlinear insertions. The text is closely written in a small version of Ammon's draft-hand, characteristic of the insertions and addenda he has inscribed in the margins of drafts **7** and **13**, to neither of which can **8** belong. It apparently was added in the margin of still another draft not otherwise represented or recognized in the Duke and Köln collections.

On the verso in Ammon's draft hand are the scarcely legible line-ends of a draft of an unidentified document apparently related to Ammon's case, no. **22** below.

The text of **8** overlaps the phrasing of **7**.32–34, **9**.19–23, **13**.44–47 and **15**.5–7. Although somewhat expanded from that of **7**, it is briefer and less developed in form and style than that of **9**, **13** and **15**. The interlinear revisions and the cancellation of words in line 4 that are reintroduced in line 6 reveal an early tentative formulation of these phrases. Indeed the sentence in 5f with third-person verb forms at 6 imply Eugeneios as subject; in the later drafts the sentence is recast in first-person with Ammon himself as subject. Since both the adversaries traveled because of what each had learned, either version was adjustable to the context.

It would be tempting to attribute this fragment to one of the lost margins of **7**, but the poorly preserved texts on the versos of **7** and **8** were written in inverse direction to each other. Such an inconcinnity on the same sheet, however unlikely, would not be impossible.

Text

- -

1 [τελε]υτήσαντ[ος ἐξ αἰτήσεως ἐσχηκέ]ναι παρὰ τῇ[ς θειότητος
τῶν]
2 καλλινίκων {ἡ[μῶν} δεσποτῶν ἡ]μῶν καὶ τετυχηκέναι ἀντι-
γρα[φῆς]

`φανείη τις ..΄`
3 οὕτως ἐχούση[ς· εἰ μή τις τούτω]ν ἀντιποιοῖτο μηδὲ ἐκδικῶν
`΄.....οντος του΄`
4 τὴν τούτων δε[σποτείαν, παραδοθ]ῆναι αὐτῶι. [ἐξετάσεως τοῦ [.].]
5 ταῦτα ἐκεῖ ἐν Ἀ[λεξανδρείαι εἰ]δὼς ἔτι μᾶλλον πρὸς τὴν ἀποδημ[ίαν]
`΄ἵγετο΄`
6 ἠπείχθη. ἀλλ[ὰ πρὸ τῆς δεῦρο π]αρουσίας ἐξετάσεως τοῦ πράγ-
μ[ατος]
(margin)

Notes

1. Restorations as supplied by **7**.33f (see note), **9**.19f, **13**,44f and **15**.4f.

2. *Eta* seems secure before the lacuna, though ἡμῶν would be out of sequence here in the formula. After the lacuna the curving stroke ligatured to *omega* conforms to *mu*, not *tau*, and ἡμῶν regularly follows δεσποτῶν. The prior ἡ[μῶν, if written, would have been a lapse awaiting correction.

2ff. While **8**.1f through ἡ]μῶν repeat the text of **7**.33f, that from καὶ τετυχηκέναι onward is absent from **7** but occurs somewhat revised at **9**. 20ff, **13**.45ff and **15**.5ff. The other drafts are lacunose here. On ἀντιγρα-φή see note on **9**.20.

3f. εἰ μή τις --- παραδοθ]ῆναι αὐτῶι : apparently the first draft to cite the imperial rescript since φανείη τις, here added above the line, is incorporated in the other drafts, while a second interlinear phrase is not represented in any other draft: `δικάζοντος τοῦ μ΄` (or η΄ or ν΄) is perhaps possible, though the ligature after κ may be αι or ασ. The first word might also possibly be read as δίκαιον. The phrase ἐκδικῶν τὴν τούτων δε[σποτείαν is transposed at **13**.46, **15**.6 and perhaps at **9**.22.

4. The phrase cancelled here because Ammon suddenly thought of another sentence he wished to insert is resumed thereafter in line 6.

5f. ταῦτα --- ἠπείχθη : cf. **9**.23, **13**.47 and (in lacuna) **11a**.7, where the clause is revised and shortened, changed from third person ἠπείχθη or impf. ἠπε`ίγετο´. At mid-5, εἰ]δὼς best fits the traces; μα]θὼν, which might be expected, or ἀκού]σας, as inserted at **13**.47, cannot be read. Maresch considers μαθ]ὼ̣ν a possible reading.

6. The phrase ἐξετάσεως τοῦ πράγμ[ατος], begun but cancelled at the end of 4, appears in no other draft. This marginal text ends here.

P.Duke inv. 18v   14.0 x 38.2 cm   Plate XX
(in Ammon's draft hand)

On a tall sheet of papyrus of which only the right half is preserved in the Duke collection, Ammon has written drafts of paragraphs for inclusion in his formal petition to the *catholicus*. Apparently he had cut a length from a roll that had the same height (27–28 cm) as **7** and **13**, which indeed may have been cut from the same roll; the length reveals two kolleseis about 17.5 cm apart, each overlapping about 2 cm. He rotated this sheet a quarter-turn so that the fibers of what had been the verso of the roll were now horizontal; making this the front of his vertical sheet on which he wrote first along the fibers, he then turned it over upside down and wrote P.Duke inv. 18r against the fibers (**10a** and **10b**).

A revised and expanded version of lines 1–30 appear in **13**.10–53 and of 30–36 in **10a**.20–25.

Text

(margin)

1   [*ca 25*   ] ἐμὸ[ς] Ἀρποκρατίων τοὔνομα
      περὶ λόγους

2   [καὶ αὐτὸς ἐσπουδακὼς ἀποδημία]ν ἔξω τ[ῆς Αἰγύπτ]ου
      τυγ[χάνει]

3   [στειλάμενος. ἐντεῦθεν δὲ ἀποδη]μῶν κατέ[λε]ιπεν ἀνδράποδα
      ἑαυτοῦ

4   [παρ' ἐμοὶ ἐνταυθοῖ τότε διατρίβ]ον[τ]ι καὶ ἄλλον τινὰ χρόνον
      προσεδόκα

5   [τὴν ἐπάνοδον γενήσεσθαι μετὰ βρα]χὺν χρόνον. ἐν δὲ τῆι
      ἀποδημίᾳ ἐκεῖνος

6   [γενόμενος καὶ ἀπὸ χώρας εἰς χώραν] ἑκάστοτε μεταβαίνων ἀπὸ
      τῆς Ἑλλάδος

7   [εἰς Ῥώμην καὶ ἀπὸ Ῥώμης εἰς Κω]νσταντινόπολιν καὶ ἀπ' ἄλλης
      εἰς ἄλλην διὰ

8   [ἐκάστης σχεδὸν χώρας καὶ ἐπὶ πολύ]ν τινα χρόνον τὴν
        ἀποδημίαν ἐξέτεινεν,
9   [ἀλλ' ἐν τῶι μεταξὺ μήτε ἐκείνου ταχ]έω[ς] ἐπανελθόντος, ἐμοῦ
        τε ἀεὶ προσδοκῶντος
10 [αὐτὸν ἐπανήξειν . . . . . δι' ὧν] ἔπεμπεν γραμμάτων τοῦτο
        δηλούντων
11 [ca 15   αὐτοὶ οἱ δοῦλοι κ]αθ' ἑαυτοὺς ζῶντες ἄνετοι καὶ
        ὥσπερ ἀπροστάτη-
12 [τοι . . . . διὰ τὴν πολυχρόνι]ον τοῦ δεσπότου αὐτῶν ἀποδημίαν.
        φήμης
13 [τοίνυν πρώην διαδοθείσης ὡς εἴη] τελευτήσας ἐκεῖνος, πρὸ
        βραχέος γὰρ χρόνου τοῦ-
14 [το ἀκήκοα, οὐ γὰρ ταχέως εἰς ἀκ]οὴν τῶν οἰκείων ἀφικνεῖται ὁ
        περὶ τοῦ θανά[το]υ
15 [τῶν ἐπὶ ξένης λόγος, παρεσκευαζόμ]ην μὲν ἐπὶ τῆι ἀκοῆι ταύτηι
        δεῦρο καταπλεῦσαι
16 [διὰ τὰ ἀνδράποδα τὰ ἐνταυθοῖ δι]α[τρ]ίβοντα. ἕως δὲ περὶ τὴν
        ἀποδημίαν ἤμην
17 [ca 13   ἐξαίφνης ἔξωθ]έν τις ἐπιστὰς Εὐγένειος τοὔνομα ἔφη
        τὰ ἐν
18 ['Αλεξανδρείαι ἀνδράποδα τοῦ ἀ]δελφοῦ μου 'Αρποκρατίωνο[ς
        ὡς νῦν ὄ]ντα ἀδέσποτα
19 [καὶ ὡς μὴ ἐπὶ κληρονόμοις ἐκείνου] τελευτήσαντος ἐξ αἰτήσεως
        ἐσχηκέναι
20 [παρὰ τῆς θειότητος τῶν καλλινίκων] δεσποτῶν ἡμῶν καὶ τε-
        τυχηκέναι ἀντιγραφῆς
21 [οὕτως ἐχούσης· vacat ?   ] εἰ μή τις τούτων ἀντιποιοῖτο μηδὲ
        φανείη τις
22 [τὴν τούτων δεσποτείαν ἐκδικῶν,] . [   ] . . . . . [   ] . [   ] .
        [ ]βειας
23 [ἀκούσας ἔτι μᾶλλον πρὸς τὴν ἀπο]δημίαν ἠπείχθην. ἀλλὰ πρὸ
        τῆς ἐμῆ[ς] παρουσίας
24 [ἐκεῖνος ἐν 'Αλεξανδρείαι γενό]μενος καὶ γνοὺς ἐκεῖνον τὸν
        'Αρποκρατίωνα κλη-
25 [ρονόμον ἔχειν ἀδελφὸν ὁμοπάτρ]ιόν τε καὶ ὁμ[ο]μήτρι[ο]ν, ἐμὲ
        δὴ τὸν Ἄμμωνα

26 [*ca 25*   ] *traces* [*ca 15*   ]
27 [ἴσως τοῦτο] πυνθάνεσθαι βουλόμενος, ἔλεγεν δὲ
          γρ[άμματα ἔχειν]
28 [παρὰ τῆς σῆς   *ca 10*   παρα]καλ[ο]ῦντά με εἰς τὴν Ἀλε-
          ξανδρέων πόλιν διὰ
29 [ταῦτα τὰ ἀνδράποδα, τὸν καὶ πρὸ τῆς τ]ο[ύ]του ἀφίξεως
          προπαρεσκευασμένον δεῦρο
30 [καταπλεῦσαι ..... καὶ ἐπειδὴ] νῦν τὰ ἀνδράποδα ταῦτα
          ἐφρουρήθη παρὰ
31 [τῆι τάξει τῆς καθολικότητος μέχρ]ι τῆς ἐμῆς παρουσίας,
          Εὐγενεί[ο]υ δὲ ἐπὶ συλ-
32 [λήψει ὑπὸ φρουρᾶς εἶναι ἀξι]ώσαντος καὶ πρὸ[ς] ἐμὲ [*ca 11*]
          .[.]
33 [*ca 13*   ἀξιῶ, δέσποτα, τ]αῦτά μοι παραδοθῆναι καὶ ἀπὸ
          τῆς φρουρᾶς
34 [*ca 18*   ἐμὲ γὰρ ν]ῦν καλοῦσιν οἱ νόμοι ἐπὶ τὴν
          τ[ο]ύτων δεσποτείαν
35 [ὄντα ἐκείνου τοῦ Ἁρποκρατ]ίωνος ὁμοπάτριόν τε καὶ ὁμο-
          μήτριον ἀδελφὸν
36 [μμένα τῆι δοθείσ]ηι Εὐγενείωι [.] ἀντιγραφὴν τὴν
          τῶν νόμων
37 [   ]...[.][..] *traces*
38 [   ] *traces*
          (*margin*)

Notes

1. This half line reappears at **12**.10f and **13**.17, which supply the restoration in the following line. It remains very doubtful whether our line begins with ἐμὸ[ς] or μο[υ] (cf. **13**.16).

2f. Since the surviving half lines are followed at **12**.11ff and **13**.18f, their ensuing lacunae are drawn from those parallels. After ἀποδη]μῶν line 3 omits the phrase ἀπὸ τῆς λαμπρᾶς ταυτησὶ πόλεως found at **12**.12 and **13**.18.

2. The lacuna allows no room for ὑπερόριον of **12**.11 and **13**.17.

4. This wording does not reappear in legible parts of the later drafts, but a revised version occurs at **7**.20, **11a**.6, **12**.21 and **13**.21f.

5–8. A colorful passage apparently reused at **11a**.23–**b**.4, somewhat reduced at **14b**.3–6, and adopted with an extensive addition at **13**.23–28. **11a**.8 is in lacuna.

8. ἐπὶ πολύ]ν --- ἐξέτεινεν is paralleled at **13**.27; cf. **11a**.20.

9. Cf. **13**.28f and **14c**.2.

10f. Possibly e.g. δηλούντων Ι [ὡς ἀπέστησαν αὐτοὶ οἱ δοῦλοι, cf. **11d**.1ff, **13**.30ff with note, and **15**.1–4.

12. Cf. **11d**.3 and **13**.32f.

13. Cf. **7**.23f, **11c**.3, **12**.27 and **13**.37, whence restoration is drawn. The length of the lacuna favors **11c**.3 τοίνυν over the δὲ of **7** and **12**. πρὸ βραχέος --- χρόνου, the more emphatic word order, is paralleled by **13**. 37; **7**.24 has the reverse order.

15. The lacuna allows insufficient space for the second half of the *sententia* given in full by **7**.24–26, **11**.4–6 and **13**.38f; see notes. For παρεσκευαζόμ]ην --- καταπλεῦσαι cf. **7**.27, **11c**.6f and **13**.39f.

16. For the content of the lacuna cf. **7**.27f and note, **11c**.8 and **13**.40f. ἕως δὲ περὶ ἀποδημίαν ἤμην : for the idiom εἶναι + περὶ c. acc. see LSJ *s.v.* περὶ C.3; here "While I was [concerned?] about (my?) absence from home," replaced at **13**.41 (cf. **7**.28 and **11c**.8f) by ἕως δὲ ταύτην ἔτι ἐν χερσὶν εἶχον τὴν φροντίδα. Ammon provides another instance in his letter to his mother (**3**.iii.9–10). Cf. Xen. *Hell.* 2.2.4 οὗτοι μὲν περὶ ταῦτα ἦσαν. For *koine* ἤμην as 1st.p.sg. impf. for Attic ἦν, see B.G. Mandilaras, *The Verb in the Greek Non-Literary Papyri* (Athens 1973) par. 103, 109; Ammon rarely uses a non-Attic form. Maresch connects ἤμην with [διανοούμενος] (l. 17; cf. W. J. Aerts, *Periphrastica*, Amsterdam 1965, p. 52, and **13**, 37n.).

17. [διανοούμενος would fit space and context.

17f. Cf. **7**.29 and **13**.42ff.

19f. Cf. **7**.33f and note, **8**.1f, **13**.44f and **15**.4f.

20f. τετυχηκέναι --- [οὕτως ἐχούσης : cf. **8**.2f, **13**.45f and **15**.5f, omitted at **7**.34; **9**'s lacuna affords space for *ca* 15 letters not found in other drafts, possibly left vacant. Eugeneios has obtained an ἀντιγραφή from the emperor, suggesting that he was connected closely to the court. U. Wilcken defined a distinction between 'direct' and 'indirect' rescripts according to whether the rescript was addressed to the petitioner himself or to the official who should be concerned with its execution; see "Zu den Kaiserreskripten,"

Hermes 55 (1920) 2. This rescript appears to have been addressed directly to Eugeneios, not to the *catholicus*. Eugeneios will have petitioned the emperor Constantius and then have himself conveyed the rescript to the *catholicus* as the competent official for this case; on the procedure see W. Williams, "The Publication of Imperial Subscripts," *ZPE* 40 (1980) 284–87. On imperial rescripts see also P. Classen, *Kaiserreskript und Königsurkunde, Diplomatische Studien zum Problem der Kontinuität zwischen Altertum und Mittelalter* (Thessaloniki 1977) 17–41; F. Dölger / J. Karayannopulos, *Byzantinische Urkundenlehre* (Munich 1968) 81f; and J.-P. Coriat, "La technique du rescrit à la fin du Principat," *Studia et Documenta Historiae et Juris* 51 (1985) 319–48, esp. 332–35.

It is of interest that the emperor Constans in the western half of the Empire sought a short time earlier to restrain abuse by *delatores* by the following order: *Cod.Theod.* X 10.7 (15 v 345) *ad Eustatium com(item) r(erum) p(rivatarum). Nulli palatino delatorios libellos de conpetentibus rei privatae nostrae rebus accipere liceat, nec delatori ad comitatum nostrum vel officium sublimitatis tuae pateat accessus, priusquam ordinarius iudex cognitione suscepta veram esse delatoris adsertionem probaverit atque tuam sublimitatem rettulerit. Dat. Id. Mai. Trev(iris) Amantio et Albino conss.*

21f. The imperial rescript; cf. **8**.3f, **13**.46f and **15**.6f with notes.

22. Possibly καὶ ταῦτα διὰ] πρ[εσ]βείας | [ἀκούσας κτλ.

23. Cf. **8**.5f and note; restored from **13**.47, where also ἠπείχθην is clear. Thereafter the phrase ἀλλὰ πρὸ τῆς ἐμῆς παρουσίας, omitted in other drafts, appeared also in **8**.6. Instead of ἐμῆ[ς], δεῦρ[ο] may possibly be read (cf. **18b**.5); cf. **16a**.3 ἀλλὰ πρὸ τῆς αὐτοῦ π[α]ρουσίας.

25f. Cf. **7**.34ff, **13**.48f and **15**.7f; here at the beginning the word order differs slightly.

26. After τὸν Ἄμμωνα one expects according to **7**.36 [παραυτίκα εἰς Θηβαίδα ἀνέδραμεν.

27. For πυνθάνεσθαι βουλόμενος cf. **7**.36f and **13**.50.

27ff. For ἔλεγεν --- πόλιν cf. **7**.37f and **13**.50f; **13** and presumably **9** here add διὰ ταῦτα τὰ ἀνδράποδα, absent in **7**. Ἀλεξανδρέων πόλιν διὰ occurs also at no. **12**.34.

29. Cf. **7**.38f and **13**.52f. From here **9** omits the remaining text of **7** and **13**.

30–32 are paralleled by **10a**.20–22, on which see note.

33f. Cf. **10a**.22f, beginning the final appeal of the petition.

35. Ammon here seems to rest his case for inheriting the slaves on his kinship to his full brother Harpocration. Perhaps he doesn't yet know of the wills, or they hadn't yet been opened.

36. Cf. **10a**.25 and note.

37. This additional line, though not preserved, may have begun with a word modified by τὴν in the preceding line; candidates that occur in this phrase in other papyri are διάταξιν, δύναμιν and ἐκδικίαν, or an adjectival form might be expected.

10A AND 10B

P.Duke inv. 18r   14.0 x 38.2 cm   Plate XXI

(in Ammon's draft hand)

About the sheet of papyrus used for this draft see the introduction to **9** above. On its recto here are written two apparently unconnected paragraphs, inverted top-to-foot from the text on the verso. The first, **a**, preserves the right half of 26 lines, of which 7–14 slightly expand the addendum in the top margin of 7.63–66 (where Harpocration's wills appear to be mentioned for the first time), while 15–19 are paralleled in **11e**.1–4, and 20–25 offer a version of the text overleaf at **9**.30–36.

Below an uninscribed space of about four lines follows the second paragraph, **b**, of which the right half of 10 lines are preserved. The content, which is not represented in the preserved and legible parts of the other drafts, appears to concern Ammon's rejection of his agreement with Eugeneios to divide the slaves when he learns of the existence of wills left by Harpocration. This matter may have figured in a final form of this petition or even in a subsequent petition.

Texts

10a

- -

1   [*ca 35*   ]...[   ]

2   [*ca 30*   ]ην τότε τα[   ]

3   [   ]ναι αὐτὸ δὴ [ ]ο[   ]

4   [   ] ἀνδραπόδων ὥρισεν ὁ τούτων
                  δεσπ[ό]της

5   [   ] αὐτὸν σκεψάμενος, τοῦτο ἐντεθύμημαι

6   [   ]μαι ὥσπερ ἐκπεπληγμένος τέλει τ[ο]ῦ

7   [πράγματος καὶ σχεδὸν οὐδ]ὲ ἐμαυτῶι εἶναι δοκ[ῶ]ν τ[ὰ
                  ἀνδράποδα ταῦτα]

8   [ὁρῶν τοὺς βουλομένους οὕτω]ς ἄγοντας καὶ φέροντας τὰ
                  ἡμέτερα ὡς ἐπαν-

9 [*ca 25*   ].[.....]...ν. διὰ τοῦτο νῦν ἀσφαλίζομαι
    ἀξιῶν

10 [*ca 4* τῆς σῆς, ὦ δέσποτα, πρὸ]ς τοὺς νόμους ἀκριβείας, εἴπερ
    ἀνάγκη με τὴν

11 [*ca 13*   ἀπάτην φέρειν] κἂν διόρθωσιν τοῦ γενομένου
    σφάλματος

12 [*ca 25*   ]σθῆναι τοῦτο ἐὰν μεθήσονται
    μετὰ τ[.]...

13 [*ca 16*   ἐπάναγκες] καὶ τοῦτον πεισθήσεσθαι τοῖς διὰ
    τῶν διαθη-

14 [κῶν δειχθησομένοις καὶ μὴ πρ]οεῖναι πρόκριμα. εἰ τοῦτο
    φαίνεται παραλελιμ-

15 [μένον   *ca 20*   ] αν [.] γενήσεται ......, ἐγγυητὴν δὲ

16 [αὐτὸν παρασχέσθαι ἄνδρα ἐν τ]ῆι πόλει ἢ περὶ Θηβαίδα
    ἔχοντα τὸ ἐφέστιον,

17 [ἵν᾽, ἤν τι μετὰ ταῦτα νῦν περὶ] τῶν ἀνδραπόδων τούτων δειχθῆι
    ὡς ἀπο

                      `ἐγγυητὴς´

18 [*ca 25*   ]ειος γένηται ὑπεύθυνος τοῦ
    δειχθησ[ο]μένου ε.

19 [*ca 25*   ] ἐν ἄλλαις χώραις διατρίβοντος καὶ
    ἐπειδὴ

20 [τὰ ἀνδράποδα ταῦτα ἐφρουρήθη παρ]ὰ τῆι τάξει τῆς καθο[λ]ι-
    κότητος μέχρ[ι τ]ῆ[ς] ἐμῆς

21 [παρουσίας, Εὐγενείου δὲ ἐπὶ συλλ]ήψει ὑπὸ φρουρᾶς εἶναι
    ἀξιώσαντος κα[ὶ]

22 [πρὸς ἐμὲ   *ca 24*   ]ειος, ἀξιῶ, δέσποτα, ταῦτά μοι
    παραδοθῆναι καὶ

23 [ἀπὸ τῆς φρουρᾶς   *ca 12*   ]ναι, ἐμὲ γὰρ νῦν καλοῦσιν οἱ
    νόμοι ἐπὶ τὴν

24 [τῶν ἀνδραπόδων δεσποτείαν, ὄντα] ἐκείνου τοῦ Ἁρποκρατί-
    ωνος [ὁμοπάτριόν τε καὶ]

25 [ὁμομήτριον ἀδελφὸν   *ca 10*   ]μμένα τῆι δοθείσηι Εὐγενείωι
    διὰ αν[.].[.]

26 [ca 25   ]τ̣α̣ρ̣ι̣α̣ τ̣ηρουντ̣ [.] traces?
                 (Free space of 4 lines)

_____

13 δ of διὰ corr. from ι pap. 14 read παραλελειμ-. 16 θηβαῗδα pap.

10b

1 [ca 25   ] μηδὲν ὧν ἐπηγγείλατο διὰ τῆς
                                    ὁποίας δη-
2 [   ] προσετέθη δὲ καὶ τοῦτο τῆι
                                    βιαιοτάτηι ἐκει-
                          [σ]αντος΄
3 [τ]ὰ συντεθειμένα τῶι ἑτέρωι
                                    πάντων τῶν ἀν-
4 [δραπόδων   κ]αὶ τοίνυν αὐτὸς τὰ συντεθει-
                                    μένα παραβεβη-
5 [   ] τὴν ἀφορμὴν αὐτοῦ κατα-
                                    κεκλεισμένων ἡμε-
6 [τέρων   ].̣ τῶι χρόνωι ποιησάμενος ὡς
                                    καὶ ἐγγράφως
7 [   ].̣η̣....̣ τὴ[ν] παράστασιν ὥστε
                                    καὶ διὰ συνθή-
8 [ματα   Ἁρποκρατίω]ν̣ο̣ς αὐτοῦ̣ βούλημα καὶ διὰ
                                    τἄλλα πάντα ..[.]̣.
9 [   ] οὕτως ἡμᾶς ἀνάγκη τὸ
                                    πρακτέον ἐκλέξασ̣θ̣αι̣
10 [τῶν ἀ]νδραπόδων τούτων κ̣ο̣ινῶ̣ν̣
                                    α̣ [...] υ̣........
11 [   ]   traces of ink
                          (margin)

_____

2 -θη corr. from -θει pap.

Notes

10a 1–5. These lines are paralleled in no other surviving draft.

3. Cf. a similar sequence at **7**.64, προσθεῖναι αὐτὸ δὴ τοῦτο τό· εἰ μὴ διέθετο κτλ.

4. At the line-end appear two faint parallel lines slanting upward to the right, perhaps marking the close of a section.

6f. For the supplement cf. **7**.63 and note.

7. Instead of ἐμαυτῶι εἶναι δοκ[ῶ]ν, **7**.63 reads ἐμαυτοῦ εἶναι ἐδόκουν. The lacuna here is ca 15 letters longer than the text of **7**.

8f. For ἄγειν and φέρειν see LSJ *s.v.* ἄγω I 3. Perhaps ὡς ἐπάν∥[ω δεδήλωται, the only common phrase beginning ὡς ἐπαν-, the unusual wordbreak attributable to lack of space at the right edge. Another possibility, suggested by N. Lewis, may be ὡς ἐπ' ἀν∥[δράποδα ἀδέσποτα. Still another, by van Minnen, ὡς ἐπαν∥[ῆλθον.

9. ἀσφαλίζομαι 'enter a protest'; cf. e.g. *P.Oxy.* XII 1557.7f (A.D. 255) ὅθεν ἐπιδιδοὺς τὰ βιβλίδια ἀσφαλίζομαι καὶ ἀξιῶ, *P.Amst.* I 39.22 (IV cent.) ἀσφαλιζόμενος καὶ ἀξιῶν, *P.Hamb.* I 29.11–13 (I cent.) πρὸς τοῦτο τὸ κήρυγμα οἱ συνηγορούμενοι ὑπ' ἐμοῦ ... ἀσφαλίζον-ται, *CPR* I 232.7f (II/III cent.) ἀσφαλισάμενοι πρὸς τὸ μὴ ἐκκεῖσ[θαι] ἐπήρεια⟨ν⟩. The object of the protestation (διαμαρτυρία **13**.11) is under-stood. Cf. **7**.64 ̣ [[τοῦτο]] καὶ ἀσφαλῶς ˊἀναγκαίωςˊ τῶι γραμματείωι.

9–10. ἀξιῶν --- ἀκριβείας is paralleled at **7**.65. Perhaps [ἐπὶ (or ἐκ or διὰ) τῆς σῆς κτλ.

11. The lacuna is *ca* 13 letters longer than the parallel text in **7**, and γενο-μένου is omitted by **7**. On κἄν see note on **7**.65.

12. But possibly δ]οθῆναι: perhaps [ἐπὶ ὑπομνηματισμῶν δ]οθῆναι, cf. **7**.65; P. van Minnen suggests the possibility of ὑπομνηματι]σθῆναι, paraphrasing **7**.65. Apparently μεθήσονται, with which ἐὰν would be con-strued with fut.indic.; for occasional occurrences of ἐὰν with indic. see R.C. Horn, *The Use of the Subjunctive and Optative Moods in the Non-literary Papyri* (diss. University of Pennsylvania 1926) 66f. At the end of the line if μετα is right, the next letter is apparently *tau*, but possibly *gamma*; if the latter, μεταγρα∥[φ- or ∥[ψ-? The text of this line is not preserved in other drafts.

13. Cf. **7**.66, which supplies ἐπάναγκες.

14. The restoration is drawn from **7**.66 but without μηδενί, for which there would be no room. At the left edge the broken letter is *omicron* (μὴ πρ]οεῖναι) or *omega* (μήπ]ω εἶναι); cf. *P.Oxy.* LIV 3759.36f. πρόκριμα perhaps used here in the sense 'prejudgement', as also at *P.Oxy.* XVIII 2187.27, *P.Cair.Masp.* I 67006.71 and *SB* I 6000 v.19; cf. further Heu-

mann/Seckel, *Handlexikon s.v. praeiudicare*. εἶναι (or πρ]οεῖναι) πρόκριμα was transposed at **7**.66, and παραλελιμ[μένον replaces σοι ἀγαθ[ὸν
(or καὶ τα []). **7**'s marginal addendum ends here.

15. Perhaps] οντ[ ] γενήσεται ρακα, not found in other drafts. In lieu
of ἐ[γ]γυητὴν δὲ **11e**.1 has καὶ ἐγγυητὴν αὐτόν.

16. Restored from **11e**.1f, which apparently has transposed ἔχοντα τὸ
ἐφέστιον.

17. Prior half restored from **11e**.2.

18. Presumably Εὐγέν]ειος. At end γε or τε. Cf. **11e**.3, which omits the
suprascript insertion ˋἐγγυητὴςˊ.

20–22. These lines repeat **9**.30–32, each supplementing the other. **9**.30
however begins νῦν, for which **10a**'s lacuna allows insufficient room.

22f. Perhaps Εὐγέν]ειος. With ἀξιῶ begins the final request of the
petition, repeated at **9**.33f (see note). Line 33 may begin -λυθῆ]ναι.

24. The first lacuna is longer than **9**'s τ[ο]ύτων can satisfy.

25. Cf. **9**.36. Perhaps κατὰ τὰ προγεγρα]μμένα, since Ammon had already established his relationship to Harpocration; or simply γεγρα]μμένα,
'according to conditions written in the rescript(?) given to Eugeneios'. At end
διὰ ἀντ[ιγρ]αφὴν would appear to fit the traces.

26. Perhaps νὸ]τάρια or ἀκ]τάρια 'official documents'. Following
τηρουντ there are some traces of ink.

10b 1f. Possibly διὰ τῆς ὁποίας δή|[ποτε γραφῆς (or ἀντιγραφῆς) ---]
προσετέθη κτλ.

2. προσετέθη δὲ καὶ τοῦτο, presumably the contract acceded to by Ammon's friends in Panopolis providing for a division of the slaves; cf. **13**.61–
62, and at 61 οὕτω βιαιοτάτην. Possibly therefore τῆι βιαιοτάτηι ἐκεί|-
[νου ἀπάτηι.

4f. Assuming that αὐτὸς refers to Eugeneios, the verb would be παρα-
βέβη||[κε or παραβεβη||[κὼς : Eugeneios has violated terms of his agree-
ment concerning the division.

5. ἀφορμὴν probably in the sense 'pretext'. κατακεκλεισμένων, a frequent form in prose literature, occurs only here in the papyri, apparently re-
ferring to the slaves held in confinement at the instance of Eugeneios, hence
perhaps ἡμε|[τέρων ἀνδραπόδων.

8. The length of the lacuna could accommodate [ματα καὶ διὰ τὸ before the hypothesized name. βούλημα here may mean simply 'wish' or 'last will, testament'; if the latter, a single will is meant, but cf. **9**.66 and **10a**.13.

10. The very doubtful κοινῶν α̣[might also be read as καὶ νυνὶ α̣[.

11 A–E

P.Duke inv. 189v   *ca* 26.8 x 43.6 cm   Plate XXII
(in Ammon's draft hand)

The poorly preserved text, on the verso of **7** but turned 90° so as to be written along the fibers, is not a continuous draft of the petition but a series of different sections or notes in nonsequential order. **11a** begins with an expanded and interpolated version echoed in **7, 9** and **13**; lines **11a**.8–20 introduce text not preserved in extant fragments of the other drafts; **a**.21 and 23 are paralleled at **13**.33 and 25 respectively; **11b** differs from all other drafts; **11c**.3–8 modify **7**.23–28 (a sequence improved in turn at **13**.38–42) and **9**.13–16, inserting the text of **c**.5–6 into **9**.15 as also do **7** and **13**; **c**.10ff offer text not found elsewhere, while **11d**.1–4 have a modified version of the content of **9**.11–12 and **13**.30–33; **11e**.1–4 parallel **10a**.15–19 until **11** breaks off at **e**.4 in mid-line. A paragraphus occurs at the left margin between lines **c**.2 and 3. Other paragraphi may have been inscribed preceding **11d** and **11e**.

Perpendicularly along the left margin, preserved only for **11c–e**, are scattered traces of ink, apparently from a marginal addendum.

Text

- -

a.1 [*ca 70*   ] .

2 [   ]...

3 [   ] ... [ ] ἐντο-

4 [λὰς   *ca 20*   ἀλλὰ ἐνταυθοῖ ἀναμεῖναι τὴν τοῦ
ἀδελ]φοῦ μου παρουσίαν καὶ

5 [*ca 50*   ] ἐκείνωι ἀποκαταστήσηι

6 [τὰ ἀνδράποδα, προσεδόκων γὰρ τὴν ἐκείνου ἐπάνοδον μετὰ
βραχύν τι]να γενήσεσθαι χρόνον.

7 [*ca 10*   ἐλάνθανε δὲ ἄρα ἡμῶν ὁ δαίμων ἐλπίσι ματαίαις τὸν]
ἡμέτερον ἀναρτῶν τότε

8 [λογισμόν.   *ca 35*   ]ων ἔχων καθ᾽
ἑκάστην σχεδὸν

9 [ἡμέραν   *ca 40*   ] *traces* τὰ ἀνδράπο[δ]α

10 [*ca 40*   ] *traces*

11 [*ca 40*   κα]ταπλέοντα εἰς τὴν
            Ἀλεξανδρέω[ν πό]-

12 [λιν   *ca 40*   τ]ῶι ἀδελφῶι ἐπανελθόντι
            δεῦρο

13 [*ca 40*   ] θαι [.....]ντος ἑαυ`τ´οῦ
            traces

14 [*ca 40*   ]   *traces*

15 [*ca 60*   ὑπη]ρετεῖσθαι

16 [*ca 60*   ] α

17 [*ca 60*   μ]εταβολὴν

18 [*ca 50*   πε]μφθέντων μοι ὑπ᾽
            ἀδελφ[οῦ]

19 [*ca 45*   ] [ ] πάντα ἀγχίνοιαν
            τὰς αἰτίας

20 [*ca 25*   τὴν ἀποδημίαν] ἐξέτεινεν καὶ ὅπως
            ἔπειθεν ἡμᾶς

21 [*ca 35*   εἰς ἐ]πάνοδον μέχρι τῆς
            τελευταίας ὥρας

22 [*ca 40*   ] οἴχεται *nac* μετὰ τὴν
            ἀνάγνωσιν *nac*

23 [*ca 40*   τὰ πλεῖ]στα τῆς οἰκουμένης
            περιῆλθεν μέρη

24 [*ca 40*   ] ...... *traces*

11a.6 χρονον· pap.

(space of eight lines vacant or expunged)

b.1 [*ca 20*   ] τινι Κόν[ωνι   *ca 35*   ] αι

2 [   ] ι οχ[   ] α [   ] *ca 8* [*ca 15*   ] ν

3 [παν]ταχοῦ θ [*ca 10*   ]

4 [τ]ῆς Ἑλλάδος πόλεσι διαυθ υ

5 [   ]   *traces?*

6 [*ca 50*   ]̣.̣[.̣]η *vacat?*
                    (*vacant line*)

c.1 [.̣.̣.̣] [.̣.̣.̣.̣] [   ]
2 *traces of ink*   [*ca 30*   ]̣.̣.̣.̣

---

3 φήμης τοίνυν πρῴην διαδοθείσης ὡ[ς εἴη τελευτήσας ἐκεῖνος, πρὸ
          βραχέος γὰρ χρόνου]
          `ˋ ´`
          ̣.̣.̣.̣.̣

4 τοῦτο ἀκήκοα, οὐ γὰρ ταχέως εἰς ἀκοὴν τῶ[ν οἰκεί]ων ἀφικνεῖται
          ὁ πε[ρὶ τοῦ θανάτου]

5 τῶν ἐπὶ ξένης λόγος διὰ τὸ μηδένα βού[λεσθαι] μετὰ τοιαύτης
          ἀγγελ[ίας προσιέναι τοῖς]

6 τῶι τ[ετ]ελευτηκότι κατ' ἀγχιστείαν δ[ιαφ]έρουσι. παρεσκευαζό-
          [μην *ca 9*   ἐπὶ]

7 τῆι ἀκοῆι ταύτηι δεῦρο καταπλεῦσαι, π[ρῶτον μὲν δι' ἐκεῖνον,
          ἔπειτα καὶ διὰ ταῦτα τὰ]
          `ˋἡμ[ῶν]´`

8 ἀνδράποδα τὰ[.̣.̣.̣.̣.̣]. ⟦ἡμέτερα⟧ ἐνταυθ[οῖ διατρίβοντα. ἕως δὲ
          ταύτην ἐν χερσὶν]

9 εἶχον τὴν φροντίδα, ἐξαίφνη[ς

10 ταῦτα δι' ἀγχιστείαν νῦν ἐμ.[

11 τὰ ἐν Ἀλεξανδρείαι ἀνδράποδα [

12 *ca 7*   [.̣.̣.̣] [.̣.̣] [

13 [δεσ]ποτῶν ἡμῶν. ἐν Ἀλεξανδρ[είαι
          ——— (?)

d.1 [*ca 15*   ]̣.̣.̣.̣ [.̣.̣.̣] .̣.̣.̣[

2 αὐτοὶ οἱ δοῦλοι καθ' ἑαυτοὺς [.̣.̣.̣] .̣.̣.̣[*ca 15*   ]̣.̣.̣.̣ [ ]
          `ˋ ι ἐκ τοῦ ἰδί[ου´`
          ̣.̣.̣.̣.̣

3 .̣[.̣] μη[δ]ενὸς αὐτῶν [.̣] [.̣] .̣.̣.̣[διὰ τὴν πολυχρόνιον
          τοῦ δεσπότου]
          `ˋ[ ]´                          ˋκαθ´´`

4 αὐτῶν ἀποδημίαν ἄνετοι ἑαυ[τοὺς

5   *ca 13*   [.̣] .̣.̣ [.̣] [.̣] [

---

e.1 καὶ ἐγγυητὴν αὐτὸν παρασχέσθαι ἄνδρα ἐν [τῆι πόλει ἢ περὶ
          Θηβαΐδα τὸ ἐφέστιον]

2 ἔχοντα, ἵν’, ἤν τι μετὰ ταῦτα νῦν περὶ [τῶν ἀνδραπόδων τούτων
　　　δειχθῆι　*ca 8*　]
3 γένηται ὑπεύθυνος τοῦ δειχθησομέ[νο]υ　[　　　*ca 25*　　　ἐν
　　　ἄλλαις]
4 χώραις διατρίβο[ν]το[ς]　　　　　　　*vacat?*

　　　　　　　　　　　(*margin*)

———

e.2 ιν’ pap.

Notes

a.3. At end apparently] ἀδελφοῦ ἐντο-, preceding which the lacuna doubtless held the text of **7**.16f and **12**.17

a.4. The restoration is drawn from **12**.18, probably also based on the lacunose **7**.17f; **13**.20 is illegible here.

a.5. The final words are restored from **7**.19 and **12**.20, but the lacuna can have held only half of the text between **12**.18 παρουσίαν and **12**.20 ἐκείνωι, which measures *ca* 100 letterspaces.

a.6. Like **7**.20, **12**.21 and **13**.21f.

a.7. Restored from **13**.22f.

a.8f. Cf. **12**.21f; καθ’ ἑκάστην σχεδὸν ἡμέραν is a familiar phrase from Philo Judaeus onward. After λογισμόν the long lacuna will neatly accommodate the clause at **7**.21 ἀεὶ δὲ τοῦ ἀνδρὸς τὴν ἄφιξιν πρὸ ὀφθαλ[μῶν repeated at **12**.21 but replaced at **13**.23ff by a quite different sequence like that at **9**.5ff and **14b**.3ff.

a.12. Or possibly ἐπανελθεῖν.

a.13f. Possibly [--- μήτε ἐκείνου ταχέως ἐ]παν[ελθό]ντος ἐμοῦ [τε ἀ]εὶ πρ[οσδο]κῶν|[τος αὐτὸν ἐπανήξειν, like **13**.28f and **14c**.2f.

a.15. Preceding *rho* only a dot of ink survives at the upper right of its letterspace, which might conform to α, γ, η, ι, κ or υ, any of which might occur morphologically; contextually the word is most probably ὑπ]ηρετεῖσθαι, although this verb does not appear elsewhere in the archive unless perhaps in the lacunae at **7**.16 = **12**.17.

a.17. While the lower half of *beta* is sometimes indistinguishable from δι, the assumed *beta* here is formed exactly like that in **11c**.5. μ]εταβολὴν 'change' might possibly be read as ἀ]ναβολὴν 'delay'. Neither occurs elsewhere in the archive, nor does] α δι’ ὅλην if *delta* were read.

a.18. Preceding πε]μφθέντων stood probably γραμμάτων, rephrasing **9**.10, **12**.23 and **13**.28.

a.19. Perhaps [ἐπ]ὶ πάντα. ἀγχίνοια 'sagacity, shrewdness' is rare in the papyri, occurring elsewhere only at *P.Vind.Tand.* 2.r.5,16 (III cent.), *P.Oxy.* LIV 3758.r.63 (A.D. 325) and LV 5793.11 (A.D. 340) as an honorific title of address to the prefect (*P.Vind.*) or a λογιστής (*P.Oxy.*); see notes *ad locc.* Here, however, the word may retain its basic meaning.

a.20. τὴν ἀποδημίαν] ἐξέτεινεν apparently corresponds to **9**.8 and **13**.27.

a.21f. Cf. **13**.33f.

a.22. The standard phrase μετὰ τὴν ἀνάγνωσιν occurs elsewhere *only* in minutes of court proceedings, 'after the reading' of a document or order officially introduced. It occurs only here in our fragments of Ammon's drafts. Perhaps a quotation had preceded.

a.23. Cf. **13**.24f, where περιῆλθεν is replaced by the participle.

b.1. Cf. **12**.15 and **13**.21, where the order of words is reversed. Across τινι a faint trace of a horizontal stroke may have cancelled the word.

b.2. The traces of ink may conform to]ος καὶ ἀπὸ χ[ώρας, as at **13**.23.

b.3. Cf. **13**.25.

b.4. The beginning of the line seems to parallel **13**.26 though differing slightly in word order, and so might be restored ἐν ταῖς ἐπισήμοις τ]ῆς Ἑλλάδος πόλεσι κτλ. After δια apparently υθ, although damaged τo may may be possible; if the former, perhaps δι' αὐθεντι *vel sim.*, if the latter perhaps διὰ τοιούτους *sc.* καιρούς.

b.6. There are traces of expunged letters after η at line end.

c.3. The genitive absolute φήμης with participle (usually of verb of motion or arrival, e.g. ἀφικομένης, διαδιδομένης, διαδραμούσης, γενομένης) introducing indirect statement, an idiom progressively more frequent in narrative from Polybius and Diodorus onward and even commoner in later philosophy and patristica, occurs only here in documentary papyri; TLG records 21 instances with διαδοθείσης, e.g. Diod. 17.88.7.1 διαδοθείσης δὲ φήμης ὅτι τετελεύτηκεν ὁ βασιλεύς. Cf. **7**.23 and **12**.27 with notes; in these parallels δὲ has replaced τοίνυν, but at **9**.12 the length of the lacuna suggests the longer τοίνυν. **13**.36f alter the passage by naming an Aurelius Aëtius as source of the φήμης.

c.4–6. Cf. **7**.24–26 and **13**.38f with notes.

c.6. Restored from **13**.39. Cf. *P.Cair.Masp*. III 67312.49f οἱ δὲ λοιποὶ πάντες, ὅσοι πρὸς γένος μοι δ[ι]ενηνόχασιν ἢ κατ᾽ ἀγχιστείαν δια-φέρειν οἴονται; also *WB* I and IV *s.v.* διαφέρω 7 or 6 respectively.

c.6f. The final lacuna of 6 allows room for an additional word not found in the parallels at **7**.27, **9**.15 and **13**.39f.

c.8f. Cf. **7**.27f, **9**.16 and **13**.40f.

c.9–13. Here the arrival of Eugeneios was probably recounted, as at **7**.29f, **9**.17f and **13**.42ff.

c.10. Cf. **7**.30, where however δι᾽ ἀγχι[στείαν is preceded by μή. At end probably either ἐμ [(ἐμοὶ?) or ἐν [.

c.11. Cf. **13**.43.

c.13. Cf. **7**.34, **8**.2, **9**.20, **13**.45.

d.1. Above the line a horizontal stroke at the margin may be a para-graphus, though it may otherwise be the only surviving trace of the tops of two or three letters. For the text cf. **7**.11, **13**.30–32 with note, and **15**.1–4.

d.2. Cf. line **d**.4 below and **9**.11 and **13**.30f. The small floating frag-ment at line-end has broken letters conforming to]τητοι [, which would yield a probable reading ἀπροστά]τητοι as at **9**.11, rather than the expand-ed though very lacunose text at **13**.32.

d.3. For the restoration see **9**.12, and cf. **13**.32f. The insertion above the line may read ʽἑαυτῶι ἐκ τοῦ ἰδίου᾽ 'for himself at his own cost', a phrase that doesn't occur in other fragments of the archive.

d.4. Cf. line **d**.2 and note above. **d**.4 appears to be a rephrasing of the same passage.

d.5. Possibly this line should be renumbered **11e**.1, but the traces are too slight to determine to which section it belongs.

e.1f. Restored from **10a**.15f. At left above the line is a remnant of a horizontal stroke that is probably a paragraphus.

e.2. Latter half restored from **10a**.17.

e.3f. Cf. **10a**.18f, where ʽἐγγυητὴς᾽ is inserted after γένηται. The re-maining four words are supplemented from **10a**.19. Here **11** ends.

12

P.Köln inv. 4532v   20.2 x 20.3 cm   Plate XXIII
+ P.Duke inv. 19v   (draft hand)

This is the first surviving draft to contain the fully elaborated preamble to the petition, which would have been preceded only by the address in a final copy. The text is further revised and expanded by **13**.

This draft is written in Ammon's draft hand on the verso of no. **5** and continues in the upper left margin of the recto, about which see its introduction. From the left edge of this side a strip is missing (by an apparently modern cut) resulting in the loss of slightly more than twenty per cent of text from the beginning of each line. This lost strip would have constituted on the recto the missing foot of no. **5**. At the end of line 11 a large blot of blue ink, doubtless a modern metallic ink, covers the end of the final word.

From line 22 forward the traces of ink are too faint to warrant confidence in the text I have tried to transcribe.

Text

(margin)

1 [*ca 18*   ] ὦ δέσποτα, καὶ ἐκεῖνον τότε τὸν χρόνον
       εὐδαιμονίας ἐνεπλήσθην .....

2 [τῆς] θεῶν προνοίας ἡγουμένης σὺν ᾿Αγαθῶι
       Δαίμονι τῆς χώρας τῆς τῶν

3 [ἄνω Αἰγυπτίων καὶ παρ]ὰ τοῖς κάτω Α[ἰγυ]πτίοις καὶ τοῖς ἄλλοις
       ἅπασιν ἀνθρώποις μακάριοι καὶ ζηλωτοὶ

4 [ἐνομίσθημεν εἶναι] δ[ι]ὰ τὸ τοιοῦ[το εὐτυχ]εῖν, ὧι παραπλήσιον
       ἕτερον ἐκείνη ἡ λῆξις κηδεμόνα

5 [καὶ προστάτην εἶχε μ]ήπω πρότερον. διάδοχοι δὲ νῦν τῆς
       εὐδαιμονίας ἡμῶν ἐκείνης οἱ τὴν

6 [λαμπροτάτην οἰκο]ῦντες πόλιν, ἀλλὰ καὶ αὐτὸς πάλιν ἐν τῶι
       παρόντι εἰς εὐδαιμονίας μέρος

7 [λογίζομαι φοιτῆσα]ι, ὡς ἐπέπρωτο κἀμοὶ δικαστηρίωι νῦν ὁμιλεῖν
       ὑπὸ τοιούτωι ἄρχοντι καὶ δι-

8 [καστῆι δικαζόμενο]ν, οὗ τὸ ἀμείμητον τῆς κρίσεως ἐν διαφόροις
       ἔθνεσι καὶ πάλαι καὶ νῦν ἡ
9 [πεῖρα ἔδειξεν. ......]ς τοίνυν τούτου τὴν ὑπόθεσιν ἄνωθεν
       ἀρξάμενος ὡς ἔχει συντόμως τῆι
10 [σῆι   ca 15   ]...ι πρὸ πολλοῦ ca 10   ἀδελφός τις ἐμὸς
       Ἀρποκρατίων τοὔνομα
11 [περὶ λόγους καὶ αὐτὸς ἐ]σπουδακὼς ἀποδημίαν ὑπερόριον ἔξω
       τῆς Αἰγύπτου τυγχάνει στειλάμεν[ος].
12 [ἐντεῦθεν δὲ ἀποδημ]ῶν ἀπὸ τῆς λαμπρᾶς ταυτησὶ πόλεως
                       ˋἑαυτοῦˊ
       κατέλειπεν ἀνδράποδα παρ' ἐμοὶ ἐν-
13 [ταυθοῖ τότε διατρίβον]τι ἐντειλάμενός μοι εἰς Θηβαΐδα, καθ' ὃν
       μέλλω καιρὸν ἀναπλεῦσαι, ἀναγαγεῖν
14 [τὰ ἀνδράποδα. ἐγὼ δὲ φοβού]μενος, μὴ ἔν τι τούτων τῶν
       ἀνδραπόδων ἀπ' ἐμοῦ δρασμῶι χρήσηται,
15 [ca 18   ἐτύ]γχανεν, παρεθέμην Κόνωνί τινι φίλωι
       ἐκείνου Ἀλεξανδρεῖ ὡς καὶ
16 [ca 20   ] traces [....] μενος δὲ τιν' ἐκ τῶν
       ἀνδραπόδων
17 [τούτων   ca 14   ] κἀμοὶ ἕπεσθαι ε[ἰ]ς Θηβαΐδα ἀνήγαγον
       κατὰ τὰς τοῦ ἀδελφοῦ ἐντολὰς
18 [ca. 15   ἐβου]λήθη, ἀλλὰ ἐνταυθοῖ ἀναμεῖναι τὴν τοῦ
       ἀδελφοῦ μου παρουσίαν
19 [ca. 15   ἀναγ]κάσαι, ἀλλὰ [π]αρὰ τῶι αὐτῶι Κόνωνι
       κατέλειπον ὁμολογίαν παρ' αὐτοῦ ἔγγρα-
20 [φον δεξάμενος ὅπ]ως ἐπανελθόντ[ι ἐκε]ίνωι ἀποκαταστήσηι
       [ca. 15   ] ἀνδρ[άπ]οδα,
21 [προσδόκων γὰρ τὴν ἐπάνο]δ[ο]ν μετ[ὰ βρα]χύν τινα
       γενήσεσθαι χ[ρόνον. ἀ]εὶ δὲ τοῦ ἀνδρὸς τὴν
22 [ἄφιξιν πρὸ ὀφθαλμῶν ἔχ]ων καὶ καθ' ἑκάστην σχεδὸν ἡμέραν
       αὐτοῦ τὴν ἐπάνοδον
23 [γρ]αμμάτων   ca 14   ἐπὶ τὰ ἀνδράποδα αὐτὸς
       ... πέμπων εἰς
24 [   ]....καὶ traces ετ.... καὶ τότε. ι τα... τὴν
       [ἀ]ποδημίαν
25 [ca 15   ] traces τὰ ἀνδράποδα κ[α]ὶ traces καιου. το
26 [ἀ]ντιποιούμενον ..[..] ρ. ι..... ἀδελφ[ca 20   ]

27 [   ]. φήμης δὲ πρώην [δια]δοθείσης ὡς εἴη τελευτήσας
              [ἐκεῖνος, πρὸ βραχέος γὰρ χρόνου]
28 [τοῦτο ἀκήκοα, οὐ γὰρ ταχέως εἰς ἀκοὴν τῶν οἰκείων ἀφικνεῖ]ται
              ὁ περὶ τοῦ θανάτου τῶν ἐπὶ ξέν[ης] λό[γος]
29 [ca 60   ] traces
30 [ca 60   ] ca 15
31 [ca 60   ] ca 15
32 [ca 60   ] traces
              (lower edge of verso)

(continued perpendicularly in the upper left margin
of the recto after loss of some lines)
33 τον δεδύνημαι διὰ τοῦτ[ο   εἰς τὴν]
34 Ἀλεξανδρέων πόλιν διὰ [   ]
35 [ ]ου[   ]
              (left edge of recto)

---

7 δικαστηριον corrected to δικαστηριωι pap.   8 ὁυ (spiritus asper type 2 Turner) pap.;
lege ἀμίμητον.   12 ταυτησϊ pap.   13 θηβαϊδα, καιρὸν pap.   14 ἐν (spir.asp. type 2)
pap.   15 ωϛ (spir.asp. type 2 over ς) pap.   17 θηβαϊδα pap.

Notes

1–8. These lines are virtually repeated at **13**.1–8, each providing restorations to its parallel. According to this unabashedly flattering preamble, Flavius Sisinnius had filled an important post in Upper Egypt where he had been
acquainted with members of Ammon's family (**7**.45–60), perhaps *magister
rerum privatarum* (see *supra* pp.53f fn.4), possibly even *praeses*, and he
seems also to have served offices outside Egypt (8 ἐν διαφόροις ἔθνεσι).
Hitherto, however, no record of Sisinnius has come to light either within or
outside Egypt. For an earlier list of known *catholici* in Egypt see Lallemand
pp.257–60 and Delmaire "Le personnel" pp.114–24 and 138 (*supra* pp.61f.
fn.4).

    1. The right half of the opening line (repeated at **13**.1) of the preamble of
the petition. It presupposes something like "The Thebaid well remembers
your magistracy there".

    2. θεῶν προνοίας ἡγουμένης : cf. *P.Laur.* II 41r.3f (iii cent.) τῆς τῶν
πατρῴων ἡμῶν θεῶν προνοίας [συναιρομέ]|νης ἡμῖν κτλ. (or [συν-

ερχομέ]ἰνης). πρόνοια occurs in pagan as well as late-antique Christian letters; see G. Tibiletti, *Le lettere private nei papiri greci del III e IV secolo d.C.* (Milan 1979) 118f, to which add *P.Neph.* 1.31, *P.Oxy.* LV 3821.12 and n., *P.Lond.* III p.lii no.1014 descr. = G.M. Parassoglou, ed., in *Miscellània papirològica Ramon Roca-Puig* (Barcelona 1987) 249. On Ἀγαθὸς Δαίμων see J. Quaegebeur, *Le dieu Shaï dans la religion et l'onomastique* (Louvain 1975) 170ff, 263f; L. Koenen, "Die Adaptation ägyptischer Königsideologie am Ptolemäerhof," in *Egypt and the Hellenistic World* (Stud. Hell. 27, Louvain 1983) 149.

3. ἄνω, κάτω : Ammon regards Egypt as divided into two distinct countries, οἱ ἄνω Αἰγύπτιοι being his homeland the Thebaid, οἱ κάτω Αἰγύπτιοι being Alexandria and Lower Egypt. He of course recognizes the jurisdiction of the prefect, the *catholicus* and the *archiereus* over all of Egypt. While governed centrally from Alexandria, from A.D. 326 to 357 Egypt comprised the two provinces.

4. Or [ἐνομίσθησαν, for at **13**.4 the source of the restoration is suspended after the *theta*. λῆξις in its late Greek figurative meaning 'sphere, province, realm' has not occurred previously in the papyri.

5. [καὶ προστάτην from **13**.4, κηδεμὼν καὶ προστάτης being common phrase especially in later Greek; doubtless εἶχε followed. μ]ήπω πρότερον 'never before' too is frequent from Cassius Dio onward. At **13**.5 this line is revised and expanded.

6. The πόλιν is of course Alexandria.

9f Restored from the beginning of **13**.9, after which up to ἀδελφὸς this passage has no parallel in other drafts, which however are lacunose.

10ff. Cf. **9**.1–3 and **13**.18f.

10. Perhaps [σῆι ἀκριβείαι; cf. on **7**.65.

12. ἑαυτοῦ, inserted here above the line, is incopoated at **9**.3 and in the cancelled half of **13**.19 but omitted in the revised half.

13–22. Cf. **7**.15–22, of which **12** offers here a revised and expanded version. **9** omits the content of **12**.13–20.

13. Cf. **7**.15, which gives ἐν]ετείλατο instead of the participle here; the traces of ink surviving in **13**.20 are illegible but that line offers only half the space required by **12**.13–15.

15. Perhaps [ὡς καὶ τῶι ἀδελφῶι ἐτύ]γχανεν. The introduction of Konon here is paralleled only at **13**.21, although **13** continues quite differently thereafter.

16. The three letters following δέ appear to be so smeared and overwritten that the proposed reading is very doubtful. The corresponding spot in the parallel text at **7**.16 is in lacuna.

17. For a possible supplement cf. notes on **7**.16 and **11a**.15.

18. Cf. **7**.17. ἐνταῦθα corrected to ἐνταυθοῖ or ἐνταυθ[α]ὶ.

19. For ἀναγκ]άσαι cf. **7**.18 and n.

20. Perhaps [τὰ ἐν Ἀλεξανδρείαι] ἀ̣ν̣δρ[άπ]οδα; **7**.19f omit the space of this lacuna.

21. Cf. **7**.20f, **11a**.5 and **13**.21f; since the lacuna is too short for the full text of **7**, ἐκείνου was probably either omitted or written above the line like ἑαυτοῦ above line 12. After χρόνον **13** has a different and expanded text.

22. This almost expunged line alone appears to parallel the text of **7**.21f, which is too lacunose to help here. After καθ' the faint traces of ink conform to the text at **11a**.8.

23–27. The text here is considerably expanded from that which the half-line lacuna of **7**.22 can have held.

23. Apparently γρ]αμμάτων πεμφθέντων μοι as probably also at **11a**. 18. γρ]αμμάτων may be compared to **9**.10 δι' ὧν] ἔπεμπεν γραμμάτων or to **13**.28 διὰ τῶν γραμμά(των); the preceding and following text here more closely parallels that of **13**. The corresponding locus of **7** is mainly in lacuna.

27. Cf. **7**.23, **9**.12f, **11c**.3 and **13**.37 with notes; after φήμης **12** reads δὲ like **7**, while the others substitute τοίνυν. From this line forward the text parallels that of **7**, **9** and **11c**, which its lacunae will accommodate, and partly that of **13**.

28f. Cf. **7**.24–26, **9**.14f, **11c**.4–6 and **13**.38f with notes.

30. The surviving traces of ink may conform to the text of **11c**.7 and **13**.40, e.g. δεῦρο καταπλε]ῦσαι, πρῶτον μὲν δι' ἐκεῖνον, but the scattered flecks of ink do not warrant any confidence.

33ff. As my colleague P. van Minnen pointed out, this addendum overleaf bears no relation to the text on the recto (no. **5**), but appears to be a continuation of **12**. A match for line 33 is found at **6**.12 οὐδὲ εὑρεῖν αὐτὸν δεδύνημαι· διὰ τοῦτο κτλ.; that text, however, offers no further parallels.

Line 34 corresponds to **7**.38, **9**.28 and **13**.51f παρακαλοῦντά με εἰς τὴν Ἀλεξανδρέων πόλιν διὰ ταῦτα τὰ ἀνδράποδα. For the formal designation of the city see note on **6**.2.

13

P.Köln inv. 4533v+r   30.9 x 25.9 cm   Plates XXIV and XVIII
[= P.Duke inv. 1278]   (draft hand)

This draft is the fullest form of the petition preserved in the archive, although it does not start at the beginning nor reach a conclusion at the end. Written in Ammon's draft hand, it fills the verso of the complete document no. **6** and continues onto the left, bottom, right and top margins of the recto, still lacking space to complete the text. Here only among the drafts (except at **7**.65) Ammon resorts to frequent suspension, curtailing word-ends especially in phrasing already familiar from earlier drafts.

At the beginning the text corresponds almost line-for-line to the text of **12**.1–8 (though amplifying **12**.5), at 9 switches to **7**.3ff, at 16 begins **9**.1ff = **12**.10ff, and after 21 adopts or revises a medley from **7**, **9** and **11**. After 60 the text continues beyond that of any other drafts.

It is in this draft that Ammon's efforts to achieve a literary style may be seen best; note especially the ingratiating prologue (lines 1–13), such rhetorical flourishes as 9f, 22f, 23ff, 39f and 57f.

Text

(margin?)

1 [*ca 20*   δέσποτα, καὶ ἐκεῖνον τότε τὸν χρόν]ον εὐδαιμονί[α]ς
ἐνεπλήσθη[ν]

2 [*ca 25*   ] τῆ[ς θ]εῶν προνοίας ἡγουμένης σὺν Ἀγαθῶι
Δαίμονι τῆς χώρας

3 [τ]ῆς τῶν [ἄν]ω Αἰγυπ[τίω]ν καὶ παρὰ τοῖς κάτω Αἰγυπτίοις καὶ
τοῖς ἄλλοις ἅπασιν ἀνθρ(ώποις) μακάριοι

4 κ[αὶ ζ]ηλ(ωτοὶ) ἐνομίσθ(ημεν) εἶναι. δ[ιὰ] τ[ὸ] τοιοῦτ(ο)
εὐτυχ(εῖν), ὧι παραπλ(ήσιον) ἕτερον ἐκείνη ἡ λῆξις
κηδεμ(όνα) καὶ προστάτ(ην)

5 *ca 8*   μήπω πρότερ(ον) μήτε ὕστερ(ον) προσδοκᾶ θεάσεσθαι.
διάδοχοι δὲ νῦν τῆς εὐδαιμ(ονίας) ἡμῶν ἐκεί(νης)

6 οἱ τὴν λαμπροτάτ(ην) οἰκ(οῦντες) πόλ(ιν), ἀλλὰ καὶ αὐτὸς πάλιν
ἐν τῶι παρόντ(ι) εἰς εὐδαιμονίας μέρο(ς) λογίζομαι

7 φοιτῆσαι, [ὡ]ς ἐ[πέ]πρω[το] κάμοὶ [δ]ικαστηρίωι νῦν ὁμιλεῖν ὑπὸ
     τοιούτωι [ἄρχον]τι καὶ δικαστῆι
8 {ἑστάναι} δικαζόμενον, οὗ τὸ ἀμίμητον τῆς κρίσεως ἐν διαφόροις
     ἔθνεσι καὶ πάλαι καὶ νῦν
9 ἡ πεῖρα ἔδειξεν. ἡσυχίαν τοίνυν ἀπράγμονα τοῖς ἐν φιλοσοφίαῑ
     καὶ λόγοις ἀνηγμένοις πρέ-
10 πειν καὶ αὐτὸς ἐπιστάμ(ενος) ἥκω καταναγ[κ]ασθ(είς), δέσποτα,
     ὑπὸ τῶν ἐν πράγμασιν ἐξετάζεσθαι ἡμᾶς
11 πεποιηκότων, προαχθεὶς ἐπὶ ταυτηνὶ [τὴ]ν διαμαρτυρίαν. εἰ μὲν
     γὰρ ἐξῆν τοῖ[ς] ν   ca 8   ῃρη-
12 μένοις κατὰ τὸ τῆς φύσεως αὐ[θ]αίρετον μέχρι τέλους ἀπολαύειν
     τῆς   traces
13 [ca 15   ]ουσης [.], ἀπειλεῖ δὲ φθόνος ἀεὶ τοῖς καλοῖς ....
     εἰ μή μοι traces
14 [ca 35   ]   ca 15
     [ca 12   ].....
15 .[.] [ca 10   ] [ca 13   ]οις .[.]χ σ[ρ]εινα .[ca 15   ]
     συγγνώμη
16 χ [.] [.] καὶ [ca 20   ] ς το .[....] πρ[ὸ] πολλοῦ τ[.....
          'μου'
     ἀ]δελφός [τις ἐμὸς]
17 Ἀρποκρατίων τοῦ[νομ]α π[ε]ρὶ λόγους καὶ αὐτὸς [ἐ]σπουδακὼς
     ἀποδημ[ίαν ὑ]περόριον ἔξω τῆς
18 Αἰγύπτου τυγχάνει στειλάμενος, ἐντεῦθεν δὲ ἀποδημῶν ἀπὸ τῆς
     λαμπρᾶς ταυτησὶ πόλεως
19 [[κατέλειπεν ἀνδράποδα ἑαυτοῦ ἐνταυθὶ]] κατέλειπεν ἀνδράποδα
     π[α]ρ' ἐμ[ο]ὶ ἐνταυθοῖ τότε διατρίβοντι
20 ....   traces of ca 50 letters   παρεθέμην
21 Κόνωνί τινι Ἀλεξανδρεῖ φίλωι ὄντι ἐκείνου, ὅπως ἐπανελθὼν
     ἀπολάβηι, προσεδόκων γὰρ
22 τὴν ἐκείνου ἐπάνοδον μετὰ βραχ(ύν) τινα γενήσ(εσθαι)
     χρόν(ον). ἐλάνθαν(ε) δὲ ἄρα ἡμ(ᾶς) ὁ δαίμων
     ἐλπ(ίσι) ματ(αίαις) τὸν
23 ἡμέτ(ερον) ἀναρτ(ῶν) τότ(ε) λογισμ(όν). ἐν γὰρ τῆι ἀποδημίαῑ
     ἐκεῖνος γενόμ(ενος) καὶ ἀπὸ χώρας εἰς χώρ(αν)
     ἑκάστοτ(ε) μεταβαίν(ων)

24 ἀπὸ τῆς Ἑλλάδ(ος) εἰς Ῥώμην καὶ ἀπὸ Ῥώμης εἰς Κωνσταντινό-
πολιν καὶ ἀπ' ἄλλης εἰς ἄλλην τὰ πλεῖστα

25 σχεδ(ὸν) τῆς γῆς περιελθ(ὼν) μέρη τῶν καλλινίκων δεσποτῶν
ἡμῶν τὰς νίκας καὶ λόγους βασιλικοὺς πανταχ(οῦ)

26 .... το ἐπιδεικνύμε[νος], αὐ[τ]ὸς γὰρ ἐν ταῖς ἐπισ(ήμοις)
πόλ(εσι) τῆς Ἑλλάδ(ος) καὶ ἐπιτρ(οπεύων) καὶ
λογισ(τεύων) ἔπραξ(ε) καὶ διὰ ταύτ(ας)

27 τὰς ἀφορμ(ὰς) ἐπὶ πολ(ύν) τινα χρόν(ον) τὴν ἀποδ(ημίαν)
ἐξέτ(εινεν), ἐμοῦ ἀεὶ προσδοκῶντ(ος) αὐτοῦ τὴν
ἐπάνοδ(ον), ἐπεὶ καὶ οὕτω γράφων

28 ἀεὶ παρεκάλε(σεν) ἡμᾶς διὰ τῶν γραμμάτ(ων), ἀλλ' ἐν τῶι
μεταξὺ μήτε ἐκείνου ταχέως ἐπανελθόντος, ἐμοῦ δὲ

29 ἀεὶ προσδοκῶντος αὐτὸν ἐπανήξειν ἔτι τε καὶ ἀσχολουμένου
περὶ τὴν τῶν δημοσίων μου

30 τελεσμάτων διάλ[υσ]ιν καὶ μὴ δυνηθέντ(ος) δεῦρο καταπλεῦσαι,
αὐτοὶ οἱ δοῦλ(οι) μηκέτι ἀνασχόμ(ενοι)

31 παρὰ ξένοι[ς] εἶν[α]ι [ca 7   κα]θ' ἑαυτ(οὺς) ὑπο[μ]έν{ειν},
πρὸ πολλοῦ ἀπέστησ(αν) τῆς τούτων οἰκ(ίας) καὶ
καθ' ἑαυτοὺς

                                                    ‛ωσ΄
32 ἔζησαν μηδενὸς αὐτῶν πρ[.] ....[.] ρ. ( ) [.].[τ]οῦ προ[τ]έρ(ου)
δεσπότου διὰ τὴν πολυχρ(όνιον) μὲν

33 ἐκείνου ἀποδημ(ίαν), ἀεὶ δὲ ὑφ' ἡμῶν εἰς ἐπάν[οδον   ca 10   ]
ι[..]ν( ) [μ]έχρι καὶ τῆς τελε[υταίας]

34 ὥρας ἐκείνης καθ' ἣν τὴν ἀνάγκ(ην) μοι [ca 30   ]

35 αρ.τ( ) [π]αντὸς τοῦ βίου τῆι τῆς ἄνω κινήσ(εως) [ca 35   ]

36 Αὐρήλ(ιος) Ἀέτιος παραγένηι ἀνελ[θ(ὼν)] καθότι [ca 30   ]

37 λέγ(ων) ὡς εἴη τελευτήσας ἐκεῖνος, πρὸ βραχ[έος γὰρ χρόνου
τοῦτο ἀκήκοα   ca 15   ]

38 οὐ γὰρ ταχ(έως) εἰς ἀκοὴ(ν) τῶν οἰκ(είων) ἀφικν(εῖται) ὁ περὶ τοῦ
θ[ανάτ(ου)] τῶν ἐπὶ ξέν(ης) λόγ(ος) διὰ τὸ μηδ(ένα)
βούλ(εσθαι) μετὰ]

39 τοι(αύτης) ἀγγελ(ίας) προσιέναι τοῖς τῶι τελευτ(ήσαντι) κατ'
ἀ[γ]χ[ιστείαν διαφέρουσι. παρεσκευαζόμην μὲν
ἐπ]ὶ τῆι

40 ἀκοῆι ταύτηι δεῦρο καταπλεῦσαι, πρῶτον μὲν δι' ἐκεῖνον, ἔπειτα
καὶ διὰ ταῦ[τα τὰ ἀνδρ]άποδ(α) αὐτοῦ

41 τὰ ἐνταυθοῖ διατρίβοντα. ἕως δὲ [[ε]]ταύτην ἔτι ἐν χερσὶν εἶχον τὴν
      φροντίδα, ἐξα[ί]φνη[ς ....]
42 ἀγγέλλων Σ[ερ]ηνιανὸς ὁ τοῦ Παλλαδίου ὡς ἔξωθέν τις ἐπιστὰς
      Εὐγένειος τοὔνομα [ ]
43 ....[ca 4   τὰ ἐ]ν Ἀλεξανδρείᾱ ἀνδράποδ(α) τοῦ ἀδελφοῦ μου
      Ἁρποκρατίωνος ὡς ὄντα [νῦν]
44 [ἀ]δέσποτα καὶ ὡς μὴ ἐπὶ κληρονόμοις ἐκείνου τελευτ[ήσαντος]
      ἐξ αἰτήσεως ἐσχηκέναι
45 παρὰ τῆς θειότητος τῶν καλλινίκων [δε]σποτῶν ἡμῶν καὶ
      τετυχηκέναι ἀντιγραφῆς

(Addendum in the left margin of the recto across the fibers)
46 οὕτως ἐχούσης· εἰ μή τις τούτων ἀντιποιοῖτο μηδὲ φανείη τις τὴν
      τούτων δεσποτείαν ἐκδικῶν,
                                  `ἀκούσας´
47 παραδοθῆναι αὐτῶι. ταῦτα παρ' ἐκείνου τοῦ Σερηνιανοῦ ἔτι
      μᾶλλον πρὸς τὴν ἀποδημίαν ἠπείχθην.
48 [ἐν Ἀ]λεξανδρείᾱ δὲ γενόμενος ἐκεῖνος καὶ γνοὺς ἐκεῖνον τὸν
      Ἁρποκρατίωνα κληρονόμον ἔχειν
                                  `Νίκης´
49 [ἀδελ]φὸν ὁμοπάτριόν τε καὶ ὁμομήτριον, ἐμὲ δὴ τὸν Ἄμμωνα
      τῆς μητρός, τούτων τῶν σωμάτων
50 [ca 27   ] [ ] [ἀ]νέδ[ρ]αμεν ἴσως τοῦτο
      πυνθάνεσθαι βουλόμενος, ἔλεγεν
51 [δὲ γράμματα ἔχειν παρὰ τῆς σῆς ...... παρακαλοῦντά με εἰς]
      τὴν Ἀλεξανδρέων πόλιν διὰ

(Addendum in the lower margin of the recto along the fibers)
52 {διὰ} ταῦτα τὰ ἀνδράποδα, τὸν καὶ πρὸ{ς} τῆς τούτου ἀφίξεως
      προπαρ[εσκευασμένον δεῦρ]ο κατα[πλε]ῦσαι
53 δι' αὐτὸ τοῦτο. ἀφικόμενος δὲ εἰς τὴν πατρίδα τὴν ἐμὴν καὶ γνο[ὺς
      τοῦ πράγματος τὴ]ν ἀκρί[βει]αν
    `πρώτου´
54 καὶ ὡς τοῦ ἐπιχειρήματος ἀποτυχών, λοιπὸν εἰς ἄλλο τι ἐτράπη
      [καὶ περὶ τὴν δεσπο]τείαν [ἐστ]ρέ-
55 φετο. φίλους γὰρ ἀξιώσας μεταξὺ γενέσθαι Πανίσκον τὸν ἀπὸ
      δικ[αιοδοτῶν καὶ Ἀπόλλωνα] τὸν π[οι]ητὴν

56 τὸν ἀδελφιδοῦν τὸν ἐμόν, ὃν καὶ ἡ σή, ὦ δέσποτα, περὶ τοὺς
       λόγους ἀρε[τή τε καὶ φιληκοΐα γιν]ώσ[κει τὴν]
57 παρὰ σοῦ, κύριε, ἐν Θηβαίδι εὐτυχήσαντα ἀκρόασιν, καὶ ἄλλα
       προσ[.] [ἀναλώματά?]
58 τινα καὶ καμάτους πρ[ο]σ[ε]λόμενος, ἕως ἂν συλλάβηι καὶ
       συνα[γάγηι τὰ ἀνδράποδα ταῦτα τῆι δ   ]
59 ἐσκορπισμένα καὶ δρασμὸν πλημμελήσαντα καὶ ὡς ἐν ἐρημί[α]ι
       [ἀδέσποτα   ca 12   ] . [.]
                   ʽτινα [ἐ]πηρεάζωνʼ
60 προισταμένου καὶ τοιαῦτα λέγων τοὺς φίλους τοὺς με[τ]αξὺ
       κατηνάγκα[σεν   ca 17   ] . [.]τον [. . . .]

       (Addendum in the right margin of the recto across the fibers)
61 οὕτω βιαιοτάτην ὥστε ἔχειν οὐ δικαίως αὐτὸς ἑαυτῶι καθ’ ἰδίαν
       κτῆσ(ιν) τῶν ἀνδραπ(όδων)
62 τὸ (ἥμισυ) αὐτ(ῶν) {ἔχειν} καὶ τὸν κληρ(ονόμον) ν[ό]μιμ(ον) τὸ
       ἄλλο (ἥμισυ), ἐμὲ [.] . την . . . . [.] . [.]ιαν
       ἐγύμνασ(εν)
63 γεν . . . . χ( ) [ca 8] . [.] . τ( ) . [. . .]του [ca 20   ]
64 [ca 22   ] . [.] . τοι γοῦν . [.] . [.]ημ[ca 20   ]
65 καὶ αὐτὸς οὗτος ὁ Εὐγένειος παρά[δ]οσ(ιν) καὶ τὴν παρά-
       στασ(ιν) τῶν δούλων τῶν . . [ ] . . . .
66 κἄν τις ἐν αὐτοῖς ἦι ἀποδεδ[ρ]ακώς   vacat
                   (margin)

       (Addendum in the upper margin of the recto along the fibers)
                            ʽτότεʼ   ʽ[ ]αουδετ[ ]υτοʼ
67 καὶ διαπλ[αναται? . . . .]μ[. υ] τοῦ ἔτι κρατουμένου, [[.]περουδε]]
       πεποίηκεν τ[.]υτ[.] παράδ[ο]σιν
68 τῶν δι’ αὐ[τοῦ τοῦ Εὐγεν]εί[ο]υ π[αρ]ὰ τῆι τάξει τῆς κα[θολι]-
       κότητος φρουρηθέντω[ν .] . τὴν παρά[στ]α-
69 σιν τοῦ πε[φ]ευγ[ότος καὶ] οὐ [π]αρόντος μοι πεποίηκ[εν. ἕτ]εροι
       ʽλοιπὸνʼ
       δὲ [[ἤδη]] δύο ἐξ οὗ εἰ[ς τήνδ]ε ἀφικόμην τὴν

70 πόλιν ἤδη διέδρα[μον ἀποδημ]ήσαντος ἐμοῦ καὶ δεινῶς ἐσχηκό-
τος, καὶ ὁ τρίτος ἤδη ἐπιστ[ ] [ἐ]νταῦθ' ἐμοὶ [α]ὐτός
                              (*margin*)

---

9 φιλοσοφιαῖ pap.   23 αποδημιαῖ pap.   28 αλλ᾽ pap.   33 ὕφημ ν pap.   43 αλεξανδρειαῖ pap.   48]λεξανδρειαῖ pap.   68 In φρουρηθεντω[*tau* corr. from *sigma*.

Notes

1. Like **12**.1, this is the first line of the body of the text.

1–9 = **12**.1–8 (on which see notes), except that **13**.5 adds the phrase
μήτε ὕστερ(ον), following perhaps μήτε εἶχε.

9–16. An expansion and elaboration of the very lacunose text of **7**.3–13.
At line 9, **13** inserts τοίνυν ἀπράγμονα.

10. This clause does not appear in **12**, and **7**.4 differs.

11. On διαμαρτυρία in the sense 'protestation, plea in protest' see E.
von Druffel, *Papyrologische Studien zum byz. Urkundenwesen* (Munich
1915) 42ff. More recent examples occur at *P.Mil.* II 61.3 (= *SB* VI 9444),
PSI XIV 1424.3, *P.Ness.* 29.3f, 163.5. προαχθεὶς ἐπὶ ταυτηνὶ [τὴ]ν
διαμαρτυρίαν : cf. *CPR* I 232.5f (II/III cent.) προήχθημε[ν   *ca 8*   ]ν
ταύτην [τὴν δια]μαρτυρίαν (cf. von Druffel p.45); perhaps here also
for]ν one should read ἐ]πὶ.

The traces at the end of the line possibly might yield τοῖ[ς] ἀναχώρησιν
ᾑρημένοις, but they are too slight to confirm this or any other conjecture.

12. τὸ τῆς φύσεως αὐ[θ]αίρετον : cf. Theodoret. *Gr. affect. cur.* 5.7.3
τῆς τῶν ἀνθρώπων φύσεως τὸ αὐθαίρετον. At line-end some word like
εἰρήνης or εὐδαιμονίας is expected.

13. After καλοῖς possibly κἀγαθοῖς, then εἰ μή μοι. The sentiment is
implied at Plut. *Mor.* 84.c ἀντὶ φθόνου ζῆλον ἐπὶ τοῖς καλοῖς and by the
Suda Φ 508.1 φθόνος· ἡ ἐπὶ τοῖς καλοῖς τοῦ πλησίον βασκανία παρὰ
τῷ Ἀποστόλῳ (St Paul).

15. At end perhaps συγγνώμη, but]ας γνώμη is also possible.

16. The ἀδελφός τις ἐμὸς at **12**.10 and apparently **9**.1 is revised by
cancellation here to ἀδελφός μου, an indication that **12** was written before
13.

17ff. Cf. **9**.1ff and **12**.10ff.

18. ἀπὸ τῆς λαμπρᾶς ταυτησὶ πόλεως : so also at **12**.12, but absent from **9**.3.

19. Cf. **9**.3f and **12**.12; **9** has ἑαυτοῦ, **12** omitted but added it above the line, **13** had it in the cancelled half-line but apparently omitted it in the substituted version, though there are faint traces of ink above π[α]ρ᾽ ἐμ[ο]ὶ̣ which may have inserted ἑαυτοῦ as at **12**.12.

20. Some of the text of **12**.13ff. might fit here, but the traces of ink are too exiguous to permit confirmation and alignment. The line apparently begins ἐ̣ν̣τ̣ειλάμ̣(ενος) following **12**.13 rather than **7**.15, and may end παρε-θέμ̣(ἡν) like **12**.15, though this word may have been cancelled by a horizontal line that may rather be a smear.

21. For the introduction of Konon cf. **12**.15 and note; the continuation differs: ὅπως ἐπανελθὼν ἀπολάβηι replaces ὅπως ἐπανελθόντι ἐκείνωι ἀποκαταστήσηι of **7**.19, **11a**.5 and **12**.20.

21f. Cf. **7**.20f and **12**.21f with notes. At line 22 the prior half-line = **7**.20 and **12**.21f, revises **9**.5 and ends like **11a**.6.

22f. The *sententia* ἐλάνθανε --- λογισμόν occurs elsewhere apparently only at **11a**.7f, replacing the different formulation of **7**.21 and **12**.21f.

23f. Like **9**.5ff up to εἰς ἄλλην, but **14b**.3ff is closer.

25. λόγους βασιλικούς : 'imperial panegyrics'; Browne cites Thomas Magister ed. Ritschl p.63.4 βασιλικὸς λόγος ἢ ὃν ἔγραψε βασιλεὺς ἢ ὃν ἔγραψέ τις εἰς βασιλέα. At end, or πανταχ(ῆ).

26. ἐπιδεικνύμε[νος, as at **14b**.7; perhaps ο̣ὺ̣κ ἐπ[αύσ]α̣τ̣ο ἐπι-δεικνύμε[νος. The corresponding passage at **11b**.3–4 is in lacuna.

27. ἐπὶ πολ(ύν) --- ἐξέτεινεν is paralleled at **9**.8 and **11a**.20.

27ff. ἐμοῦ δὲ ἀεὶ προσδοκῶντος occurs at both 27 and 28f, though the constructions differ. It is unlike Ammon to repeat a phrase. The lacunose **12**.22 may have been parallel.

28f. Cf. **9**.9 and **14c**.2, after which **14** breaks off. From ἀσχολουμέ-νου through καταπλεῦσαι in 30 no parallels have survived.

30. διάλ[υσ]ιν Hagedorn; but διάδ[οσ]ιν is also palaeographically possible. At this time διάδοσις could mean not only 'division, allotment' but in transferred sense also 'delivery of the allotment' (so L. Mitteis on *P.Lips.* 97 xii 18ff, p.287). On διάδοσις see most recently H. Brandt, "*P.Rein.* I 56 (= *W.Chr.* 419): die διαδόται und das Problem der Adäration," *ZPE* 68 (1987) 87–97, with further literature cited there.

30–32. Beginning αὐτοὶ οἱ δοῦλοι, **13** provides the fullest account of the flight of the slaves; cf. **9**.11, **11d**.1f and **16**.1–4. Most different from all other versions is **15**, which therefore is possibly the earliest.

31. Perhaps ὑπο[μ]έν(ειν).

32. Possibly μηδὲ παρ᾽ ἑαυτῶν and [τ]υῦ προ[τ]έρου δεσπότου.

33. ὑφ᾽ ἡμῶν : Perhaps Ammon wishes to stress that the slaves continued under family control despite their 'living apart'. Equally possible palaeographically is ἀεὶ δ᾽ εὐφημῶν 'being careful of my words'.

33f. For μέχρι --- ὥρας cf. **11a**.21.

35. ἀρετ(ῆι) Browne.

37. Cf. **7**.23 with note, **9**.12f, **11c**.3 and **12**.27. For the *koine* periphrastic εἴη τελευτήσας, see Smyth-Messing 1962 par.2091 (use of εἰμι with "the aorist participle is chiefly poetic"), Mandilaras 890, and especially W.J. Aerts, *Periphrastica* (Amsterdam 1965) pp.76ff. It is a case of the fusion of εἴη τετελευτηκώς and τελευτήσειεν. Apparently all drafts employed the same form, to judge from lacunal space in **7** and **11c**.3. With βραχ[έος --- χρόνου] **13** follows the word order of **9**.13, not **7**.24.

39. τωι τελευˋτ´ pap. : **7**.26 and **11c**.6 have the perfect participle τῶι τετελευτηκότι. Here the apparent aorist participle τῶι τελευτ(ήσαντι) probably results from omission of the reduplication by haplography. This apparently original *sententia* is guaranteed by the non-overlapping lacunae in **7**, **11c** and **13**; **9** omits the latter half διὰ --- διαφέρουσι, **12** is in lacuna.

39f. Cf. **7**.27, **9**.15, and **11c**.6f with note.

40f. Cf. **7**.27f, **9**.16 and **11c**.7f; 'our slaves' at **7** and **11** is here revised to 'his slaves'.

41. First τ of ταύτην written over ε. At line-end perhaps ἧκεν], παρῆν], or (Maresch) ἐπέστη].

42. A Serenianos is listed as a householder of Panopolis at *P.Berl. Bork.* 1.3.23 in early IV century. Only here is he named as source of the news of Eugeneios' arrival; elsewhere merely φήμης at **7**.23, **9**.12, **11c**.3 and **12**.27.

43. At the beginning possibly ἀξι[ῶν .

44f. Cf. **7**.33f and note, **8**.1f, **9**.19f and **15**.4f.

45f. τετυχηκέναι --- ἐχούσης : cf. **8**.2f, **9**.20f (see n.), and **15**.5 where the indicative replaces the infinitive.

46f. The imperial rescript; cf. **8**.3f, **9**.21f and **15**.6f with notes.

47. Cf. **8**.5f and **9**.23 with notes. Only **13** (at 42) has mentioned Serenianos.

48f. Cf. **7**.34ff, **9**.24f and **15**.7f. Eugeneios is referred to as οὗτος by **7**, here as ἐκεῖνος despite the ensuing ἐκεῖνον for Harpocration.

49. In her yet unpublished *apographai* at Duke the Egyptian name of Ammon's mother is recorded as Senpetechensis; only here in the archive is her Greek name given, Νίκη, specially mentioned perhaps as a person known to Sisinnius. She was still living, recipient of Ammon's letter no. **3** and matriarch of the family; Ammon's father the priest Petearbeschinis had died presumably some years earlier. P. van Minnen suggests an alternative reading, Νίκης τῆς μητρὸς τούτων τῶν σωμάτων [γενομένων "these slaves [having belonged] to our mother Nike."

50f. With the aid of **7**.36f and **9**.26f the line might be restored as follows: [ἕνεκεν παραυτίκα εἰς Θηβαΐδα ἀ]νέδ[ρ]αμεν ἴσως τοῦτο πυνθάνε- σθαι βουλόμενος. For ἔλεγεν --- ἀνδράποδα cf. **7**.37f and **9**.27ff with notes.

51. Such honorific terms of address as ἀρετή τε καὶ φιληκοΐα (line 56 = **7**.52ff and n.) or ἀκρίβεια (**7**.36) are hardly suitable to the context here. For the remainder, cf. **7**.37f, **9**.28f and **12**.34 with notes.

52f. Cf. **7**.38f and **9**.29; for πρὸ **13** erroneously has πρὸς, and in lieu of **7**'s διὰ ταῦ]τα τὰ ἀνδράποδα **13** reads δι' αὐτὸ τοῦτο.

54f. Cf. **7**.41 καὶ περὶ τοῦτο ἐστρέφετο.

55f. Πανίσκον τὸν ἀπὸ δικ[αιοδοτῶν καὶ Ἀπόλλωνα] τὸν π[οι]η- τὴν τὸν ἀδελφιδοῦν τὸν ἐμόν : cf. **7**.42–45, cast in the nominative and naming only Apollon, concerning whom see note on **6**.5. Paniskos was named also at **6**.4 Πα[ν]ίσκ[ο]υ ἀπὸ δικαιο[δ]ότου, about whom see the note *ad loc*. Maresch considers that Πανίσκος ὁ (article) ἀπὸ δικαιοδότου may have been a subordinate of the Iuridicus. On compromise of a dispute out-of-court (διάλυσις) with the aid of friends see note on **6**.3f; cf. further *P.Haun.* III 57 with introduction and notes, also *PSI* XII 1256.10 φίλοι μεταξὺ γενόμενοι.

56f. ὃν καὶ --- ἀκρόασιν : cf. **7**.45–59, where at 54f τοῦ ἐμοῦ δεσ- πότου is here replaced by κύριε. See also note on **7**.50f.

57. Possibly πρὸς [ἀλλήλους ̣ ̣ διάλυσιν, *vel sim*.

58. π[ρο]σ[ε]λόμενος : at the corresponding place at **7**.60, επ[. At line- end perhaps δεσποτείαι; cf. **7**.61 and note.

60. προισταμένου --- κατηνάγκα[σεν : **15**.10f is too indistinct and lacunose to confirm a parallel; in any case the remainder of **15** had a quite different text.

61f. Here evidently the interim agreement between Ammon and Eugeneios reached in Panopolis (cf. **6**.2–8) was cited and Ammon's complaint against Eugeneios' ἀπάτη was registered. An equivalent passage occurs at **16b**.2ff; cf. also **10b**.2.

62. Perhaps τὴν ﹍﹍ δεσ[π]οτ[ε]ίαν.

64. Perhaps either] οὗτοι or] αὐτοί.

65. At line-end possibly φρουρηθέντων

66. Since at mid-line the margin becomes too narrow for further use, Ammon presumably now continues in the upper margin.

67–70. These lines are paralleled in no other surviving draft, but their implications seem to be implied also at **18b**.6f on which see notes.

67. Assuming a direct continuation from the truncated line 66 in the right margin, καὶ διαπλ[ανῆται seems probable. The three or four letters after]ν appear to be cancelled by blobs of ink rather than by the usual horizontal bar; perhaps the word was μεταξὺ and the deferred suprascript τότε replaced it. τοῦ ἔτι κρατουμένου implies that one of the slaves was then still in custody. The ensuing cancelled phrase was perhaps [καί]περ οὐδὲ replaced by suprascript [ἀλλ]ὰ οὐδὲ τ[ο]ῦτο, then πεποίηκεν τ[ο]ύτ[ω]ν παράδοσιν, in the general sense "but not even in this regard (the case of the slave still under ward) has Eugeneios made a restitution of these" and continuing at 68 "who are in custody, etc."

68. Cf. **15**.12. After φρουρηθέντω[ν possibly κα]ὶ or οὔ]τε, though neither fits the traces well.

69. Perhaps πε[φ]ευγ[ότος κα]ὶ οὐ [π]αρόντος μοι. ⟦ἤδη⟧ is revised to λοιπὸν above the line. In late Greek these words are synonymous (see D. Tabachovitz, *Études sur le grec de la basse époque* [Uppsala/Leipzig 1943] 32).

69f. δύο and ὁ τρίτος evidently denote the δοῦλοι, two of whom had already fled before Ammon's arrival in Alexandria. The definite article with τρίτος suggests that only three slaves are in question, presumably the same three mentioned in Ammon's letter to his mother (**3**.11–14); cf. **15**.1 and note. In 69 and 70 the script grows smaller and more compressed.

70. Or possibly ὁμοῦ καὶ δεινῶς ἐσχηκότες, modifying δύο and explaining why they had run away. Perhaps ἐπιστ[ὰ]ς, modifying ὁ τρίτος who had not fled. The petition remains incomplete, but Ammon has filled all the spaces available in the margins of this papyrus.

14

P.Duke inv. 188r   frr. a (5.6 x 1.7), b (4.8 x 5.6), c (5.3 x 1.7)   Plate VI a

Written rather hastily in Ammon's formal hand across the fibers on the original recto of the papyrus, the three fragments preserve only small parts of one, seven and two lines respectively. The text appears to overlap the text of **9**.5–9 and **13**.23–29, though too little survives to attest variations. In frr. **b** and **c** the lacunae between lines seem to average 45–50 letters, so that the original line-length was approximately 60 letters. The allotment of words to the lacunae in lines 5 and 6 is *exempli gratia*.

On the verso is no. **18**, a draft of a text other than the petition but clearly related to the same judicial process.

Text

Fr. **a**

1 [   ]   *traces*   [   ]

[ἀπὸ Παν]ὸς πόλεως τῆς Θ[ηβαίδος.   ]

- - - - - - - - - - - - - - - -

[several lines lost]

Fr. **b**   - - - - - - - - - - - - - -

1 [   ]ͺος δε *traces*   [   ]

[   ]ͺμε   *traces*   [   ]

[ἐν τῆι ἀποδη]μίᾳ ἐκεῖνος γεν[όμενος   ]

4 [μεταβαίνων ἀπὸ] τῆς Ἑλλάδος εἰς [Ῥώμην   ]

[καὶ ἀπ'ἄλλης εἰ]ς [ἄ]λλη[ν τὰ] πλεῖστ[α σχεδὸν τῆς   ]

[γῆς περιελθὼν μέρη τ]ῶν καλλινίκω[ν δεσποτῶν ἡμῶν   ]

[   ] ἐπιδεικνύμε[νος   ]

- - - - - - - - - - - - - - - -

[three lines lost]

Fr. **c**   - - - - - - - - - - - - - -- -

1 [   ]ͺͺͺͺ[   ]

[τῶι] μεταξὺ μήτε ἐκεί[νου   ]

[αὐ]τὸν ἐπανήξειν ἔ[τι τε   ]

- - - - - - - - - - - - - - - -

Notes

a.1f. No doubt as at **6.**1–3 and **7.**1–3 Φλαυίωι Σισιννίωι τῶι διασημοτάτωι καθολικῶι παρὰ Αὐρηλίου ῎Αμμωνος Πετεαρβεσχίνιος
σχολαστικοῦ ἀπὸ Πανὸς πόλεως τῆς Θηβαίδος. Of line 1 there are only faint surviving traces of ink.

b.1f. The traces of ink do not seem to fit the corresponding text of either **9**
or **13**.

b.3. Cf. **9.**5f and **13**.23. ἀποδη]μίᾳ is a rare instance of a dative
without an *iota*-adscript which Ammon regularly writes.

b.4. Cf. **9.**7 and **13**.24.

b.5. Here apparently begins the version to be followed by **13**.24ff, an addition inserted into the text of **9**, amplified somewhat more at **13**.25f.

c.2f. Cf. **9.**9 and **13**.28f.

15

P.Duke inv. 217r and P.Köln inv. 4547r   fr. **a** (7.0 x 8.8 cm) and (8.5 x 9.8)
P.Duke inv. 217r   fr. **b** (3.8 x 6.8)

Plate VII

Three poorly preserved fragments of a draft of part of a petition, roughly written in an irregular example of Ammon's draft hand on what is apparently the original verso of the papyrus since the quality of the surface is poor. Standing at the left, the Duke fr. **a** carries the beginnings of eleven lines, with margins at top and left. At the right, leaving an interval varying from about 4 to nearly 8 cm stands the second fragment, consisting of Duke fr. **b** and the Köln fragment joined together; it bears interrupted continuations of the eleven lines of fr. **a** plus part of a twelfth line. On the other side is no. **17**.

While the text clearly concerns the case of Ammon *vs.* Eugeneios, its first four lines use language distinctly different from that describing the slaves' escape in the other drafts. Lines 4–10 are paralleled by **7, 8, 9** and **13**, but the scant remains of 11–14 again differ. **15** is probably a very early draft (though later than **8**), but might possibly be a draft of an entirely different petition, as is its verso no. **17**.

Text

(margin)

6 εἰ μή [τ]ις τούτων ἀντι[ποιοῖτο μηδὲ φανείη τι]ς τὴν τούτων
       δεσποτείαν [ἐκ]δικῶν, πα[ρα]-
7 δοθῆναι αὐτῶι. ταῦτ[α   ἐν Ἀ]λεξανδρείαι δὲ
       γε[ν]όμε[νο]ς [οὗ]τος καὶ γν[οὺς]
8 ἐκεῖνον τ[ὸν Ἀρποκρατίωνα κληρονόμον ἔχε]ιν ἀδελ[φὸν
       ὁμοπά]τριόν τ[ε] καὶ ὁ[μ]ομήτρι[ον]
9 ἐμὲ δὴ τὸ[ν Ἄμμωνα   τοῦ πρά]γματος τὴν ἀ[κρίβειαν]
       καὶ [ ]   ca 9   [ ]
10 ἐτράπη κ[αὶ   ]δι ca 9 [ ]   ca 8
       π[ροι]-
11 σταμ[ένου   ] ς, περὶ τούτου δὲ καὶ
       περὶ τ[   ] [
12 [   ]υ δι' αὐτοῦ Εὐγενείου
       ἀπεστάλη ὅπως [
13 [   ] [
14 [   ] [

            (margin)

Notes

1–4. Cf. **13**.31–32 and note.

1. After οιπ, the letters αρθε (and possibly faded ν) appear to have been deleted by a cross-stroke, and damaged υ changed to χ so as to result in ἔχονται. The supralinear insertion (to replace παρθεν-?) may possibly be read as οὗτοι ʿοἱʾ δοῦλοι τρεῖς. If so, these slaves are probably those mentioned in Ammon's letter to his mother (**3**.iv.11–14); cf. also **13**.70f and note. At end, perhaps παρθενεύονται [ἔτι 'they are still girls'.

2. Cf. **13**.31; here perhaps ἀπέστησαν τῆ[ς οἰκίας ἑαυτῶν ἄνευ δεσποτ]είας οὔσης or τῆ[ς οἰκίας τῆς ἑαυτῶν δουλ]είας.

3. Possibly [πάν]τες or [ἀπο]δρά[ντε]ς. Perhaps ὥσπερ δε[σπότας.

4. For latter half cf. **7**.33, **8**.1, **9**.19, **13**.44; after αἰτήσεως the faint traces would conform to [ἐ]σχηκένα[ι The doubtful interlinear insertion is assumed to be gen.pl. of ἀφηνιαστής 'the rebellious ones'.

5ff. Restored from **8**.1–4, **9**.20–22, **13**.45–47; at line 5 the indicative has replaced the infinitive found in the other drafts.

6f. For the rescript see also **8**.3f, **9**.21f and **13**.46f with notes.

7ff. Restored from **7**.34–36, **9**.24f, **13**.48f; cf. **8**.5. If [οὖ]τος is right at 7, **15** anticipates **7** rather than **13** (see notes *ad locc.*).

9f. Cf. **7**.40f and **13**.53f. Perhaps π[ροι]στᾳμ[ένου from **13**.60.

11. Not matched in other drafts.

12. After skipping the text of **13**.61–67, line 12 partly parallels **13**.68. Traces of two more lines are too slight to read.

Composite Translation of 7–15

As explained above, the following is a translation of no single or actual document but of a medley of the nine disparate and fragmentary drafts **7–15** of the petition, arranged in a hypothetical order of their developing argument. It is intended only to show the editor's understanding of these texts; suggested connecting words or phrases italicized within square brackets are not attested anywhere and are given *exempli gratia*.

7¹⁻³=**14**¹⁻² [To Flavius Sisinnius,] *rationalis, vir perfectissimus,* [from Aurelius Ammon son of Petearbeschinis,] advocate, from Panopolis of the Thebaid.

12¹⁻⁸=**13**¹⁻⁹ [*The Thebaid well remembers your magistracy there*], my lord, and throughout that time I was filled with true happiness [---] while the goodwill of the gods together with Agathos Daimon was guiding the land of the Upper Egyptians, and among the Lower Egyptians and all the rest of mankind [*we*] were considered to be blessed and enviable because of such good fortune like unto which [*neither*] before did that province [*have*] nor hereafter may it expect to behold another (such) kindly guardian. Now the inhabitants of the most splendid city are successors to that prosperity of ours; but I myself too reckon that at present I have again come into a share of good fortune since it has been allotted to me too that I appear in court pleading my case before so great a magistrate and judge, whose unmatched judgement among diverse peoples both hitherto and now experience has shown.

7³⁻⁷ ~ **13**⁹⁻¹³ While I myself, to be sure, know that a quiet life free from business befits those educated in philosophy and rhetoric, I have come, my lord, constrained by those who have caused us to be investigated in this affair, and provoked to this present protestation. For if it were possible for those who have chosen [*seclusion*] according to the dictates of their nature to enjoy to the end [---]. But envy ever threatens the honorable [---]

12^9 Starting from the beginning, therefore, [*I shall recount*] to your [*acuity*] as succinctly as I can the thrust of this case.

$[7^{10-13}]\sim$
$9^{1-4} \sim$
$12^{10-13} =$
13^{16-19} [*As you doubtless knew during your magistracy in the Thebaid*] long ago, a brother of mine, Harpocration by name, himself also proficient in rhetoric, undertook an extended journey outside Egypt. While absent from

this splendid city he left his his slaves with me since I was sojourning here at that time,

15^{1-4} My brother Harpocration owned `these three? slaves´ who are [*still*]

12^{13-15} directing me to take them up to the Thebaid on the occasion when I was going to sail upriver. [*But I, fear*]ing lest one of these slaves might resort to flight from me [---] happened,

girls [---] they left the [*house since it was without a master?*] and turning restive [---] they fled for refuge to [---] receiving and

$12^{15}=13^{21}$ entrusted them to a certain Konon, an Alexandrian who is a friend of his,

as if [---] to these [---] `of the restive ones´ [---]

13^{21} in order that 12^{15} as also [---] 7^{15} [---]
on his return $12^{16-17}=$]μενος ...... of these slaves [---]
he might take 7^{16-17} to follow me to the Thebaid, I took
them back.   (*or* would have taken?) them up according to my brother's instructions

7^{17-18} [--- as] he wished to compel $12^{18-19}=$ [*did not*] wish to compel
(them) no longer to follow [$11a^4$] [---] but to await here
before my brother's arrival,   my brother's arrival,
$7^{18-21} \sim$ but I left (them) with the same Konon, receiving from him
$12^{19-22}=$ a written agreement that he restore the slaves to him (Harpo-
$11a^8$ cration) when he returned.

For I kept expecting that 9^{4-5} and for another period he kept
his return would happen   expecting that his return would
after a brief time.   happen after a brief time.

$7^{21-22}=$ Ever keeping before my   [$11a^7$]= But then imperceptibly Provi-
$11a^8=$ eyes the man's arrival 13^{22-23} dence kept our reckoning in

12^{21-22} and virtually each day   suspense with vain expecta-
          anticipating his return   tions at that time.
          to the Thebaid? [---]

9^{5-6} = For being in that absence abroad and moving each time from coun-
$12b^3$= try to country, from Greece to Rome and from Rome to Constanti-
13^{24} nople and from one country to another

13^{24-25} traversing virtually 9^7 through $11a^{23}$ [---] he traversed most
$=14b^{5-6}$ most parts of the   [---]   parts of the inhabited
          earth   (earth) [---]

13^{25-26} he did not cease (?) proclaiming the victories of our gloriously tri-
$=14b^{6-7}$ umphant emperors and (delivering) royal orations everywhere [---],
$[11b^4]$ = for he himself had served as procurator and curator in the
13^{26} notable cities of Greece

13^{26-27} and because of these undertakings he $11a^{20}$ [---] he extended
$=9^8$ extended his absence abroad a rather   and how he per-
          long time,   suaded us [---]

13^{27} while I always kept expecting 12^{22-23} [---] his return, [---]
          his return, since also in   letters [---] on the
          writing thus he ever urged us   matter of the slaves
          through his letters,   [---] he himself sending

$9^9=14c^{2-3}$ but in the meantime since he had not returned soon and I was
$=13^{28-29}$ always expecting that he would come back,   (**14** *breaks off*)
9^{10} [---] through letters that he had sent making this clear [---]

13^{29-30} and furthermore I was occupied with the payment of my public
          taxes and was not able to sail downriver hither,

13^{30-31} the slaves themselves no longer $11d^1$ the slaves themselves
          enduring to be among strangers   by themselves [---]
          [---] to abide by themselves

13^{31-32} had earlier decamped from 9^{11} living by them- $11d^2$ `private´
          their house and lived by   selves uncon-   none of
          themselves, none of them   strained and as   them [---]
          [---] their former master   if without a   unconstrained
                                       guardian [---]   by themselves

13^{32-33} because of his lengthy $9^{12}=11d^3$ because of their master's
          travel abroad,   lengthy travel abroad,

13^{33-34} but ever under our control until his return [---] even up to
$=11a^{21}$ that final hour at which the necessity for me [---]

11a^{22} [---] he (or they?) had gone. After the reading [---]

13$^{35-36}$ [---] through all of life by the [---] of upward movement [---]

(that) Aurelius Aëtius arrive,   **7**^{23}=**9**^{12} A rumor therefore had

having come up because [---] =**11c**^{3}=^{27} just been spread round

7$^{23-26}$ =**9**$^{12-14}$ =   saying that he (Harpocration) had died. For (only) a

11c$^{3-6}$ =**12**$^{27-28}$ =   short time earlier had I heard this, for not swiftly

13$^{37-39}$ does the report of the death of those in a foreign

land come to the ears of their relatives

(**9** *omits*)   because no one wishes to approach with such a message

those especially close to the deceased.

7$^{27-28}$ =**9**$^{15-16}$ At this news I prepared to sail downriver hither,

=**11c**$^{6-8}$ =**13**$^{39-41}$ (**9** *omits*) first on his account,

then also because of our (**13** his) slaves residing there.

7^{28}=**11c**^{9} While I was (**13** still) engaged   **9**^{16} While I was [thinking]

=**13**^{41} with this concern,   about my journey,

13$^{41-42}$ suddenly [*came*] Serenianos   **7**^{29} suddenly arriving from abroad

son of Palladios reporting that   Eugeneios, imperial secretary,

9^{17}~**13**^{42} a certain Eugeneios by name   [---] demanded to gain

arriving suddenly from abroad   possession [*of the slaves*]

claiming (?)   [*claimed?*] by him not by

reason of kinship [---] and

not because of their sale

7$^{32-33}$ =**9**$^{18-19}$ my brother Harpocration's slaves in Alexandria as being

8^{1} **11c**^{11} **13**$^{43-44}$ ownerless and since he had died without heirs

7$^{33-34}$ =**8**$^{1-2}$ =   he (Eugeneios) had acquired by request from the divinity

9$^{19-20}$ =**13**$^{44-45}$ (**7** divine fortune) of our gloriously victorious

=**15**$^{4-5}$ sovereigns

8$^{2-3}$ =**9**^{20}=   and was in possession of a rescript providing as follows:

13$^{45-47}$ =**15**$^{5-6}$ If no one should lay opposing claim to them and no one

should appear proving legal claim to their ownership,

they are to be handed over to him.

8$^{4-6}$ [[investigation of the]]   **13**^{47} On hearing this from   **15**^{7} this [---]

learning this there in   the aforementioned

Alexandria he was still   Serenianos I was   **9**^{23} [---] I was

more impelled to the   still more impelled   still more

journey. But [*before*   to the journey.   impelled to

his] arrival on investi-   the journey.

gation of the matter   But before

(**8** *breaks off*)   After   my arrival

7³⁴⁻³⁶ =**9**²⁴⁻²⁵ he (**13** ἐκεῖνος, *cet.* οὗτος) had arrived in Alexandria

=**13**⁴⁸⁻⁴⁹   and discovered that the said Harpocration had an heir,

 =**15**⁷⁻⁸   a (full) brother sharing the same father and mother,
                          namely me, Ammon,

13⁴⁹   whose mother is Nike, (while) these slaves [---]
                          (*or* my mother Nike [having owned] these slaves)

7³⁶⁻³⁸ =**9**²⁷⁻²⁸ at once he (Eugeneios) hastened up to the Thebaid, doubt-

=**13**⁵⁰⁻⁵¹   less wishing to enquire about this. He said that he had doc-
                          uments from your [*highness*] summoning me to Alexandria

[**9**²⁸⁻²⁹]=**13**⁵²   because of these slaves,

7³⁸⁻³⁹ =**9**²⁹=   me who was prepared even before his arrival to sail down-

13⁵²⁻⁵³   river hither

                          13⁵³ for this very reason. **7**³⁹ because of these slaves.

7³⁹⁻⁴⁰ =**13**⁵³   On arriving at my own native land

7⁴⁰⁻⁴¹=**13**⁵³⁻⁵⁵ and finding out the fact of the matter and that he had

=**15**⁹⁻¹⁰   failed of his first attempt, he then resorted to another
                          and busied himself about the ownership (**7** this).

7⁴¹=**13**⁵⁵   For he, having asked friends to intervene,

13⁵⁵   Paniskos, former *juridicus*, **7**⁴²⁻⁵⁹ (*insert from margin*)

13⁵⁵⁻⁵⁷=   and Apollo the poet, my own nephew, whom your refinement and

7⁴²⁻⁵⁹   appreciation for literature knows, my lord, since he had the good
                          fortune to obtain from you, my lord (**7** τοῦ ἐμοῦ δεσπότου,
                          13 κύριε), an audience in the Thebaid,

7⁶⁰⁻⁶² ~   and having claimed in addition certain [*expenses?*] and toils

13⁵⁷⁻⁵⁹   until he should capture and bring back these slaves to
                          [*judgement?*] that were dispersed and had wrongfully taken
                          to flight and were as if ownerless in abandonment [---]

13⁶⁰⁻⁷⁰   coming forward?, and by saying **15**¹¹⁻¹² coming forward? [---]
                          such things (˚making abusive   about this and [---]
                          threats˚) he compelled the friends   sent away through Eu-
                          who were mediating [---] so very   geneios himself in
                          aggressive as to have for himself   order that [---] ‖
                          unjustly for his personal possession   (**15** *breaks off*)
                          half of the slaves and me, the lawful
                          heir, the other half; me [---] he stripped

[---] and this Eugeneios himself [---] restitution and appearance
of the slaves that [*are in custody?*] even if some one among them
may have run away [---?] and be wandering? [---] the one `then´
being still in custody. But not even in this(?) has he made
restitution of those detained (through the agency of Eugeneios
himself) at the *catholicus'* office nor has he produced the one
that has fled and is not present here for me. From the time
that I arrived in this city the other two had already run away
while I was out-of-town and in difficult circumstances, and
the third having already appeared here for me   (**13** *ends*)

10a$^{4-5}$ [---] of the slaves, their master appointed [---] after
investigating him, I pondered this [---]

10a$^{6-8}$ =**7**^{63} as if thunderstruck at the outcome of this matter and I almost
imagined that [*these slaves were*] not even my own on seeing
whoever wished thus plundering and carrying off our possessions
as [*recounted*] above? [---]

7^{64} [---] but he by-passed us [*and demanded?*] firmly `compel-
lingly´ to add to the document this very clause: "if he had
not willed anything other than [---]"

10a^{9} For this reason I now make certification

7^{65}~**10a**$^{9-10}$ [and I ask] of your acuity toward the laws, my lord, that, if
indeed I must endure his deceit, at least you make a correction of

7^{65} the (fraudulent) error   **10a**$^{11-12}$ that has occurred [---] this
in the proceedings   be [*recorded*] if they will
                                                            allow

7^{66}=**10a**$^{13-14}$ [---] necessary that he too obey the provisions set forth
in the wills and there be no prejudice ⟦**7** to anyone⟧.

7^{66} If this seems to you good [---]   **10a**^{14} If this seems (to
(**7**'s *marginal addendum may end here*)   have been) omitted
                                                            [---] will be [---],

10a$^{15-19}$=   him as guarantor to nominate a man having his residence in

11e$^{1-4}$ the city or in the Thebaid in order that, if hereafter anything concerning these slaves now be shown as from [---]
he be held liable for what will be shown [---] while (Harpocration) was residing in other lands   (**11** *breaks off*)

9$^{30-36}$=   and since these slaves were held under guard at the *catholicus'*

10a$^{19-25}$ office up to the time of my arrival, since Eugeneios demanded

that they be held under arrest and toward me [---], I request,
my lord, that they be surrendered to me and [*released*] from
detention [---], for the laws now summon me to the ownership
of them, since I am the full brother of that Harpocration [---]
[the ---] granted to Eugeneios because of the rescript that

936   the [---] of the laws [---] **10a**26 [---] observing(?) [---]

(9 *ends*)   **(10a** *ends*)

10b1–10   (*The initial lacuna of each line is half the line-length.*)

[-----] none of which he proposed through whatever
[-----] but this too was added by his most aggressive
[-----] the compacts with the other party of all the slaves
[-----] and therefore he himself has violated the compact
[-----] his assault(?) (*on*) our sequestered property
[-----] at the time having made as if also in writing
[-----] their production so that because of the compact
[*and because of*] the wish of Harpocration himself and because
of all the other [---]
[-----] thus we must select what must be done
[-----] of these slaves shared in common(?) [---]   **(10b** *ends*)

16. DRAFT OF A PETITION, PERHAPS TO THE PREFECT

P.Duke inv. 186r (↑)   frr. **a** (10.0 x 10.7), **b** (9.0 x 6.0)   Alexandria, A.D. 348
c (6.3 x 2.8), **d** (3.9 x 2.5)   Plate VIII

There are four disconnected fragments of the draft of a different petition concerned with this case written by Ammon not to Sisinnius, since he is mentioned in lines **a**.4 and **a**.7, but possibly to the prefect himself, Flavius Nestorius, although no trace of the addressee survives. In fr. **a** Ammon speaks of himself in first-person (**a**.10) and and of Eugeneios in third-person (**a**.12). It cannot therefore be part of a subjectively or objectively styled agreement between these two parties. The prefect may be conjectured as the addressee, for Ammon had already thought of approaching him as revealed at **5**.13ff.

At what point he might have composed this petition one can only speculate. Since the agreement between Eugeneios and Ammon is mentioned at fr. **b**.2, it must have been written after the slaves had decamped, after Eugeneios' journey to Panopolis where 'among friends' a compromise was agreed to, and after Ammon himself had arrived in Alexandria in compliance with the summons to attend Sisinnius' court (cf. **6**). Even while composing for the *catholicus* the full account of his position (the διαμαρτυρία **7–15**), Ammon may have thought it prudent to state his case to the prefect so as to gain his support in case of need. If so, whether this appeal to the prefect was ever completed or dispatched we do not know.

The text is inscribed against the fibers *charta transversa* in Ammon's draft hand. Frr. **a, b** and **c** preserve the left margin, **a** and **b** a width of up to 10 cm. If the roll were as wide as that of **6** or **7**, *ca* 25.5 cm, at least 15.5 cm are lost at right, enough to allow a line-length of *ca* 50 letters. The lacunae would thus accommodate the proposed supplements to **b**.2 and 3. The location of the isolated small fr. **d** is indeterminate, placed in the plate for convenience; its left edge may be a narrow survival of the margin.

No. **19** is found on the verso. Too little text is legible to reveal its relation to the text on the recto.

Text

Fr. a -

1 [*ca 5*   ] α̣ν ι̣[ ]   δίκαιον [   ]

   τούτοις γὰρ ἐν Θηβαίδι οὕτως [   ]

   ἀλλὰ πρὸ τῆς αὐτοῦ π[α]ρουσίας [Φλαουίου]

4 Σισιννίου ὑπεβλ̣[   ]

   νης ὁ αὐτὸς οὔτε [   ]

   ἀδελφὸς περὶ τοῦ δ[Φλαουίου]

   Σισιννίου διὰ τοῦ [   ]

8   ̣[̣] Ἀρποκρατί[ων-   εἰς τὴν Ἀλεξάν]-

   δρειαν διὰ ταῦτα τ̣[ὰ ἀνδράποδα   τοῦ]

   ἐμοῦ ἀ̣δε[λ̣]φ̣ο̣ῦ τελ̣ευ̣[τή]σ̣αντ̣[ος   ]

   ἐδέξατο παρὰ τούτων ἀναφ[   ]

12 μετ' Εὐγενείου ἀπήντηκεν [   ]

   ε ̣[̣] ̣[̣] ̣[   ]

   λ̣[   ]

   -

Fr. b -

1 ἀφηνιάσαντα καὶ ⟦ ̣⟧ τοιαῦτ[α   ]

   εἰς διάλυσιν ⟦με⟧ ῾τοῦτον᾿ πρὸς αὐτὸ̣ν [ὥστε ἔχειν οὐ δικαίως

         αὐ̣]-

   τὸς ἑαυτῶι τῶν ἀνδραπ[όδων τούτων τὸ ἥμισυ καὶ τὸν κληρο-

         νόμον νό]-

4 μιμον τὸ ἄλλο ἥμισυ τούτ[ων   ]

   [ἀ]γν̣ω̣μ̣ο̣σύνης πλέ̣[ο]νος ειτε̣ [   ]

   νῦν καὶ ὁμολογ[   ]

   [̣] ̣[̣] ̣ ̣ ̣ ̣[   ]

   -

2 *pi* in προς corr. from *nu* pap.

Fr. c - - - - - - - - -

1 [̣] ̣[̣] ̣[   ]

   παρὰ̣ τ̣ο̣ύτωι [   ]

   λαβεῖν ἑαυτῶι [   ]

4 τῶι ἐν [̣] ̣ ̣[   ]

[ ].ρ[   ]

- - - - - - - - -

Fr. **d** - - - - - - - -
1   ....[.].[με]-
       ταξὺ γενέσθα[ι   ἕως ἂν]
       συλλάβηι κα[ὶ   ]
4   ....[   ]

- - - - - - - - -

Notes

a.2. Possibly refers to Eugeneios' visit to Panopolis when he negotiated the compromise with Ammon's friends, after which Ammon departed for Alexandria to answer his summons from the *catholicus*.

a.3f. Perhaps ἀλλὰ πρὸ τῆς αὐτοῦ π[α]ρουσίας [πρὸς τὴν ἐνδο-ξότατον τοῦ Φλαουίου]Ι Σισιννίου ὑπέβλ[εψα ὑπεροχήν, "but before his (Eugeneios') arrival [I looked to the most honored authority of Flavius] Sisinnius." Elsewhere in papyri, however, ὑποβλέπειν occurs only at *P. Meyer* 26.4 (III cent.), while ὑποβάλλειν is quite frequent; ὑπεροχή as an honorific title occurs first in the VI century and refers only to the *dux* (see J. Gascou, *ChrÉg* 52 [1977] 363).

a.4f. ὑπεβλ[ήθην is suggested by van Minnen. At turn of line, perhaps ἐξαίφ]Ινης, frequent in Ammon's vocabulary, though ἐξαί]Ιφνης would be a more natural wordbreak; in any case no personal names ending -νης occur elsewhere in the archive. At the end of line 5 possibly ὁ ἐμὸς], or perhaps οὔτε] correlative with the preceding οὔτε in the sense that ὁ αὐτὸς (presumably Eugeneios) is neither [---] nor a brother (of Harpocration).

a.9. Presumably the reference is to Ammon's intention to sail to Alexandria when he learned of Harpocration's death (cf. **7**.27f, **9**.15f, **11c**.6ff, **13**.39ff, from which the supplement is drawn).

a.11. Van Minnen suggests ἀναφ[ορὰν.

a.14. The *lambda* might also be read as *chi*.

b.1. ἀφηνιάσαντα *sc.* ἀνδράποδα, cf. **15**.2.

b.2ff. The supplement is derived from **13**.61f.

b.6. νυν might also have been τοί]Ινυν 'therefore'.

c.3f. Between lines 3 and 4 a paragraphus extends into the left margin. Cf. Ammon's practice in **11**.

d.2. Cf. **13**.55, φίλους γὰρ ἀξιώσας μεταξὺ γενέσθαι. If correct here, the friends named in **7** and **13** are not named in this draft.

d.3. Cf. **13**.58, ἕως ἂν συλλάβηι καὶ συνα[γάγηι τὰ ἀνδράποδα.

Translation

Fr. **a**

[---] just [---] For to(?) these in the Thebaid thus [---] but before his (Eugeneios') arrival [--- of Flavius] Sisinnius .... [--- suddenly?] the same (person) neither [---] brother concerning the [--- of Flavius] Sisinnius through the [---] Harpocration [---] to Alexandria because of the [slaves ---] since my brother had died [---] he received from them .... [---] met with Eugeneios [--- ---]

Fr. **b**

(the slaves) becoming restive and such [---] ʽhimʼ ⟦me⟧ for a settlement with him (Eugeneios) [so that he himself have unjustly] for himself [half] of [these] slaves [and the law]ful [heir] the other half of them [---] of greater arrogance(?) whether [---] now also (an) agree[ment?] [--- ---]

Fr. **c**

[--- ---] with him [---] to take for himself [---].
paragraphus For the [---]

Fr. **d**

[--- ---] come in between [--- until?] he should capture and [bring back these slaves?] [--- ---]

17. DRAFT OF A PETITION

P.Duke inv. 217v, fr. **a** (7.0 x 8.8 cm) and   A.D. 348

P.Köln inv. 4547v (8.5 x 9.8) + P.Duke inv. 217v, fr. **b** (3.8 x 6.8)   Plate IX

How this text, written *transversa charta* like **16**, may relate to Ammon's other petitions of A.D. 348 is not clear, since its phrasing so far as it is preserved provides no parallels with other texts in the archive. That it is a petition (probably to the prefect, see line 11 n.) is assured by ἀξιῶ at line 11. That it is related to the case concerning Harpocration's slaves seems indicated by Ammon's familiar draft-hand and by the presence on the verso of a section of Ammon's principal petition to the *catholicus* (**15**). The cause of this appeal is not apparent.

The text, beginning *in medias res*, appears to be a paragraph or section drafted for insertion or addition to a longer text, like the separated sections of **10b** and **11**, for there are margins on all four sides with traces of an addendum running vertically along the fibers in the left margin and of another along the right margin. Between the left and right fragments is a gap of *ca* 18–25 letters, a space that accommodates our supplements to the text on the recto (**15**.5,6,8).

Text

(*margin*)

κἀμὲ δεῦ[ρο		ca 25	]ιγίγνεσθαι ἄνδρα μηδεμίας
2	αἰτίας μηδ[ὲ	⟦	] καὶ ⟧ διαμισθῶν δὲ α[ ]
	τησιν ἀπρα[		] ε καὶ θέαμα ἰδεῖν οὐδαμ[ῶ]ς
4	οὔτε τῶι πάσχοντ[ι οὔτε τοῖς		] ωμένοις ἀνεκτὸν πρα[ ]
	ἐνεγκεῖν ἐν σιωπῆ[ι		] τινος ὀφικιαλίου ἄνδρα
			φ[ι]λ[ ]
	`[ ] [´		
6	[ca 5]⟦ ⟧ [		]μοσύνην ἀσκοῦντα ὑβρι[ ]
	[ ] καὶ ἐναγια [		ἐ]κεῖσε περιαγομένους ἐκ[ ]
8	[-μ]ενον μηδε[		]τες οἱ περιεστῶτες α [ ]
	[ ] μὴ καρτερουν[τ		]ν τὴν τοιαύτην θέαν δι [ ]

                                           `κέ´ `μαι´

10 [   ]η τοίνυν [   ]ἀλλ᾽ ἐφέσει χρη⟦σάμενος⟧
                                           πρ[ὸς]

[τὸ   ]τατον η[   ] δικαστήριον, ἐφ᾽ οὗ ἀξιῶ,
                                           εἰ τ[ ]

12 [   ]. [....]. [] *traces*   [   ]
                           (*margin*)

(*in left margin along the fibers*)
] δουσιν ἐξετα[

Notes

1. Perhaps δεῦ[ρο καταπλεύσαντα or παραγενόμενον *vel sim.* ἐπ] or περ]ιγίγνεσθαι.

2. Perhaps διαμισθῶν relates to the contract which Ammon had made with Konon (see at **7**.18f). Then perhaps α[ἴ]Ιτησιν.

3. With θέαμα cf. at line 9 τὴν τοιαύτην θέαν; neither term occurs elsewhere in the archive, and the nature of the 'spectacle' remains unknown.

4. Possibly θ]εωμένοις. Preceding it there would be room for τοῦτο. At end perhaps πρᾶ[γμ]α or πρά[γμ]ατα.

6. ἀπραγ]μοσύνην is suggested by ἀπράγμονα at **13**.9f.

10. ἐφέσει κέχρημαι : ἔφεσις (*appellatio*) is an appeal to a higher court, on which see F.J.A. Hoogendijk and P. van Minnen, "Drei Kaiserbriefe Gordians III an die Bürger von Antinoopolis (P.Vindob. G 25945)," *Tyche* 2 (1987) 45f.

11. Probably ἡ[γεμονικὸν] δικαστήριον, the prefectural court, to which **16** also was probably addressed; cf. *CPR* XVIIA 9b.2.21, *P.Col.* VII 171. 20, *P.Oxy.* XVIII 2187r.12 and *SB* VI 9192.14,16, all of the IV-cent. If this supplement is right, we may infer that the lower court was that of the *catholicus*, by which Ammon's petition (**7–15**) would have been denied.

Translation

and me [*on arriving*] here [--- that] a man follow/prevail/escape (?) without cause/blame nor [---], but farming out [---]τησιν [-----] and to see a spectacle not at all either for the one suffering [*it or for those witness*]ing (it) bearable to endure in silence [-----] friend of a certain officer [-----] one practising a quiet life [*to suffer?*] an outrage [---] and atrocities (?) [-----]

(those) being led about there [---] nor [-----] the bystanders [---] not enduring [-----] such a sight [---]. Therefore [-----] but I have appealed to [the ---]est court of the [prefect], before which I ask, if [---]

18. DRAFT

P.Duke inv. 188v

fr. **a** (5.6 x 1.7)
fr. **b** (4.8 x 5.6)
fr. **c** (5.3 x 1.7)

A.D. 348
Plate VI b

Three fragments on the reverse side of **14 a**, **b**, **c**, written in Ammon's draft-hand along the fibers. The text appears to be related to **6**, perhaps as a preliminary draft of sections of that document, for fr. **a** line 2 partly resembles **6** line 11. The paragraphus between lines **b**.6 and 7 appears to indicate that the text is divided into separate sections for insertion into a longer draft, as is **11**. The position of the paragraphus suggests that few letters were lost together with the left margin.

Text

Fr. **a** - - - - - - - - - - - - - - - - -

    [   ]   *traces*   [   ]

2 [   ] πρὸ δύο ἡμερῶν τῆι ση[   ]

    [   ]ντος κἀμοῦ περὶ ἀν[   ]

4 [   ]..... ..[   ]

- - - - - - - - - - - - - - - - -

Fr. **b** - - - - - - - - - - - - - - - - -

    [   ]..δ.[   ]

2 [   ]νον ...... ου [εἰς τὴν]

    [Ἀλε]ξάνδρειαν εὐθέω[ς   ]

4 [   ] ἐκ τούτων δὲ τ[ῶν   ]
           ˋδεῦρο´

    [   ]ν πρὸ τῆς παρουσ[ίας   ]

6 [   ]εἶχον τὴν φροντίδα ε[   ]
    [ˋ].....

    [   ].... συντεθειμ[   ]

8 [   ] ἀνδραπόδου .[   ]

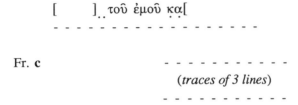

[   ] τοῦ ἐμοῦ κα[   ]

Fr. c

(traces of 3 lines)

Notes

a.2. Cf. **6.**11 π[ρ]ὸ ἄλλων δύο ἡμερῶν, also line 12. At end probably τῆι σή[μερον ἡμέραι.

a.3. Cf. **6.**6 ὁμολογίαν --- περὶ ἀνδ[ρ]απόδων, and **b.**7 below.

b.3. εὐθέως does not occur elsewhere in the archive.

b.4. Perhaps ἐκ τούτων δὲ τ[ῶν ἀνδραπόδων : cf. **12.**16f ἐκ τῶν ἀνδραπόδων [τούτων.

b.6. The poorly written beginning may conceal εἶχον τὴν, as at **11c.**9 and **13.**41, followed in both cases by ἐξαίφνης.

b.6f. A paragraphus extends from the lost left margin between lines 6 and 7.

b.7. The interlinear insert above 7 is illegible. Cf. **10b.**4 and 5 τὰ συντεθειμένα 'the compact', and note on **a.**3 above.

b.8. The singular of ἀνδράποδον occurs nowhere else in the archive but is implied by **13.**66-70.

Translation

Fr. a [-----] two days earlier, today [-----]ντος while I too concerning (the) slaves (?) [-----]

Fr. b [--- to Ale]xandria straightway [-----] from these [slaves? ---] before (my? his?) arrival ʼhereʼ [-----] I was engaged with this (?) concern, suddenly (?) [-----] *(paragraphus)* made a compact [-----] slave [-----] of my [brother? ---]

19. Draft

P.Duke inv. 186v (—>)   frr. **a** (6.3 x 2.8), **b** (9.0 x 6.0)   A.D. 348
                          c (10.0 x 10.7), **d** (3.9 x 2.5)   Plate X

Four fragments in Ammon's draft-hand written along the fibers on the verso of **16**. As on **16**, the left margin is preserved along with the beginnings of lines, most of which are expunged or abraded and illegible, so that the relation of this text to **16** or other texts in the archive is obscure. On fr. **a** (the verso of **16c**) are traces of the beginnings of four lines; on **b** (backing **16b**) after traces of three lines a bold *ancora* pointing downward stands in the left margin beside an apparently expunged fourth line, followed by a fairly legible line 5; on **c** (verso of **16a**) after traces of five lines are three clear lines, then an uninscribed space equal to three lines (unlikely to be a lower margin since no corresponding margin appears on the recto of this fragment). Fr. **d** (verso of **16d**) is not aligned with the other fragments.

Text

Fr. **a**   - - - - - - - - - - - - -

              traces of four lines

              - - - - - - - - - - - - -

Fr. **b**   - - - - - - - - - - - - -

              traces of four lines

5   *ancora*   *traces of ink possibly expunged*

              καίτοι φαίνε[ται] μηδὲ [   ]

              .. [   ]

              - - - - - - - - - - - - -

Fr. **c**   - - - - - - - - - - - - -

              traces of six lines

7   ὁμολογίας γραμματ[   ]

              τοῦτο ὅτι ἀπὸ πρώτης λ[   ]

              ἐν αὐτῶι διατετη[ρη-   ]

              (*margin?*)

Fr. d   - - - - - - - - - - - - -

traces of two lines

[   ]͵͵ παραβα[   ]

[   ]͵͵͵͵͵ ͵͵͵[   ]

- - - - - - - - - - - - -

Notes

b.5. Before the line, which appears to have been expunged, stands a bold *ancora* in the left margin, pointing downward. At **7**.42 an *ancora* pointing upward marks the start of an intercolumnar addition (cf. note *ad loc.*). Perhaps here the *ancora* points to a text below (**c**.7–9?) to be substituted for this expunged line.

c.7. γράμματ[α or γραμματ[εῖον?, 'deed of contract'.

c.8. τοῦτο stands in the left margin preceding the line.

Translation

Fr. **b** 6:   [-----] and yet it seems (that) not even [-----]

Fr. **c** 6ff: [-----] a deed of agreement [-----] this, that from the first [-----] observed(?) in it [-----]

20. DRAFT

P.Duke inv. 229r   3.9 x 7.5 cm   A.D. 348

Plate XI a

The writing in Ammon's draft-hand runs against the fibers, and except for lines 1 and 7 the surface is so abraded as to yield no parallels with other texts. On the verso is **21**.

Text

```
            - - - - - - - -
   [        ἀ]ναλέγων πι [              ]
   [        ] α    τατον [              ]
   [        ]ιαν παρὰ σοῦ  [            ]
4  [        ]  ν νόμιμον [              ]
   [        ]  traces                   ]
   [        ]  ια   [                   ]
               γα  ο ['
   [        ]ειν ἐπὶ τουτο [            ]
8  [        ]  Εὐγένειος [              ]
   [        ] vac? ε [                  ]
            - - - - - - - -
```

Notes

1. ἀναλέγω does not occur elsewhere in the archive.

3. More likely παρὰ σοῦ than τοῦ.

4. Possibly]ον νόμιμον [, cf. **13**.62 τὸν κληρ(ονόμον) ν[ό]μιμ(ον) and **5**.17 and **16b**.3f; but perhaps]ιν, as if from ἔχε]ιν.

7. τούτου[or τούτοι[ς. The small bold but very doubtful letters written above the line might be read ἐπεὶ γὰρ του[or κατήγαγον [.

8. Probably either] Εὐγένειος [or] Εὐγένειον [.

21. DRAFT

P.Duke inv. 229v   3.9 x 7.5 cm   A.D. 348

Plate XI b

Written in Ammon's draft-hand along the fibers on the verso of **20**. Only one line is legible, and its words are too commonplace in the archive to permit identification.

Text

- - - - - - - - - - -

1   [   ] *traces of one line* [   ]
     [   ].... ν .... [   ]
3   [   ] ν ἐν Ἀλεξαν[δρείαι   ]
     [   ] *vacat ca 7 lines, or* [   ]
                        margin?

Note

2f. The faint traces before and after *nu* may conceal the ἐσ]χηκέναι παρὰ τ[of **7**.33. If so, these lines may parallel the text of no. **7**; with line 3 cf. ἡμῶν. ἐν Ἀλεξανδρείαῑ at **7**.34.

22. DRAFT

P.Duke inv. 187v   frr. **a** (3.0 x 3.5), **b** (3.1 x 7.3)   A.D. 348
Plate XII a

On the verso of **8** the two separated fragments bear the line-ends of a text written along the fibers in a small version of Ammon's draft-hand. The two fragments are separated by a space equivalent to about six lines as determined by the lacuna supplements to the text on the recto. A narrow right margin is preserved on both fragments. The surface of the papyrus is abraded and discolored.

Text

Fr. **a**   (*margin*)

    [   ] *traces*
    [   ] *traces*
    [   ] *traces*
4 [   ]̣ δρασμ̣
    [   ]̣̣̣̣̣ ̣̣̣

- - - - -

(*about 6 lines lacking*)

Fr. **b**   - - - - - -

    [   ]̣ [̣̣̣]̣ [̣]̣
    [   ] *traces*
    [   ] *traces*
4 [   ]̣ πρότερον̣
                                 `σ]θαι ἀπο´`
    [   ] σαι τινι
    [   ]̣ αι ̣̣̣ [ ]̣
    [   ]ει ταύτῃ
8 [   ]ὐκ ἠθέλησα
    [   ]σθαι τὴν
    [   ] ἀδελφῶι
    [γ]ὰρ ἐκεῖνον

12   [   ]...[.]....
     [   ]..
                                                           - - - - - -

Notes

a.4. Cf. **7**.61 καὶ δρασμὸν.

b.4. Cf. **12**.5 and **13**.5 μήπω πρότερον.

b.5. In drafts **11b**.1, **12**.15 and **13**.21, τινι accompanies only Κόνωνι.

b.6. Perhaps] καὶ.

b.8. This form of ἐθέλω occurs nowhere else in the archive.

The following fragments offer too little text to permit recognition of their context. All are written by Ammon's hand.

23. DRAFT

P.Köln inv. 4551r   frr. **a** (3.5 x 3.7 cm), **b** (3.2 x 4.2)   Plate XIII
[=P.Duke inv. 1279]   **c** (3.8 x 10.2)

Written against the fibers in what begins as a smaller example of Ammon's formal hand but in fr. **c** becomes hastier and more careless. Very little of the vocabulary is found in other drafts. The verso is uninscribed.

Text

Fr. **a**   - - - - - - - -

]..[
] *traces* [
] ̣αμενον [
4   ]ς καὶ αὐτὸς α̣[

- - - - - - - -

Fr. **b**   - - - - - - - -

].[...].̣.[
] παρ' ἑαυτῶι ̣[
`].̣.[̣]ην´
] αὐτὸς κατεσ[
4   ] τῶν δούλω[ν
].̣ρ..̣.[
]α δὲ ὕστερον [
]κην δύο ημ[

- - - - - - - -

Fr. c

```
        - - - - - - - -
]ηι πρ[.]σεδρ.[.].[
] αὐτῶι κατεσκ[
]τονασοντασ.[
  ']αφε..'
```
4   ⟦   ]ματα ἔχων⟧.[
```
].χεν καὶ ἐπι[
].ἐκει..[
] traces
```
8   ].....[
```
]μενος ει...[
] σεμνοτατο[
].εσθαι ἐχον..[
```
(*margin*)

Notes

a.4. Cf. **13**.65] καὶ αὐτὸς οὗτος.

b.4. Cf. **13**.65 παράστασιν τῶν δούλων.

b.5. Perhaps] γάρ με ...[.

b.7. Perhaps δύο ἡμ[ερῶν .

c.1. Possibly τ]ῆι πρ[ο]σεδρε[ία]ῑ 'close attention, assiduity'.

c.2. κατεσκ[ευα-.

c.3. *e.g.* κρείτ]τονας ὄντας.

c.4. The correction above the line may begin]λφ as if ἀδε]λφὸς but is more likely]αφε as if from γρ]αφεὶς, or γρ]αφέντ[α] alternative to *e.g.* ⟦γράμ⟧ματα immediately below.

c.6. Apparently a form of ἐκεῖνος.

c.9. Perhaps ἐκ τῆς ...[.

c.10. Cf. **4**.56 σεμνότατον τ[ο]ῦτο δικαστήριον, preceded in **4**.55 by ἡγούμε[ν]ο[ς] καὶ προσδώσει [*ca ?*] ι ἐπὶ τὸ.

24. DRAFT

P.Köln inv. 4554   3.2 x 3.2 cm   IV cent.
[= P.Duke inv. 1280]   Plate XIV

A small fragment inscribed on both sides in Ammon's draft-hand; his script on the recto (against the fibers) is bolder and better preserved than that on the verso.

Text

Recto

    - - - - - - -

    ] ̣ ̣αρνωνε[
    ]νον εὐνομί[αν
    ]κοῦ ἡμῶν [
4   ]ων προυστη ̣[
      ]υνειναι [

    - - - - - - -

Verso

    - - - - - -

     ] ̣ ̣ ̣β[
    ] ̣ ̣[̣] ̣τατ[
    ]ναι ̣χοντα[
4   ]τατην οὐπ[
     ] ̣π ̣κρατ[

    - - - - - - -

Notes

recto   2. εὐνομία is not preserved elsewhere in the archive.

       5. Perhaps σ]υνεῖναι.

verso   3.]ν ἀνεῖχον or]ναι ἔχοντα[.

       4. Perhaps οὔπ[ω, although οὐ γὰ[ρ is possible.

       5. Probably Ἁ]ρποκρατ[ίων-.

25. PETITION

P.Duke inv. 6r   6.4 x 3.4 cm   IV cent.
                                  Plate XII b

A fragment of apparently the close of a petition, as suggested by the vocabulary and phrasing. Four well-written lines in Ammon's hand running against the fibers on the recto, closely resembling the script and line-spacing of **9** and **10**. The verso is uninscribed.

Text

- - - - - - - - - - - - - -

```
1  [                    ].[
   [          ]ν οἱ νόμοι βούλονται καὶ [
   [          ] νῦν ἑαυτοὺς ἀπατῶντες [
4  [          ].ε ους γενόμενα ἐκν[
   [          ]υ[ ]..... ιωνο....μ[
```

- - - - - - - - - - - - - -

Notes

2. Perhaps νῦ]ν or τοίνυ]ν. Cf. **9**.34 and **10a**.23f ἐμὲ γὰρ νῦν καλοῦσιν οἱ νόμοι ἐπὶ τὴν [τῶν ἀνδραπόδων] δεσποτείαν.

3. Of course τοί]νυν is equally possible. ἀπατῶντες : ἀπάτην is complained of at **7**.65 and **10a**.11.

5. Along the lower ragged edge, traces of ink from the tops of broken letters would conform to το]ῦ ['Α]ρποκρατίωνος ..μ[. Cf. n.2, continued at **9**.35 [ὄντα ἐκείνου τοῦ Ἀρποκρατ]ίωνος ὁμοπάτριον κτλ.

Translation

[-----] the laws want [---] and [-----]
(those) now deceiving themselves [-----]
things that have occurred ? [-----]
of Harpocration ? [-----]

ANHANG
KOMPOSITTEXT ZU 7–15

Zum Nutzen des deutschsprachigen Lesers folgt hier ein Komposittext der Eingabe des Aurelius Ammon aus Panopolis an den Katholikos (Rationalis) in Alexandria, zu der Konzepte in **7–15** vorliegen. Zur leichteren Orientierung seien die Ereignisse, auf die Bezug genommen wird, zusammengefaßt.

Ammons Bruder, der Rhetor Aurelius Harpokration, hatte vor einiger Zeit von Alexandria aus eine Vortragsreise angetreten, die ihn in weite Teile des römischen Reiches führte. Vor seiner Abreise ließ er Sklaven in der Obhut seines Bruders zurück. Dieser übergab sie – oder zumindest einen Teil von ihnen – Konon, einem Freund des Harpokration. Harpokration starb in der Fremde. Ammon erfuhr dies mit einiger Verspätung; danach hörte er, daß in Alexandria Eugeneios, ein memorarius, aufgetreten war, welcher versuchte, sich die Sklaven anzueignen. Nach dessen Ansicht war Harpokration ohne Erben gestorben und sein Erbe als bonum vacans (ἀδέσποτον) zu betrachten, das der res privata des Kaisers zustand. Da solche bona einem Delator, der auf sie hingewiesen hatte, häufig zugesprochen wurden, hatte sich Eugeneios mit einer entsprechenden Eingabe an den Kaiser gewandt und tatsächlich erwirkt, daß die Sklaven ihm gehören sollten, wenn sonst niemand dagegen Einspruch erhebe oder das Eigentum an den Sklaven für sich beanspruche. Als nun Eugeneios nach Alexandria kam, gelang es ihm, die verstreuten Sklaven zu finden und dem Katholikos zu übergeben. Dabei mußte er allerdings erfahren, daß Harpokration in Ammon einen erbberechtigten Bruder hatte, worauf er diesen Bruder in der Thebais aufsuchte. Durch **5** wissen wir, daß Ammon bereits vorher beabsichtigt hatte, einen gewissen Aurelius Faustinus nach Alexandria zu schicken, der vor dem Präfekten bezeugen sollte, daß Ammon der Erbe der Sklaven sei. Dieser Reise kam aber offenbar Eugeneios durch sein Erscheinen zuvor. Mit der Begründung, daß er sich in den Besitz von entlaufenen und herrenlosen Sklaven gesetzt habe, erhob Eugeneios auf sie Anspruch. Man einigte sich, die Sklaven zu teilen. In der Folge erhielt Ammon die Aufforderung, sich beim Katholikos in Alexandria zu melden, reiste dorthin und setzte einen Schriftsatz auf, in dem er erklärte, fristgerecht in Alexandria eingetroffen zu sein (erhalten in dem διασφαλισμός Nr. **6**). In unserer Eingabe lesen wir nach einer rhetorisch stilisierten Einleitung, mit der Ammon das Wohlwollen des Katholikos zu gewinnen sucht, und nach dem Referat der hier zusammengefaßten Ereignisse schließlich noch von ungeöffneten Testamenten des Harpokration, deren Existenz zunächst offenbar unbekannt geblieben war und die nun wohl eine rasche Entscheidung des Streits verhinderten. Ammon fordert abschließend die Auslieferung der Sklaven an ihn – wahrscheinlich unter dem Vorbehalt, daß erst nach der Öffnung der Testamente die Angelegenheit endgültig zu entscheiden sei.

KOMPOSITTEXT ZU **7–15**

Um die Orientierung zu erleichtern, sind nur die am besten erhaltenen Textpartien berücksichtigt, aus denen sich jedoch der intendierte Text erkennen läßt. Für eine Synopse, die die erhaltenen Fragmente möglichst vollständig präsentiert, verweisen wir auf die oben abgedruckte „Composite Translation of **7–15**", S. 136 ff.

7

1 [Φλαυίωι Σισιννίωι   *vacat*   ] τῶι διασημ[οτάτωι] καθολικῶι
2 [παρὰ Αὐρηλίου Ἄμμωνος Πετεαρβεσχίνιος] σχολαστικο[ῦ ἀπὸ
             Παν]ὸς πόλεως τῆς
3   Θ[ηβαίδος.

13

1 [*ca 20*   δέσποτα, καὶ ἐκεῖνον τότε τὸν χρόν]ον εὐδαιμονί[α]ς
             ἐνεπλήσθη|ν]
2 [*ca 25*   ] τῆ[ς θ]εῶν προνοίας ἡγουμένης σὺν Ἀγαθῶι Δαίμονι
             τῆς χώρας
3 [τ]ῆς τῶν [ἄν]ω Αἰγυπ[τίω]ν καὶ παρὰ τοῖς κάτω Αἰγυπτίοις καὶ τοῖς
             ἄλλοις ἅπασιν ἀνθρ(ώποις) μακάριοι
4 κ[αὶ ζ]ηλ(ωτοὶ) ἐνομίσθ(ημεν) εἶναι δ[ιὰ] τ[ὸ] τοιοῦτ(ο) εὐτυχ(εῖν), ὧι
             παραπλ(ήσιον) ἕτερον ἐκείνη ἡ λῆξις κηδεμ(όνα) καὶ
             προστάτ(ην)
5 *ca 8*   μήπω πρότερ(ον) μήτε ὕστερ(ον) προσδοκᾷ θεάσεσθαι. διάδοχοι
             δὲ νῦν τῆς εὐδαιμ(ονίας) ἡμῶν ἐκεί(νης)
6 οἱ τὴν λαμπροτάτ(ην) οἰκ(οῦντες) πόλ(ιν), ἀλλὰ καὶ αὐτὸς πάλιν ἐν
             τῶι παρόντ(ι) εἰς εὐδαιμονίας μέρο(ς) λογίζομαι
7 φοιτῆσαι, [ὡ]ς ἐ[πέ]πρω|το] κἀμοὶ [δ]ικαστηρίωι νῦν ὁμιλεῖν ὑπὸ
             τοιούτωι [ἄρχον]τι καὶ δικαστῆι
8 {ἑστάναι} δικαζόμενον, οὗ τὸ ἀμίμητον τῆς κρίσεως ἐν διαφόροις
             ἔθνεσι καὶ πάλαι καὶ νῦν
9 ἡ πεῖρα ἔδειξεν. ἡσυχίαν τοίνυν ἀπράγμονα τοῖς ἐν φιλοσοφίαῑ καὶ λόγοις
             ἀνηγμένοις πρέ-

Übersetzung des Komposittextes zu 7–15

In eckige Klammern sind nur jene Ergänzungen gesetzt, die sich aus keinem der Konzepte gewinnen lassen.

7

[An Flavius Sisinnius], rationalis, vir perfectissimus, [von Aurelius Ammon, Sohn des Petearbeschinis], Rechtsanwalt, aus Panopolis, Thebais.

13

[In Oberägypten erinnert man sich gut an Deine Amtszeit], Herr, und zu jener Zeit war ich erfüllt von Glückseligkeit [- - - und da] die Fürsorge der Götter zusammen mit Agathos Daimon[1] Oberägypten regierte, galten wir bei den Bewohnern von Unterägypten und bei allen anderen Menschen als glücklich und beneidenswert wegen eines solchen Glücks, angesichts dessen jene Provinz einen vergleichbaren Beschützer und Vorsteher, [da] er vorher nicht [erschienen war], auch in Zukunft nicht zu sehen erwartet. (5) Nachfolger aber jenes Glücks, das wir genossen, sind nun die Bewohner der glänzensten Stadt, aber auch ich selbst glaube jetzt wieder Anteil an diesem Glück zu erlangen, da es auch mir bestimmt war, nun einem Gericht beizuwohnen und gerichtet zu werden unter einem solchen Herrscher und Richter, für dessen unvergleichliches Urteil der Beweis bei verschiedenen Völkern früher und jetzt erbracht worden ist.

(Erweiterung, die in 12 fehlt:)
(9) Freilich, da ich auch selbst weiß, daß Friede und Ruhe jenen ziemt, die in Philosophie

---

[1] Agathos Daimon ist die Schutzgottheit Alexandriens, die nach Gründung der Stadt in Schlangengestalt erschien.

10 πειν καὶ αὐτὸς ἐπιστάμ(ενος) ἥκω καταναγ[κ]ασθ(είς), δέσποτα, ὑπὸ τῶν ἐν
        πράγμασιν ἐξετάζεσθαι ἡμᾶς
11 πεποιηκότων, προαχθεὶς ἐπὶ ταυτηνὶ [τὴ]ν διαμαρτυρίαν. εἰ μὲν γὰρ ἐξῆν τοῖ[ς]
        .ν ca 8 ηρη-
12 μένοις κατὰ τὸ τῆς φύσεως αὐ[θ]αίρετον μέχρι τέλους ἀπολαύειν τῆς   Spuren
13 [ca 15   ] ουσης [.] , ἀπειλεῖ δὲ φθόνος ἀεὶ τοῖς καλοῖς .... εἰ μή μοι
        Spuren

12

9 [πεῖρα ἔδειξεν. .....]ς τοίνυν τούτου τὴν ὑπόθεσιν ἄνωθεν
        ἀρξάμενος ὡς ἔχει συντόμως τῆι
10 [σῆι   ca 15   ] .... ι πρὸ πολλοῦ ca 10   ἀδελφός τις ἐμὸς
        Ἁρποκρατίων τοὔνομα
11 [περὶ λόγους καὶ αὐτὸς ἐ]σπουδακὼς ἀποδημίαν ὑπερόριον ἔξω
        τῆς Αἰγύπτου τυγχάνει στειλάμεν[ος].
12 [ἐντεῦθεν δὲ ἀποδημ]ῶν ἀπὸ τῆς λαμπρᾶς ταυτησὶ πόλεως
                                        ʼἑαυτοῦʼ
        κατέλειπεν ἀνδράποδα παρʼ ἐμοὶ ἐν-
13 [ταυθοῖ τότε διατρίβον]τι ἐντειλάμενός μοι εἰς Θηβαίδα, καθʼ ὃν
        μέλλω καιρὸν ἀναπλεῦσαι, ἀναγαγεῖν
14 [τὰ ἀνδράποδα. ἐγὼ δὲ φοβού]μενος, μὴ ἔν τι τούτων τῶν
        ἀνδραπόδων ἀπʼ ἐμοῦ δρασμῶι χρήσηται,
15 [ca 18   ἐτύ]γχανεν, παρεθέμην Κόνωνί τινι φίλωι
        ἐκείνου Ἀλεξανδρεῖ ὡς καὶ (wie dieser Finalsatz fortgesetzt
        wurde, erkennt man aus 13, 21:)

13

21 Κόνωνί τινι Ἀλεξανδρεῖ φίλωι ὄντι ἐκείνου, ὅπως ἐπανελθὼν ἀπο-
        λάβηι, προσεδόκων γὰρ (unten fortgesetzt nach 12, 16–20)

Gegenüber 13 erweiterte Fassung von

12

16 [ca 20   ] Spuren [.....] μενος δὲ τιν' ἐκ τῶν ἀνδραπόδων
17 [τούτων   ca 14   ] κἀμοὶ ἔπεσθαι ε[ἰ]ς Θηβαίδα ἀνήγαγον κατὰ τὰς τοῦ
        ἀδελφοῦ ἐντολὰς
18 [ca. 15   ἐβου]λήθη, ἀλλὰ ἐνταυθοῖ ἀναμεῖναι τὴν τοῦ ἀδελφοῦ μου
        παρουσίαν

und Rhetorik unterrichtet sind, bin ich nur deshalb da, weil ich, Herr, von den Beamten, die unsere Untersuchung bewirkten, dazu gezwungen und zu dieser Protestation veranlaßt worden bin. Denn wenn es denen, die nach dem Willen der Natur leben wollen, erlaubt wäre, bis an ihr Ende [Friede und Glück] zu genießen, [- - -]. Der Neid jedoch bedroht immer die Rechtschaffenen [- - -]

12

[So werde ich] also den Hergang des Streites, von vorne beginnend, so wie er sich verhält, Deiner - - - (Ehrentitel) kurz [darlegen]. Vor langer Zeit - - - mein Bruder Harpokration, der auch Rhetorik studiert hat, bereitete gerade eine Reise ins Ausland vor. Als er daraufhin von dieser glänzenden Stadt abreiste, ließ er seine Sklaven bei mir, der ich mich damals hier (in Alexandria) aufhielt, zurück und trug mir auf, die Sklaven zu dem Zeitpunkt, an dem ich in die Thebais zurückkehren sollte, mitzunehmen. Da ich jedoch [fürchtete], daß mir einer dieser Sklaven entlaufen könnte, - - - , übergab ich sie einem gewissen Konon, einem alexandrinischen Freund meines Bruders, damit auch - - - .

Zur Fortsetzung des Satzes vergleiche:

13

(21) Konon, einem alexandrinischen Freund meines Bruders, damit dieser (Harpokration) bei seiner Rückkehr die Sklaven zurücknimmt, denn ich erwartete ... *(fortgesetzt unten nach 12, 16–20)*

Gegenüber 13 erweiterte Fassung von

12

- - - einige von den Sklaven - - - [unwillig,] mir zu folgen, - - - führte ich [nur wenige?] nach dem Auftrag meines Bruders in die Thebais hinauf, [?wobei jene ausgenommen blieben, die Alexandria nicht verlassen] wollten, sondern dort die Rückkehr meines Bruders erwarten [wollten (?)]. [Denn ich brachte es nicht über mich],

19 [*ca. 15*   ἀναγ]κάσαι, ἀλλὰ [π]αρὰ τῶι αὐτῶι Κόνωνι κατέλειπον
                ὁμολογίαν παρ' αὐτοῦ ἔγγρα-
20 [φον δεξάμενος ὅπ]ως ἐπανελθόντ[ι ἐκε]ίνωι ἀποκαταστήσηι [*ca. 15*   ]
                ἀνδρ[άπ]οδα,

13

         προσεδόκων γὰρ
22 τὴν ἐκείνου ἐπάνοδον μετὰ βραχ(ύν) τινα γενήσ(εσθαι)
         χρόν(ον). ἐλάνθαν(ε) δὲ ἄρα ἡμ(ᾶς) ὁ δαίμων
         ἐλπ(ίσι) ματ(αίαις) τὸν
23 ἡμέτ(ερον) ἀναρτ(ῶν) τότ(ε) λογισμ(όν). ἐν γὰρ τῆι ἀποδημίαι
         ἐκεῖνος γενόμ(ενος) καὶ ἀπὸ χώρας εἰς χώρ(αν)
         ἑκάστοτ(ε) μεταβαίν(ων)
24 ἀπὸ τῆς Ἑλλάδ(ος) εἰς Ῥώμην καὶ ἀπὸ Ῥώμης εἰς Κωνσταντινό-
         πολιν καὶ ἀπ' ἄλλης εἰς ἄλλην τὰ πλεῖστα
25 σχεδ(ὸν) τῆς γῆς περιελθ(ὼν) μέρη τῶν καλλινίκων δεσποτῶν
         ἡμῶν τὰς νίκας καὶ λόγους βασιλικοὺς πανταχ(οῦ)
26 .... το ἐπιδεικνύμε[νος], αὐ[τ]ὸς γὰρ ἐν ταῖς ἐπισ(ήμοις)
         πόλ(εσι) τῆς Ἑλλάδ(ος) καὶ ἐπιτρ(οπεύων) καὶ
         λογισ(τεύων) ἔπραξ(ε) καὶ διὰ ταύτ(ας)
27 τὰς ἀφορμ(ὰς) ἐπὶ πολ(ύν) τινα χρόν(ον) τὴν ἀποδ(ημίαν)
         ἐξέτ(εινεν), ἐμοῦ ἀεὶ προσδοκῶντ(ος) αὐτοῦ τὴν
         ἐπάνοδ(ον), ἐπεὶ καὶ οὕτω γράφων
28 ἀεὶ παρεκάλε(σεν) ἡμᾶς διὰ τῶν γραμμάτ(ων), ἀλλ' ἐν τῶι
         μεταξὺ μήτε ἐκείνου ταχέως ἐπανελθόντος, ἐμοῦ δὲ
29 ἀεὶ προσδοκῶντος αὐτὸν ἐπανήξειν ἔτι τε καὶ ἀσχολουμένου
         περὶ τὴν τῶν δημοσίων μου
30 τελεσμάτων διάλ[υσ]ιν καὶ μὴ δυνηθέντ(ος) δεῦρο καταπλεῦσαι,
         αὐτοὶ οἱ δοῦλ(οι) μηκέτι ἀνασχόμ(ενοι)
31 παρὰ ξένοι[ς] εἶν[α]ι [*ca 7*   κα]θ' ἑαυτ(οὺς) ὑπο[μ]έν(ειν),
         πρὸ πολλοῦ ἀπέστησ(αν) τῆς τούτων οἰκ(ίας) καὶ
         καθ' ἑαυτοὺς
                 ῾ωσ῾
32 ἔζησαν μηδενὸς αὐτῶν πρ[.] .... [.] ρ ( ) [.] [τ]οῦ προ[τ]έρ(ου)
         δεσπότου διὰ τὴν πολυχρ(όνιον) μὲν
33 ἐκείνου ἀποδημ(ίαν), ἀεὶ δὲ ὑφ' ἡμῶν εἰς ἐπάν[οδον   *ca 10*   ]
         .ι[. .]ν( ) [μ]έχρι καὶ τῆς τελε[υταίας]

Zwang auszuüben, sondern ließ diese bei demselben Konon zurück, wobei ich von ihm einen schriftlich abgefaßten Vertrag erhielt, daß er jenem bei seiner Rückkehr die Sklaven übergeben werde ...

13

Denn ich erwartete, daß jener (mein Bruder) bald zurückkehren werde. Aber der Daimon ließ uns, ohne daß wir es merkten, unsere damalige Überlegung auf leere Hoffnungen gründen. Denn nachdem sich jener auf die Reise begeben hatte, wanderte er überall umher von einem Land ins andere, von Griechenland nach Rom, von Rom nach Konstantinopel und von einer Stadt zur nächsten. So bereiste er beinahe den größten Teil der Erde und [hörte nicht auf], überall in Prunkreden von den Siegen unserer herrlich triumphierenden Herren zu sprechen und über die Könige zu berichten. Und er übte in den bedeutenden Städten Griechenlands das Amt des Epitropos und Logistes aus. Und wegen dieser (27) Möglichkeiten dehnte er seine Reise auf lange Zeit aus. Ich jedoch erwartete fortwährend seine Rückkehr, da er auch in diesem Sinn schrieb und uns immer brieflich tröstete. Aber in der Zwischenzeit, als auch jener (sc. Konon) sich nicht beeilte heraufzukommen, ich jedoch fortwährend seine Ankunft erwartete und außerdem mit der Zahlung der in meine Zuständigkeit fallenden öffentlichen Abgaben beschäftigt war und nicht hierher herunter kommen konnte, da ertrugen es die Sklaven selbst nicht länger, bei Fremden zu sein - - - und [da] sie für sich bleiben [wollten], waren sie seit langem aus dem Haus dieser Leute verschwunden und lebten für sich, wobei keiner von ihnen - - - des früheren Herrn wegen seiner langen Abwesenheit, immer aber von uns zur Rückkehr - - - bis zu jener

34 ὥρας ἐκείνης καθ' ἣν τὴν ἀνάγκ(ην) μοι [*ca 30*   ]
35 αρ τ( ) [π]αντὸς τοῦ βίου τῆι τῆς ἄνω κινήσ(εως) [*ca 35*]
36 Αὐρήλ(ιος) Ἀέτιος παραγένηι ἀνελ[θ(ὼν)] καθότι [*ca 30*]
37 λέγ(ων) ὡς εἴη τελευτήσας ἐκεῖνος, πρὸ βραχ[έος γὰρ χρόνου
   τοῦτο ἀκήκοα *ca 15*]
38 οὐ γὰρ ταχ(έως) εἰς ἀκοὴ(ν) τῶν οἰκ(είων) ἀφικν(εῖται) ὁ περὶ τοῦ
   θ[ανάτ(ου) τῶν ἐπὶ ξέν(ης) λόγ(ος) διὰ τὸ μηδ(ένα)
   βούλ(εσθαι) μετὰ]
39 τοι(αύτης) ἀγγελ(ίας) προσιέναι τοῖς τῶι τελευτ(ήσαντι) κατ'
   ἀ[γ]χ[ιστείαν διαφέρουσι. παρεσκευαζόμην μὲν
   ἐπ]ὶ τῆι
40 ἀκοῆι ταύτηι δεῦρο καταπλεῦσαι, πρῶτον μὲν δι' ἐκεῖνον, ἔπειτα
   καὶ διὰ ταῦ[τα τὰ ἀνδρ]άποδ(α) αὐτοῦ
41 τὰ ἐνταυθοῖ διατρίβοντα. ἕως δὲ ⟦ε⟧ταύτην ἔτι ἐν χερσὶν εἶχον τὴν
   φροντίδα, ἐξα[ί]φνη[ς ....]
42 ἀγγέλλων Σ[ερ]ηνιανὸς ὁ τοῦ Παλλαδίου ὡς ἔξωθέν τις ἐπιστὰς
   Εὐγένειος τοὔνομα [.]
43 .... [*ca 4* τὰ ἐ]ν Ἀλεξανδρείᾱ ἀνδράποδ(α) τοῦ ἀδελφοῦ μου
   Ἁρποκρατίωνος ὡς ὄντα [νῦν]
44 [ἀ]δέσποτα καὶ ὡς μὴ ἐπὶ κληρονόμοις ἐκείνου τελευτ[ήσαντος]
   ἐξ αἰτήσεως ἐσχηκέναι
45 παρὰ τῆς θειότητος τῶν καλλινίκων [δε]σποτῶν ἡμῶν καὶ
   τετυχηκέναι ἀντιγραφῆς

(Addendum am linken Rand des Recto)
46 οὕτως ἐχούσης· εἰ μή τις τούτων ἀντιποιοῖτο μηδὲ φανείη τις τὴν
   τούτων δεσποτείαν ἐκδικῶν,
              `ἀκούσας`
47 παραδοθῆναι αὐτῶι. ταῦτα παρ' ἐκείνου τοῦ Σερηνιανοῦ ἔτι
   μᾶλλον πρὸς τὴν ἀποδημίαν ἠπείχθην.
48 [ἐν Ἀ]λεξανδρείᾱ δὲ γενόμενος ἐκεῖνος καὶ γνοὺς ἐκεῖνον τὸν
   Ἁρποκρατίωνα κληρονόμον ἔχειν
              `Νίκης`
49 [ἀδελ]φὸν ὁμοπάτριόν τε καὶ ὁμομήτριον, ἐμὲ δὴ τὸν Ἄμμωνα
   τῆς μητρός, τούτων τῶν σωμάτων
50 [*ca 27*   ] [ ] [ἀ]νέδ[ρ]αμεν ἴσως τοῦτο
   πυνθάνεσθαι βουλόμενος, ἔλεγεν

letzten Stunde, durch die die Notwendigkeit mir - - - des ganzen Lebens
durch (?) - - - der Bewegung nach oben - - - (36) sich Aurelius Aetius
einfand, als er heraufkam, wie - - -, und berichtete, daß jener tot sei. Denn
erst vor kurzer Zeit habe ich das gehört. - - - Nicht schnell nämlich dringt die
Nachricht vom Tod derer, die sich in der Fremde aufhalten, an das Ohr der
Verwandten, da niemand mit einer solchen Nachricht herantreten will an die,
die dem Toten als Nächstverwandte angehören. Auf diese Nachricht hin
bereitete ich mich vor, hierher herunter zu fahren, zuerst seinetwegen, dann
aber auch wegen seiner Sklaven, (41) die sich hier aufhielten. Als ich noch
mit dieser Sorge umging, da [fand sich] plötzlich Serenianus, der Sohn des
Palladius, [ein], und brachte die Nachricht, daß von auswärts ein gewisser
Eugeneios aufgetreten sei [- - - und behauptete], von der Göttlichkeit unserer
herrlich siegenden Herren die in Alexandria befindlichen Sklaven meines
Bruders Harpokration auf Grund einer Eingabe erhalten zu haben, da sie jetzt
herrenlos und nicht bei Erben seien, nachdem jener gestorben ist, und er be-
hauptete, ein Reskript bekommen zu haben,

(Addendum am linken Rand des Recto)
(46) das wie folgt lautet: „Wenn nicht jemand dagegen Einspruch erhebt und
auch niemand erscheint, der das Eigentum an diesen Sklaven beansprucht,
(47) so sollen sie ihm überlassen werden."
Als ich dies von jenem Serenianus erfahren hatte, da drängte ich noch mehr
zur Reise. Als jener (sc. Eugeneios) jedoch in Alexandria eintraf und erfuhr,
daß jener Harpokration einen leiblichen Bruder als Erben habe, mich,
Ammon, den Sohn der Nike, da begab er sich sofort [wegen] dieser Sklaven
[in die Thebais - - -] und wollte vermutlich dies auskundschaften. Er erklärte

51 [δὲ γράμματα ἔχειν παρὰ τῆς σῆς . . . . . παρακαλοῦντά με εἰς]
       τὴν Ἀλεξανδρέων πόλιν διὰ

(Addendum am unteren Rand des Recto)
52 {διὰ} ταῦτα τὰ ἀνδράποδα, τὸν καὶ πρὸ{ς} τῆς τούτου ἀφίξεως
       προπαρ[εσκευασμένον δεῦρ]ο κατα[πλε]ῦσαι
53 δι' αὐτὸ τοῦτο. ἀφικόμενος δὲ εἰς τὴν πατρίδα τὴν ἐμὴν καὶ γνο[ὺς
       τοῦ πράγματος τὴ]ν ἀκρί[βει]αν
       `πρώτου΄
54 καὶ ὡς τοῦ ἐπιχειρήματος ἀποτυχών, λοιπὸν εἰς ἄλλο τι ἐτράπη
       [καὶ περὶ τὴν δεσπο]τείαν [ἐστ]ρέ-
55 φετο. φίλους γὰρ ἀξιώσας μεταξὺ γενέσθαι Πανίσκον τὸν ἀπὸ
       δικ[αιοδότου[1] καὶ Ἀπόλλωνα] τὸν π[οι]ητὴν
56 τὸν ἀδελφιδοῦν τὸν ἐμόν, ὃν καὶ ἡ σή, ὦ δέσποτα, περὶ τοὺς
       λόγους ἀρε[τή τε καὶ φιληκοῖα γιν]ώσ[κει τὴν]
57 παρὰ σοῦ, κύριε, ἐν Θηβαίδι εὐτυχήσαντα ἀκρόασιν, καὶ ἄλλα
       προσ[.] [ἀναλώματά?]
58 τινα καὶ καμάτους πρ[ο]σ[ε]λόμενος, ἕως ἂν συλλάβηι καὶ
       συνα[γάγηι τὰ ἀνδράποδα ταῦτα τῆι δ   ]
59 ἐσκορπισμένα καὶ δρασμὸν πλημμελήσαντα καὶ ὡς ἐν ἐρημί[α]ι
       [ἀδέσποτα   *ca 12*   ] . [.]
       `τινα [ἐ]πηρεάζων΄
60 προϊσταμένου καὶ τοιαῦτα λέγων τοὺς φίλους τοὺς με[τ]αξὺ
       κατηνάγκα[σεν   *ca 17*   ] . [.]τον . [. . . .]

Textlücke unbekannter Größe,
in welche offenbar folgende zwei Randnotizen auf 13 gehören:

13

(Addendum am rechten Rand des Recto)
61 οὕτω βιαιοτάτην ὥστε ἔχειν οὐ[2] δικαίως αὐτὸς ἑαυτῶι καθ' ἰδίαν
       κτῆσ(ιν) τῶν ἀνδραπ(όδων)

---

[1] δικ[αιοδότου : δικ[αιοδοτῶν Willis.
[2] Lesung unsicher; εὖ? Kaum αὖ.

aber, ein Schreiben von Deiner [- - -] (Ehrentitel) zu haben, das mich nach
Alexandria

(Addendum am unteren Rand des Recto)
wegen dieser Sklaven rufe, mich, der ich bereits vor dessen Ankunft Vorbe-
reitungen getroffen hatte, gerade deswegen dorthin zu fahren.
 (53) Als er jedoch in meine Heimatstadt kam und die genaue Sachlage erfuhr,
änderte er, weil er in seinem ersten Anlauf gescheitert war, in der Folge seine
Vorgangsweise und insistierte auf der Frage des Besitzers. Ich hatte nämlich
Freunde gebeten, sich einzuschalten, Paniskos, den Untergebenen des
Iuridicus[1], und den Dichter Apollon, meinen Neffen, den auch Deine, o Herr,
der Literatur gegenüber bewiesene Vortrefflichkeit und Aufmerksamkeit
kennt, da er vor Dir, o Herr, in der Thebais bei einer Lesung reüssierte. - - -
[Er (Eugeneios) führte dabei ins Treffen, daß er keine Kosten gescheut] und
Mühen auf sich genommen habe, bis er diese Sklaven, die - - - zerstreut
waren und sich der Flucht schuldig gemacht hätten und gleichsam wie in der
Wüste herrenlos gewesen wären, gesammelt hatte - - - (60) - - - und solches
redend überwältigte er meine Freunde, die sich eingeschaltet hatten - - -

Textlücke unbekannter Größe,
*in welche offenbar folgende zwei Randnotizen auf **13** gehören:*

13
(Addendum am rechten Rand des Recto)
(61) - - - so daß er selbst (Eugeneios) für sich in ungerechter Weise[2] zu eige-

---

[1] oder: „Paniskos, den früheren Iuridicus".
[2] oder „in guter, gerechter Weise".

62 τὸ (ἥμισυ) αὐτ(ῶν) {ἔχειν} καὶ τὸν κληρ(ονόμον) ν[ό]μιμ(ον) τὸ
   ἄλλο (ἥμισυ), ἐμὲ [̣] την ..... ̣ ̣[̣] ̣[̣]ιαν
   ἐγύμνασ(εν)
63 γεν..... χ( ) [ca 8] ̣[̣] ̣τ( ) ̣.[....]του [ca 20   ]
64 [ca 22   ] ̣[̣] ̣τοι γοῦν ̣[̣] ̣[̣]ημ[ca 20   ]
65 καὶ αὐτὸς οὗτος ὁ Εὐγένειος παρά[δ]οσ(ιν) καὶ τὴν παρά-
   στασ(ιν) τῶν δούλων τῶν ...[̣]..... ....
66 κἄν τις ἐν αὐτοῖς ἦι ἀποδεδ[ρ]ακώς   vacat
                    (Rand)

               (Addendum am oberen Rand des Recto)
                          ʿτότεʾ   ʿ[ ]αουδετ[̣]υτοʿ
67 καὶ διαπλ[αναται? ...]μ[[̣ ̣ ̣υ]] τοῦ ἔτι κρατουμένου, [[̣[̣ ̣]περουδε]]
   πεποίηκεν τ[̣]υτ[̣] παράδ[ο]σιν
68 τῶν δι᾽ αὐ[τοῦ τοῦ Εὐγεν]εί[ο]υ π[αρ]ὰ τῆι τάξει τῆς κα[θολι]-
   κότητος φρουρηθέντω[ν ̣ ̣] ̣ τὴν παρά[στ]α-
69 σιν τοῦ πε[φ]ευγ[ότος κα]ὶ οὐ [π]αρόντος μοι πεποίηκ[εν. ἕτ]εροι
                       ʿλοιπὸνʾ
   δὲ [[ἤδη]] δύο ἐξ οὗ εἰ[ς τήνδ]ε ἀφικόμην τὴν
70 πόλιν ἤδη διέδρα[μον ἀποδημ]ήσαντος ἐμοῦ καὶ δεινῶς ἐσχηκό-
   τος, καὶ ὁ τρίτος ἤδη ἐπιστ[̣] [̣ ἐ]νταῦθ᾽ ἐμοὶ [α]ὐτός
                    (Rand)

               Textlücke unbekannter Größe

                        10a
1 [ca 35   ] ̣[   ]
2 [ca 30   ]ην τότε τα[
                                     ]
3 [   ]ναι αὐτὸ δὴ [̣]ο[   ]
4 [   ] ἀνδραπόδων ὥρισεν ὁ τούτων
   δεσπ[ό]της
5 [   ] αὐτὸν σκεψάμενος, τοῦτο ἐντεθύμημαι
6 [   ]μαι ὥσπερ ἐκπεπληγμένος τέλει τ[ο]ῦ
7 [πράγματος καὶ σχεδὸν οὐδ]ὲ ἐμαυτῶι εἶναι δοκ[ῶ]ν τ[ὰ
   ἀνδράποδα ταῦτα]

nem Besitz habe die eine Hälfte der Sklaven und der gesetzliche Erbe die
andere Hälfte, mich - - - entblößte er (?) - - - (65) und gerade Eugeneios
selbst die Übergabe und Bereitstellung der Sklaven - - - (66) wenn auch einer
unter ihnen weggelaufen sei - - -

(Addendum am unteren Rand des Recto)

(67) - - -, der damals noch verfangen (festgesetzt?) war und nicht hat er
durchgeführt - - - die Übergabe der (Sklaven), die durch Eugeneios selbst im
Officium des Rationalis festgehalten wurden, [noch] hat er mir herbeige-
schafft den, der flüchtig und nicht anwesend war. Die beiden anderen (?) aber
waren, als ich in diese Stadt kam, bereits entlaufen, da ich noch fern der Stadt
weilte und mich in schwierigen Umständen befand, und der dritte war dort
bereits zur Stelle (?ἐπιστ[ὰ]ς) und selbst - - - mir - - -

Textlücke unbekannter Größe

10a

- - - (5) bin ich in Zorn geraten und - - - wie betäubt [durch den Ausgang]
dieser Sache, (7) und ich bekam den Eindruck, daß diese Sklaven kaum

8 [ὁρῶν τοὺς βουλομένους οὕτω]ς ἄγοντας καὶ φέροντας τὰ
ἡμέτερα ὡς ἐπαν-[1]
9 [ca 25   ] [ ] ν. διὰ τοῦτο νῦν ἀσφαλίζομαι
                            ἀξιῶν
10 [ca 4 τῆς σῆς, ὦ δέσποτα, πρὸ]ς τοὺς νόμους ἀκριβείας, εἴπερ
                            ἀνάγκη με τὴν
11 [ca 13   ἀπάτην φέρειν] κἂν διόρθωσιν τοῦ γενομένου
                            σφάλματος
12 [ca 25   ]σθῆναι τοῦτο ἐὰν μεθήσονται μετὰ
                            τ[ ]
13 [ca 16   ἐπάναγκες] καὶ τοῦτον πεισθήσεσθαι τοῖς διὰ
                            τῶν διαθη-
14 [κῶν δειχθησομένοις καὶ μὴ πρ]οεῖναι πρόκριμα, εἰ τοῦτο
                            φαίνεται παραλελιμ-
15 [μένον   ca 20   ] αν [ ] γενήσεται   , ἐγγυητὴν δὲ
16 [αὐτὸν παρασχέσθαι ἄνδρα ἐν τ]ῆι πόλει ἢ περὶ Θηβαίδα
                            ἔχοντα τὸ ἐφέστιον,
17 [ἵν᾽, ἤν τι μετὰ ταῦτα   περὶ] τῶν ἀνδραπόδων τούτων δειχθῆι ὡς
                            ἀπο
                                        ˋἐγγυητὴςˊ
18 [ca 25   ]ειος γένηται ὑπεύθυνος τοῦ
                            δειχθησ[ο]μένου ε
19 [ca 25   ] ἐν ἄλλαις χώραις διατρίβοντος καὶ
                            ἐπειδὴ
20 [τὰ ἀνδράποδα ταῦτα ἐφρουρήθη παρ]ὰ τῆι τάξει τῆς καθο[λ]ι-
                            κότητος μέχρ[ι τ]ῆ[ς] ἐμῆς
21 [παρουσίας, Εὐγενείου δὲ ἐπὶ συλλ]ήψει ὑπὸ φρουρᾶς εἶναι
                            ἀξιώσαντος κα[ὶ]

---

1   *An dieser Stelle hat 7 in Z. 6 zusätzlich eingeschoben:*
63   ὁρῶν τοὺς βουλομένους οὕτως ἄγοντας καὶ φέροντας τὰ ἡμέτερα ὡ[ς]
                                ˋ   ˊ   ˋἀναγκαίωςˊ
64 [πα]ρῆλθεν δὲ ημ[   ]μιν   [[τοῦτο]] καὶ ἀσφαλῶς τῶι γραμματείωι
            προσθεῖναι αὐτὸ δὴ τοῦτο τό· εἰ μὴ διέθετο ἐκει   η[ ] ἀλλ
            π[   ]
65   [τῆ]ς σῆς, ὦ δέσποτα, π[ρὸς τοὺ]ς νόμους ἀκριβείας, εἴπερ ἀνάγκη
με τὴν ἀπάτην φέρειν κἂν διόρθωσιν τοῦ σφάλματος ἐπὶ ὑπομνημ(ατισμῶν) δόσθαι   [

mehr mir gehörten, als ich sah, wie jeder Hergelaufene auf diese Weise unser Eigentum plünderte - - - [1]

(9) deswegen lege ich nun bei Deiner, o Herr, gegenüber den Gesetzen bewiesenen Gewissenhaftigkeit Verwahrung ein und fordere, wenn ich schon die [- - -] Täuschung ertragen muß, wenigstens die Berichtigung der geschehenen Täuschung (*oder vielleicht:* des geschehenen Irrtums) [zu Protokoll zu geben][2] - - -

(13) daß auch dieser (Eugeneios) gezwungenermaßen sich dem, was durch die Testamente bewiesen werden wird, füge, und daß niemandem ein Rechtsnachteil entstehe, wenn dies verabsäumt erscheint - - - (15) [und ich fordere], daß [er] für sich als Bürgen einen Mann stellt, der in Alexandria oder in der Thebais seinen Wohnsitz hat, (17) damit, wenn etwas danach in Hinblick auf die Sklaven ans Licht gebracht wird - - - ,

[Eugen]eios [?oder der] Bürge haftbar ist für erwiesene [- - -] in anderen Ländern sich aufhaltend. (19) Und da diese Sklaven bis zu meiner Ankunft im Officium des Rationalis in Gewahrsam waren und Eugeneios bei ihrer

---

[1] *An dieser Stelle hat* **7**, 64 *noch zusätzlich:*
- - - trat (Eugeneios) [an uns] heran [und forderte], dem Vertrag gerade dies sicher (zwingend) hinzuzufügen: "außer jener verfügte letztwillig etwas anderes (?) [- - - "
[2] Vgl. **7**, 65 κἂν διόρθωσιν τοῦ σφάλματος ἐπὶ ὑπομνημ(ατισμῶν) δόσθαι

22 [πρὸς ἐμὲ   *ca 24*   ]ειος, ἀξιῶ, δέσποτα, ταῦτά μοι
    παραδοθῆναι καὶ

23 [ἀπὸ τῆς φρουρᾶς   *ca 12*   ]ναι, ἐμὲ γὰρ νῦν καλοῦσιν οἱ
    νόμοι ἐπὶ τὴν

24 [τῶν ἀνδραπόδων δεσποτείαν, ὄντα] ἐκείνου τοῦ Ἁρποκρατί-
    ωνος [ὁμοπάτριόν τε καὶ]

25 [ὁμομήτριον ἀδελφὸν   *ca 10*   ]μμένα τῆι δοθείσηι Εὐγενείωι
    διὰ ἀν[.].[.]

26 [*ca 25*   ]ταρια τηρουντ.[.]   *Spuren?*

Ergreifung gefordert hat, daß sie festgehalten werden, und da zu mir - - -, bitte ich, Herr, daß diese mir übergeben und aus der Haft [freigelassen werden], denn mich rufen nun die Gesetze zur Herrschaft über die Sklaven, da ich der leibliche Bruder jenes Harpokration bin - - -

IV. INDICES

SUBJECT INDEX

Lightface numbers denote pages; boldface denote Greek texts followed by their
line numbers or commentary notes

WORD AND NAME INDICES

I. List of Scholarchs

ἀδελφιδοῦς **1** ii [6]
Ἀθηναῖος **1** i 9; ii [5],[8]
Ἀκαδημία **1** ii 11,16
Ἀναξαγόρας **1** i [7]
Ἀναξίμανδρος **1** i 4
Ἀναξιμένης **1** i [6]
Ἀντίοχος **1** ii 14
ἀπό **1** ii 19
Ἀπολλωνία **1** i [12]
Ἀριστοτέλης **1** ii 22
Ἀρκεσίλαος **1** ii 9
Ἀρχέλαος **1** i [9]
ἀρχηγέτης **1** i [1]; ii [15]
Ἀσκαλωνίτης **1** ii [14]

Βοιώτιος **1** ii 20

Διογένης **1** i [12]; ii 18
δουλία **1** ii 19

ἐκ, ἐξ **1** i 7,[12]; ii [9],13,24
Ἐλεάτης **1** i 11

Ζήνων **1** ii 28

Θαλῆς **1** i [3]
Θεόφραστος **1** ii 23

Ἴων **1** ii 23

Καρνεάδης **1** ii 10
Καρχηδόνιος **1** ii [12]
Κλαζομεναί **1** i 7-8
Κλιτόμαχος **1** ii 12
Κράτης **1** ii 20
Κριτόλαος **1** ii [26]
Κυνικοί **1** ii 17,27

Κυρηναῖος **1** ii [10]

Λάμψακος **1** ii 24
Λάρισσα **1** ii [13]

μέσος **1** ii [11]
μετά **1** ii 27
Μιλήσιος **1** i 3,[5],6
Μόνιμος **1** ii 19

Ξενοκράτης **1** ii 7

ὁ **1** ii 18; τῆς **1** ii [15]; τῶν **1** ii 15,27

Παρμενίδης **1** i [11]
Περιπατητικοί **1** ii 21
Πιτάνη **1** ii [9]
Πλάτων **1** ii 6
Πολέμων **1** ii 8
Πραξιφάνης **1** ii [25]

Ῥόδιος **1** ii 25

Σινωπεύς **1** ii [18]
Σπεύσιππος **1** ii 5
Σταγειρίτης **1** ii 22
Στράτων **1** ii [24]
Στωικοί **1** ii [27]
Σύριος **1** i 10

τρίτος **1** ii 16

Φασηλίτης **1** ii 26
Φερεκύδης **1** i [10]
Φιλίων **1** ii 13
φιλόσοφος **1** i 1

Χαλκηδόνιος **1** ii [7]

II. Emperors, Consuls

Διοκλητιανός **3**.iv 24,25

ὑπατείας Φλαυίου Φιλίππου τοῦ
λαμπροτάτου ἐπάρχου τοῦ [ἱεροῦ

προιτωτίου κ]αὶ Φλαυίου Σαλιᾶ τοῦ
λαμπροτάτου μαγίστρου ἱππέων (AD
348) **6**.18-19

III. Months

Ἀθύρ **6**.9
Μεσορή **3**.iv 10
Παχών **3**.iv 10

Φαμενώθ **3**.iii 10
Φαρμοῦθι **3**.iii 11
Χοιάκ **6**.13,19

IV. Personal Names

Ἀέτιος see Αὐρήλιος Ἀέτιος
Ἄμμων see Αὐρήλιος Ἄμμων
Ἀπίων **3**.iv 4
Ἀπόλλων poet, ἀδελφιδοῦς of Aurelius
Ammon **6**.5; **7**.42; **13**.[55]
Ἁρποκρᾶς = Ἁρποκρατίων, brother of
Aurelius Ammon **3**.iii 15
Ἁρποκρατίων brother of Aurelius
Ammon **5**.12,16; **6**.7; **7**.35;
9.1,18,24,[35]; **10a**.24; **10b**.[8];
12.10; **13**.17,43,48; **15**.1,[8]; **16a**.8
Αὐρήλιος Ἀέτιος **13**.36
Αὐρήλιος Ἄμμων **4**.[2],59; **5**.1,17;
6.2,3,20; **7**.[2],36; **9**.25; **13**.49; **15**.[9]
Αὐρήλιος Φαυστῖνος councillor of
Panopolis **5**.2
Αὐρήλιος Ὡρίων son of Horion, the
archiprophetes of the Panopolite nome
4.[2],59
Διοκλητιανός see Index II
Εὐγένειος μεμοράριος **6**.3,11; **7**.29;
9.17,31,36; **10a**.[21],25;
13.42,65,[68]; **15**.12; **16a**.12; **20**.8
Κα[**3**.vi 20
Κόνων **7**.18; **11b**.1; **12**.15,19; **13**.21
Μακαρία **3**.vi 13,20
Νεστόριος see Φλάυιος Νεστόριος
Νίκη mother of Aurelius Ammon

13.49
Παλλάδιος father of Serenianus **13**.42
Πανίσκος ἀπὸ δικαιοδότου **6**.4; **13**.55
Πεκῦσις **3**.iii 23
Πετεαρβεσχῖνις father of Aurelius
Ammon **4**.[2],[59]; **5**.1; **6**.2; **7**.[2]
Πολυκράτης **3**.v 22, vi [23]
Σαλιᾶς] Φλάυιος Σαλιᾶς, see Index II
Σαραπόδωρος **3**.v [5],[29], vi 19
Σερηνιανός son of Palladius **13**.42,47
Σισίννιος see Φλάυιος Σισίννιος
Ταυρῖνος **3**.v 35
Φαυστῖνος see Αὐρήλιος Φαυστῖνος
Φίλιππος] Φλάυιος Φίλιππος, see Index
II
Φλάυιος Νεστόριος ἔπαρχος τῆς
Αἰγύπτου **4**.[1]?; **5**.15
Φλάυιος Σαλιᾶς see Index II.
Φλάυιος Σισίννιος καθολικός **6**.1;
7.[1]; **16a**.[3]-4,[6]-7
Φλάυιος Φίλιππος, see Index II
Ὡρίων archiprophetes of the Panopolite
nome and half-brother of Aurelius
Ammon, father of Aurelius Horion **3**.iv
21; **4**.[2],59
Ὡρίων ὁ νεώτερος **3**.vi 20
Ὡρίων] ἄλλος Ὡρίων **6**.5

V. Geographical

Αἰγύπτιοι] οἱ ἄνω Αἰ., οἱ κάτω Αἰ.
  12.3; 13.3
Αἴγυπτος 4.[1]; 5.15; 9.[2]; 12.11;
  13.18
Αἰθίωψ. Αἰθίοπες 3.iii 21,25,26
Ἀλεξάνδρεια 3.iii 11; 5.11; 6.6,10;
  7.34,70; 8.[5]; 9.[18],[24]; 11c.11,13;
  13.43,48; 15.7; 16a.[8]-9; 18b.3;
  21.3
Ἀλεξανδρεύς 12.15; 13.21
Ἀλεξανδρέων πόλις 7.38; 9.28;
  11a.11; 12.34; 13.51

Ἀραβία 3.v 29
Ἑλλάς 9.6; 11b.4; 13.24,26; 14b.4
Θηβαίς 4.[2],[59]; 5.2,18; 6.3;
  7.[3],15,[16],36,56; 10a.16; 11e.[1];
  12.13,17; 13.57; 14a.[2]; 16a.2;
Κωνσταντινόπολις 9.7; 13.24
Πανοπολιτῶν πόλις 6.4
Πανὸς πόλις 3.iv 10,12,15,20;
  4.[2],[59]; 5.1; 6.2; 7.[2]; 14a.[2]
Ῥώμη 9.[7]; 13.24; 14b.[4]
Φοίνικες 3.iv 12

VI. Religion

Ἀγαθός Δαίμων 12.2; 13.2
ἀρχιερατικός 4.21
ἀρχιερεύς 3.iii 10, iv 16,17,19,24,[25];
  4.[19],49
ἀρχιπροφητεία 4.[33]
δαίμων 11a.[7]; 13.22
ἔνθεος 7.33
ἑορτή 3.iii 11,12
θειότης 8.[1]; 9.[20]; 13.45; 15.5
θεός 3.iii 14,16, iv 9.22,27, v [16], vi

16; 4.17,34,58; 12.2; 13.2
θρησκ[4.17
ἱερατικός see Index VII
ἱερός 6.[18]
πρόνοια 12.2; 13.2
προφητεία 3.iv 23
προφήτης 3.iv 21
τύχη 3.ii [8],[14],16,[18], iii 16, iv 22;
  7.[33]

VII. Official and Military Terms and Titles

ἄρχω] ἄρξας 5.2
ἄρχων 12.7; 13.[7]
αὐτοκράτωρ 4.56
βασιλεύς 3.iv 17,19; 4.32
βασιλικός 3.iv 23,27; 4.30,32; 13.25
βουλευτής 5.3
δημόσιος 5.7,21; 6.12,[16]; 13.29
διασημότατος 4.[1]; 5.14; 6.1; 7.1
δικαιοδότης 6.4; 13.[55]
δικαστήριον 4.56; 12.7; 13.7; 17.11
ἔπαρχος 4.[1]; 5.14; 6.18
ἐπιτροπεύω 13.26

ἡγεμονεύω 3.iv 4
ἡγεμών 3.iii 21; 4.[13]
ἱερατικός] ἱερατικὸν ταμεῖον 4.43;
  ἱερατικὸς λόγος 4.47
ἱππεύς 6.19
καθολικός 6.1; 7.1
καθολικότης 9.[31]; 10a.20; 13.68
κομιτᾶτον 3.iii 26
λαμπρός 6.6; 12.12; 13.18
λαμπρότατος 6.18,19; 12.[6]; 13.6
λογιστεύω 13.26
μάγιστρος 6.19

μεγαλεῖον **6**.16
μεμοράριος **6**.3; **7**.29
ὀφικιάλιος **17**.5
πραιτώριον **6**.[18]
προστάτης **3**.iv 26, v 23; **12**.[5]; **13**.4

στρατηγός **3**.iii 6
ταμεῖον **4**.43
τάξις **3**.iv 16,17,20; **4**.[25],29,48;
  9.[31]; **10a**.20; **13**.68

VIII. Professions, Trades, Occupations, and Status Designations

ἀνδράποδον **5**.11; **6**.6; **7**.16,19-
  20,23,[27],[31],39,[61];
  9.3,[16],[18],[29],30;
  10a.4,[7],17,[20],[24]; **10b**.3-[4],10;
  11a.[6],9; **11c**.8,11; **11e**.[2];
  12.12,14,16,20,23,25;
  13.19,40,43,52,[58],61; **16a**.[9];
  16b.3; **18b**.8
δοῦλος **9**.[11]; **11d**.2; **13**.30,65; **15**.1;

  23b.4
ναυτικός? **3**.iv 7
παιδίον **3**.iv 11, vi [22],[24]
ποιητής **6**.5; **7**.43; **13**.55
σταθμοῦχος **3**.iv 13
σχολαστικός **4**.2,[59]; **5**.1; **6**.2; **7**.2
σῶμα **13**.49
ταβουλάριος **6**.17

IX. Taxes

εἰσκριτικόν **4**.[48]
εἰσφορά **5**.7

τέλεσμα **5**.21; **13**.30
φόρος **3**.v 21,[29]

X. General Index of Words

ἀγαθός **3**.ii [10]-11; **7**.66
ἀγγελία **7**.26; **11c**.5; **13**.39
]αγγέλλω **13**.42
ἀγνωμοσύνη **16b**.5
ἀγχίνοια **11a**.19
ἀγχιστεία **7**.[26],30; **11c**.6,10; **13**.[39]
ἄγω **3**.iii 4; **4**.51; **7**.63; **10a**.8;
ἀδελφ[**3**.vi 3
ἀδελφιδοῦς **4**.43; **7**.44; **13**.56
ἀδελφικός **3**.vi 2
ἀδελφός **3**.iv [28], v 28, vi 18,[21],23;
  5.12,15; **6**.7; **7**.17,[17]-18,32,35;
  9.18,[25],35; **10a**.[25]; **11a**.[4],12,18;
  12.10,17,18,26; **13**.16,43,[49]; **15**.1,8;
  16a.6,10; **22b**.10
ἀδέσποτος **5**.12; **7**.33,[62]; **9**.18;
  13.44,[59]

ἀδι[κ **7**.9
ἀδικία **3**.iii 3
ἀδίκως **4**.[32]
ἀεί **3**.iii 16, v 15; **4**.34; **7**.[7],21; **9**.9;
  12.[21]; **13**.13,27,28,29,33
ἀθυμ[**3**.ii 5
ἀθυμέω **3**.ii 16,22
ἀθύμως **3**.vi 11
αἰδέομαι **3**.ii 29
]αιρέω **7**.[5-6]; **13**.11-12
αἰσθ[**3**.ii 7
αἴτησις **7**.33; **8**.[1]; **9**.19; **13**.44; **15**.4
αἰτία **11a**.19; **17**.2
ἀκοή **7**.[24],27; **9**.[14],15; **11c**.4,7;
  12.[28]; **13**.38,40
ἀκολουθέω **7**.18
ἀκούω **4**.53; **5**.9; **7**.24; **9**.[14],[23];

V. Plates

Plate I:
No. 1. Ammon's List of Scholarchs
(reduced 92%)

b) *Odyssey* 11.273–82
   (Fr. B, *recto*) (original size)

a) *Odyssey* 9.295–309
   (Fr. A, *recto*) (original size)

Plate II: ·
No. 2. Homer, *Odyssey*

b) (Fr. B, *verso*) (original size)

a) *Odyssey* 9.344–84
   (Fr. A, *verso*) (original size)

Plate III:
No. 2. Homer, *Odyssey*

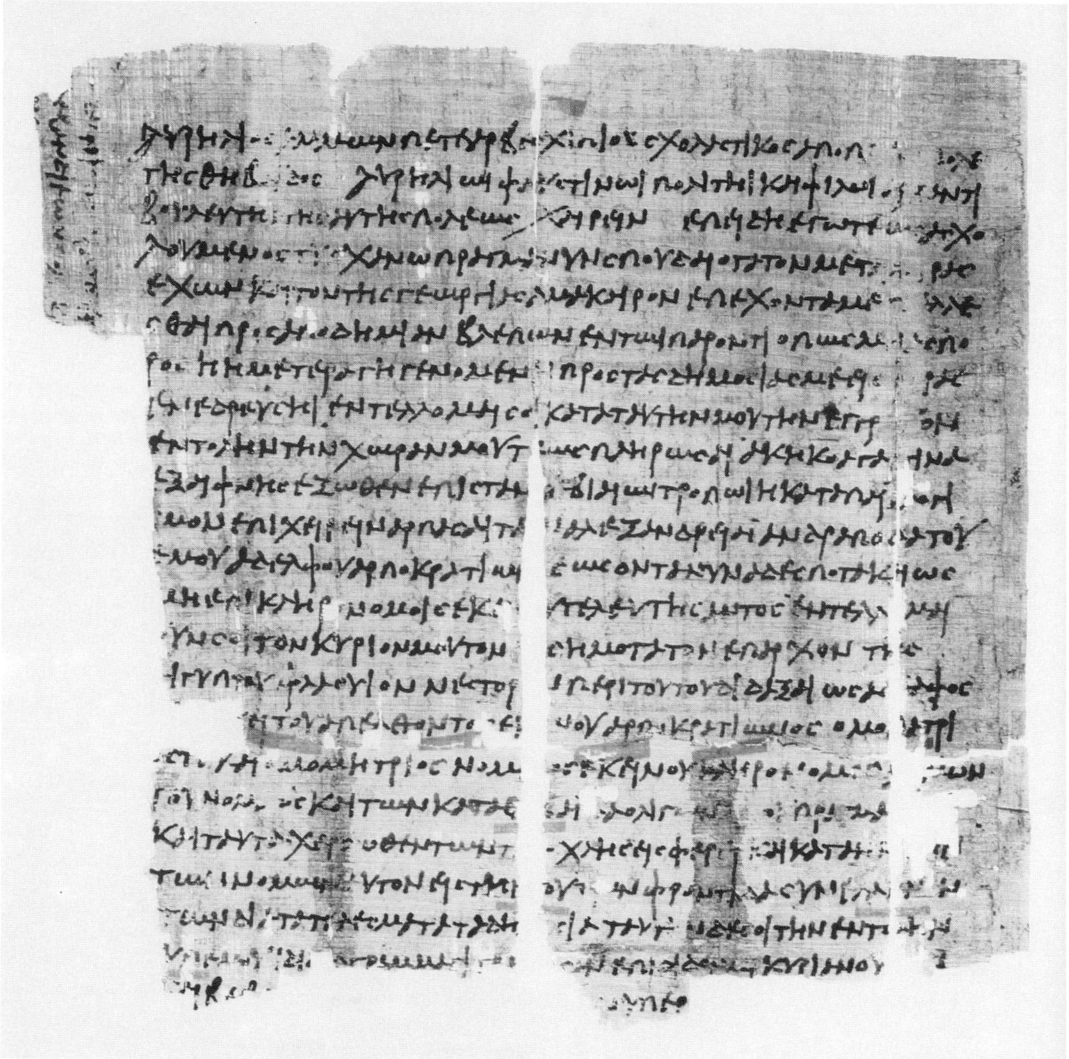

Plate IV: No. 5. Deputation (reduced 65%)

Plate V: No. 8. Ammon's Petition to the *Catholicus*, Draft 2 (original size)

Plate VI

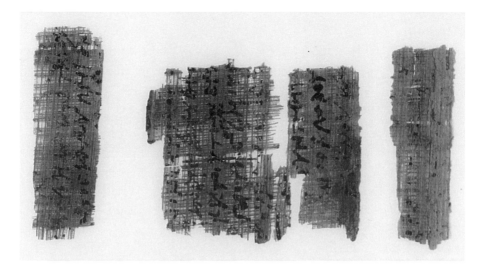

b) No. 18.
Fragments
of a Draft
(original size)

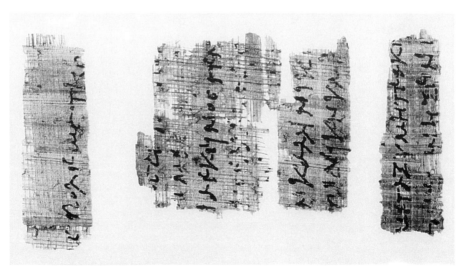

a) No. 14. Ammon's
Petition to the
Catholicus, Draft 8
(original size)

Plate VII: No. 15. Ammon's Petition to the *Catholicus*, Draft 9 (enlarged 108%),

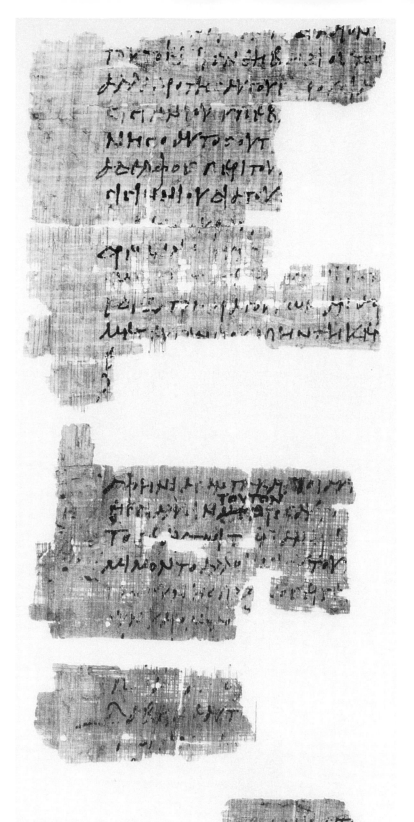

Plate VIII:
No. 16.
Draft of a Petition
(reduced 93%)

Plate IX: No. 17. Draft of a Petition (enlarged 108%)

a) No. 20. Draft Fragment (original size)

b) No. 21. Draft Fragment (original size)

Plate XI

◁ Plate X: No. 19. Fragments of a Petition (reduced 93%)

Plate XII

a) No. 22. Fragments of a Draft (original size)

b) No. 25. Fragment of a Petition
(original size)

Plate XIII: No. 23. Fragments of a Draft (enlarged 108%)

a) recto (original size)   b) verso (original size)

Plate XIV: No. 24. Draft Fragments

Plate XVI: No. 3. Ammon's Letter to his Mother (right half, cols. iv, vi, vi) (reduced 69%)

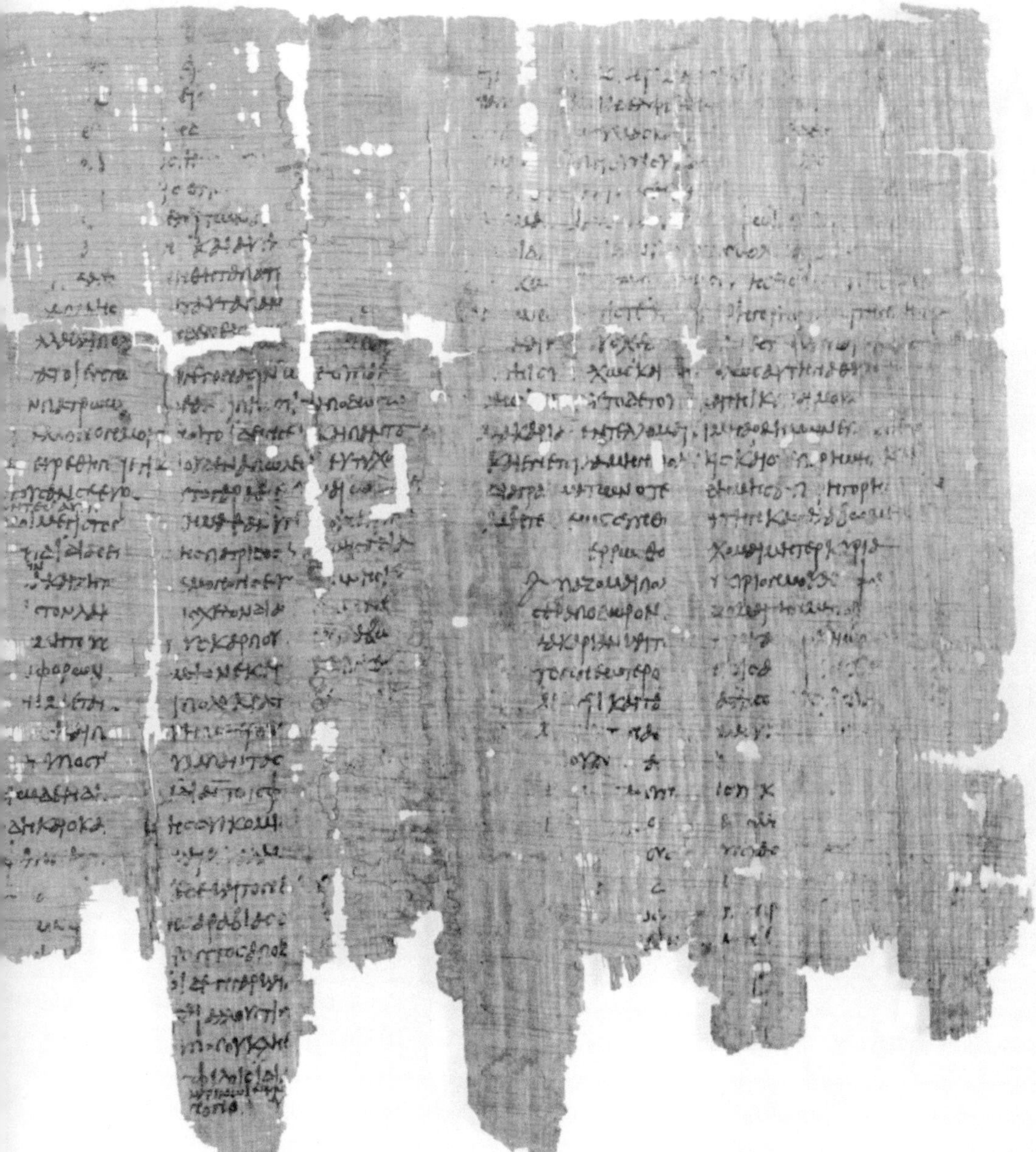

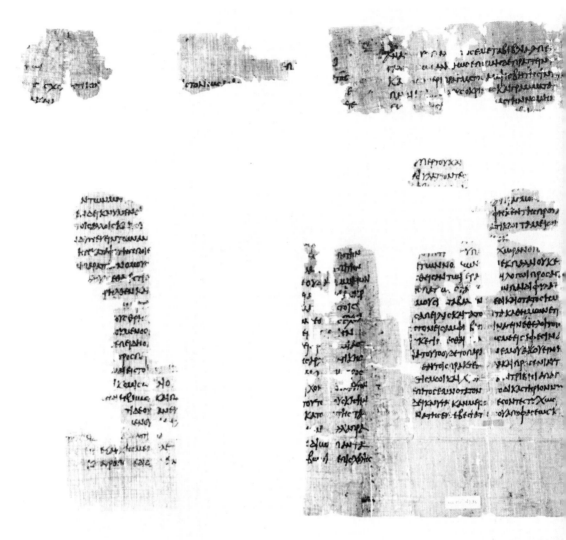

Plate XVII: No. 4. Horion II's Petition to the Prefect (reduced 50%)

XIX: No. 7. Ammon's Petition to the *Catholicus*, Draft 1 (reduced 71%)

Plate XXII: No. 11. Ammon's Petition to the *Catholicus*, Draft 5 (reduced 70%)

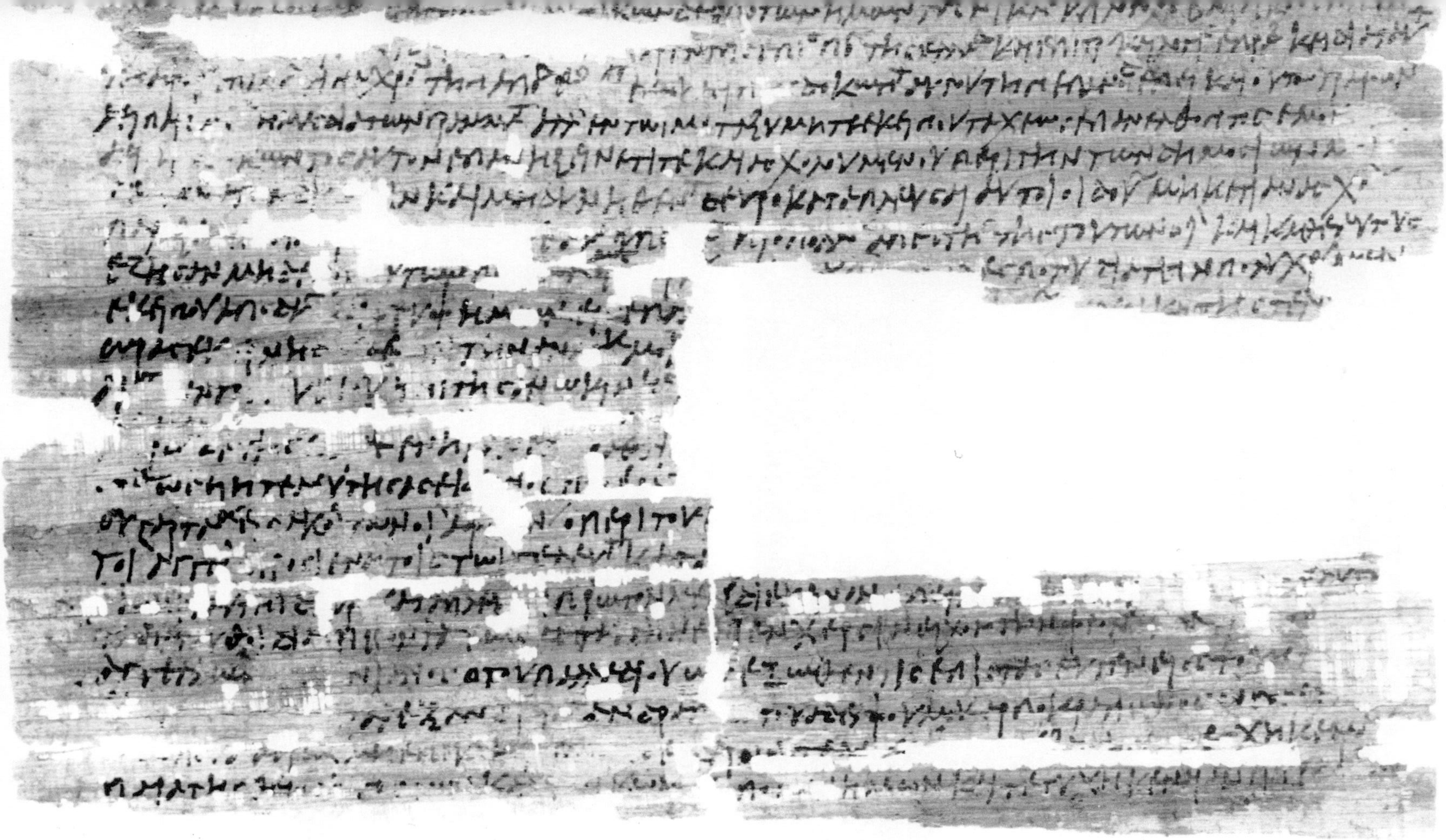

Plate XXIV: No. 13. Ammon's Petition to the *Catholicus*, Draft 7, ll. 1–45 (reduced 88%)